D1478353

We Dance for the Virgen

NUMBER 19

CLAYTON WHEAT WILLIAMS
TEXAS LIFE SERIES

We Dance for the Virgen

Authenticity of Tradition in a San Antonio Matachines Troupe

ROBERT R. BOTELLO

Foreword by Megan Biesele

TEXAS A&M UNIVERSITY PRESS
COLLEGE STATION

This paper meets the requirements of ANSI/NISO Z39.48–1992
(Permanence of Paper).
Binding materials have been chosen for durability.
Manufactured in the United States of America by Versa Press, Inc.

Library of Congress Cataloging-in-Publication Data

Names: Botello, Robert R., author. | Biesele, Megan, writer of foreword.
Title: We dance for the Virgen: authenticity of tradition in a San Antonio
matachines troupe / Robert R. Botello; foreword by Megan Biesele
Other titles: Clayton Wheat Williams Texas life series; no. 19.
Description: First edition. | College Station: Texas A&M University Press,
[2022] | Series: Clayton Wheat Williams Texas life series; Number 19 |
Includes bibliographical references and index.
Identifiers: LCCN 2021055928 (print) | LCCN 2021055929 (ebook) | ISBN
9781648430473 (cloth) | ISBN 9781648430480 (ebook)
Subjects: LCSH: Botello, Robert R. | Our Lady of Guadalupe Church (San
Antonio, Tex.) | Matachines (Dance) | Religious dance—Texas—San
Antonio. | Folk dancing, Mexican—Texas—San Antonio. | Guadalupe, Our
Lady of—Cult. | Folk dancers—Texas—San Antonio—Biography. | San
Antonio (Tex.)—Social life and customs.
Classification: LCC GV1796.M35 B57 2022 (print) | LCC GV1796.M35 (ebook)
| DDC 793.3/19764351—dc23/eng/20211122
LC record available at https://lccn.loc.gov/2021055928
LC ebook record available at https://lccn.loc.gov/2021055929

In Memoriam:
Pablo Olivares Sr., Crecensio Ernesto Aguilar,
Rose Violet Botello, Francisca O. Aguilar

Contents

Foreword

Megan Biesele

Like many others who live in the southwestern United States, I have been bewildered by the symbolism of ritual dances and pilgrimages that exist somewhere in the interstices between indigenous cultures of the Americas and the Spanish Catholic colonizers. Using the wastebasket word "syncretism" to deal with this symbolism seems often to mask the varied origins, histories, and ongoing creative transformations of these artistic and devotional forms. Robert Botello presents in this book a comprehensive portrait of one such dance, *La Danza Guadalupana de Pablo Olivares Sr.*, that overturns false syncretic assumptions. Chief among these assumptions is that the dance is about discarding old traditions in passive acquiescence to conquest. Instead, as he shows, this dance and others like it are about quietly holding fast to tradition by means of resilient openness to some forms of innovation. Botello's portrait is compiled only partly from meticulous research on *danzas de matachines*. Mostly it comes from his own thirteen years as a *matachín* in the *danza* (dance troupe) brought by Pablo Olivares Sr. from Monterrey, Mexico, to San Antonio, Texas, in the 1970s.

We Dance for the Virgen: *Authenticity of Tradition in a San Antonio Matachines Troupe*, presented as Botello's personal narrative of experience becoming a *matachín*, can quickly involve readers and carry them along in its strong flow. First we are told of his familiarity with the devotion to the *Virgen de Guadalupe* and matachines troupes and his upbringing in a

Catholic Hispanic family in San Antonio. Then follows the story of his training in the intricate disciplines of the specific dance troupe he was invited to join in 2006. His discriminating and nuanced reading of historical sources, from which he provides a historical account of this *danza* among other *danzas de matachines*, is also embedded in his personal narrative. The captions of the illuminating photographs spaced through the book, most taken by Botello himself, read like a synopsis of the narrative—and of the poignant chronicle of an attempted appropriation of the Danza Guadalupana de Pablo Olivares Sr. that took place in San Antonio during the years 2013–15.

The narrative structure Botello has chosen allows him to wed description of this specific dance seamlessly to his documentation of its continuity and authenticity. This book could only have been written by someone who is both a writer and a native to the relevant culture in all its complexity. Botello is not only a native of San Antonio, with ancestral and cultural roots in this historic city, but also a participant in the dance under discussion, a skilled bilingual translator, a sensitive and unassuming observer, and an educated person who is not a "scholar" in the usual sense of advanced degrees and career. His position is unique: he is an authentic authority of his own experiences as a *matachín*. It is this authenticity that makes it unnecessary for his observations and experiences to be validated through a theoretical filter. This book is one of the rare but valid instances in the social sciences in which the insider (a.k.a. "subject, native") of the dance is allowed to speak to the reader directly. Therefore, there is no need for any running commentary by an outside "expert" to qualify or "interpret" what is said. Many folklorists and other scholars see that idea as audacious, but there is a growing trajectory of this type of writing in anthropology, one I think bears watching.

Botello's involvement in documentation of his experiences in the *danza* came about organically; as he says, he had "no informants, but only peers who came to accept me as family." Being a native speaker of Spanish and holding a degree in that language contributed to his ability to articulate the nuances of important Spanish terms. I feel personally grateful that Botello, who has exquisite translation skills, chose to write the book in English. He gracefully and capaciously fulfills his triple role as *matachín*, documentarian, and interpreter.

In the course of his narrative, Botello generously shares the story of his own increased spiritual consciousness through participating in the Danza Guadalupana de Pablo Olivares Sr. He includes selected, highly illustrative extracts from his personal journal during his years of training and dancing as a *matachín*. They include a moving chronicle of the transformative dreams that accompanied his training and his participation in the various roles of the *danza*. This documentation of his personal experience offers the world of scholarship dimensions of understanding that could be obtained in no other way. As he states in the book, he was well along in his training before he realized his own experience could contribute to research about the *danza*. He participated as a radically open, natural observer; he didn't know what he was looking for, so he wrote down everything, including his own experiences as a *matachín*. To me, he seems to have been perfectly poised between the private and the public—as both a dancer and a kind of natural ethnographer of dance.

I'm writing this foreword to Botello's book partly because I am myself an ethnographer. One of the things I research and write about is the ritual healing dance of African San people of Botswana and Namibia. The healing dance is a continent away from *la danza de matachines*, but they have striking similarities. Both function to serve spiritual needs of communities rather than to serve secular needs of entertainment. Many passages in Botello's book have strong parallels to experiences I have had with the San and their healing dance, and to words I have chosen in my attempt to convey them to readers. Such passages emphasize the time-transcendence and sense of spiritual completion felt by participants when the true purposes of dances are met. To illustrate the richness of description in Botello's sharing of his personal experiences, I list a few of these passages:

"The late afternoon sun had a way of shining into the cathedral's dim recesses and onto its roughly hewn limestone pillars, bridging past centuries with the moment."

"My experiences in that *danza* would gradually enable me to identify with the devotees of the *Virgen* who would walk in to light votive candles to her almost as if nothing else mattered."

"To me, time and space, past and present, are merged into a single event that at once *is* happening and has happened and continues even when we stop. Ideally, what happens in the best *danzas* is the summoning of the transcendental and ethereal sense of the past not being the past."

"The intimacy of space afforded by the darkness meant that we danced with no hesitating but only immediate responses to Molly's drumming and single-hearted intention that made our dancing a deftly timed expression of devotion we had waited almost all year to express. It seemed anything could happen."

Two-thirds of *We Dance for the* Virgen is composed of in-depth discussions of the history, form, continuity, and authenticity of *danzas de matachines*, the San Antonio–based Danza Guadalupana de Pablo Olivares Sr., in particular. Woven into this discussion are the experiences Botello had since encountering that *danza* in 2005, soon after which he became an initiate and participating dancer. By the time the narration reaches the year 2013, when a period of supposed cooperation of the *danza* with church and municipal entities gradually leads to a misappropriation of its purpose and meaning, the reader has been brought closely into the story and thus feels, along with the author, a jarring sense of violation. At that point I also felt a sense of tragedy, of heartbreak, as I believe will all thoughtful readers who have been paying attention.

The final third of the book is devoted to how this violation played out and to lessons that can be drawn from it. Botello presents detailed documentation of a period during which the media in San Antonio, along with some church officials, misrepresented the *danza de matachines* in their city-wide attempt to have parts of San Antonio declared a UNESCO World Heritage Site. Such an intimate community chronicle could not have been written by anyone but a deeply involved participant. It ends with heart-warming evidence that the strong, quiet flow of flexible *matachín* tradition nevertheless carried on undeterred throughout this period.

In short, Botello presents us with a nuanced vision of contemporary cultural flexibility. The Danza Guadalupana de Pablo Olivares Sr. exemplifies what components of a true multiculturalism, if not misconstrued and misappropriated, could look like in a city like San Antonio. Botello shows how indigenous traditions sometimes preserve themselves by quiet and dignified withdrawal: "the archdiocese's appropriation of the dance pilgrimage did not compromise the tradition's resilience because the dance is fluid and *matachines* know how to maneuver through institutional machinations and imposed limitations. . . . *Matachines* have been sidestepping such maneuvers since the Spanish Colonial Period." Botello's sharing of his experiences is generous and wholehearted. His critique of prior scholastic methodologies used in the study of the *danza* are clearly and authoritatively articulated. May this opportunity for dialogue he offers be embraced and lead to greater insights into the resilience of this dance tradition.

Preface

The *danza de matachines* is a tradition that is intricately tied to the story of Our Lady of Guadalupe in Mexico (where she is known as *La Virgen de Guadalupe* or simply *La Virgen*). It is also a dance that is a narrative of the colonization of Mexico by the Spanish through the eyes of devotees of *La Virgen de Guadalupe* (Our Lady of Guadalupe). These devotees trace their religious roots back to that period in Mexican history. The dance tells of the *Virgen*'s repeated appearances to an Aztec Indian as she asks for a church to be built. Because of that history, it is tightly connected to present-day Mexico, and, due to northward colonization and immigration, it has spread to parts of the southwestern United States.

During most of the latter part of the 1990s, I lived near Our Lady of Guadalupe Church on the working-class, mostly Chicano West Side of San Antonio. I often walked to mass there on Sundays, playing guitar in two choirs and serving as a lector for one of its Spanish masses. The twelfth of December has always been a highly important day at that church, as it is the feast day of its patroness, *La Virgen de Guadalupe*. On the night of December 11, there was always a vigil inside the church consisting of—as I remember it—prayer, music, and different types of regional *danza* (dance) carried out by dancers wearing regalia reflecting native cultures of present-day northern Mexico and southwestern United States. Initially I only *heard* these *danzantes* (dancers) from my bedroom at the corner of Trinity and Chihuahua. I could hear their drumming, *sonajas* (rattles), and, in some cases, the *ayoyotes* (large rattling hulls) they wore on their ankles. On one occasion I saw a group, which, in hindsight, consisted of a *danza conchera* (shell dancer) troupe dancers or perhaps similarly dressed *azteca*

La Danza Guadalupana de Pablo Olivares Sr. outside Our Lady of Guadalupe Church. San Antonio, Texas. December 12, 2005.

(Aztec) dancers. In either case, they had traveled from Monterrey, Mexico, under the auspices of a parishioner. On another occasion, I saw a local matachines group preparing to dance.

Though I had been familiar with local *danzas* for many years, I became aware of the *study* of native and Chicano dance honoring *La Virgen de Guadalupe* through a captivating photojournalistic book about dance traditions of northern New Mexico that I came across by chance. On December 12, 2005, the feast day of the *Virgen*, I thought to photograph the traditional dance groups who danced at Our Lady of Guadalupe Church. This proved to be a momentous decision for me, as I happened to arrive at a time when one such group called La Danza Guadalupana de Pablo Olivares Sr. was dancing. I was moved by the devotion, solemnity, dignity, and celebratory aspects of the group. I had the sense that I was not only observing a centuries-old tradition but that I was witnessing the centuries of this dance in the echoes of the drum in the church and in the stamping of the feet, the sonorous rattles, and the small bells attached to the short rows of cut reeds and bamboo that were sewn onto the regalia. These sounds summoned for me the presence of generations of ancestral dancers. At that moment I felt that they had never gone but were still dancing somewhere beyond living perception and were simply being made perceptible by the dance. I returned to Our Lady of Guadalupe Church a second time that day and photographed the troupe again, this time as they danced outside the church.

Photographing these traditional dancers became an urgent matter for me. To me they seemed to embody part of San Antonio's essence beyond anything touted for promotional, secular purposes. Because of their devotion and collective presence, I felt they were too important a part of San Antonio's cultural history to remain undocumented. This narrow window of opportunity caused me to feel that, even if I produced only the grainy images of an amateur photographer, it would be far better than not documenting the troupe. But for whom or for what should I document? In the recesses of my mind, these issues were minor details of no concern at the time; the important thing was to create a record.

My role as a documentarian, however, began to shift when I contacted the coordinator of the troupe, Amalia "Molly" Aguilar, by phone in early 2006 to find out where the group would be dancing again. She invited me to train as a dancer in the group. It was an invitation I was slow to accept due to an already full schedule and a number of ongoing projects, but I nonetheless agreed to begin practicing with the troupe. I began to wonder how I was later able to coordinate photographing this *danza* while actively participating in it. Despite my uncertainty about how to coordinate my roles as *matachín* and documentarian, my desire to document this *danza de matachines* troupe persisted. In fact, I began taking notes immediately after practice—often on whatever scrap of paper I could find in my car— not realizing at the time that I would later be encouraged by the group's leaders to write a book on the family that continues to be the core of this dance. This note-taking, and more importantly, participation in the dance led me to an understanding of the dance on a spiritually deeper level than I had anticipated. It also facilitated my understanding of compromises made within the troupe that occurred when tradition was altered—to varying degrees—in the interest of sustaining the vitality, and therefore, the continuity, of the *danza*. In this book, I contrast these compromises with concessions initiated by institutions outside the troupe, especially after an unforeseen situation arose, setting into motion a series of equally unexpected events. I discuss the deleterious effect of those compromises and events on our dance traditions. And consequently, I am forced to explain my troupe's authenticity in that context, those unforeseen circumstances that arose and that I had not anticipated in the least.

Molly Aguilar, as I soon learned, was a niece and goddaughter of the late Pablo Olivares Sr., a native of Monterrey who began a *danza de matachines* troupe as a teenager. As a child in the late 1970s, Molly, her siblings,

Pablo Olivares in Monterrey, Mexico, plays an *arco* and *sonaja* (rattle) while dancing. His sister, Janie, a *Malinche*, at his side plays a *sonaja*. Middle–late 1960s. Photo courtesy of Amalia Aguilar.

and cousins learned the *danza de matachines* from her uncle after he immigrated to San Antonio. Later, as an adult, she undertook the coordination of the group with the assistance of her husband Antonio, known to his family as "Tony." The rootedness of her familial lineage in its ancestral traditions provided me with my core experience as a *matachín*. It has been an experience that, among other things, has led me to understand aspects of the dance in larger society.

Acknowledgments

I would like to thank all members of the Aguilar and Olivares families who have danced in La Danza Guadalupana de Pablo Olivares Sr. They welcomed me into their ranks and counted me as family. However, I would especially like to thank Molly (Amalia) Aguilar, Tony (Antonio) Aguilar, Pablo Olivares Jr., and Manuel Aguilar. I am honored by and indebted to their generosity and *confianza* (trust). I have been greatly humbled by the kindness with which they have taught me about the *danza* (dance) on so many important levels. It is my great hope to have done well by them in this endeavor. I should also thank all the family for their patience, as I have taken much longer in writing this book than I expected. Molly's mother, the late Francisca Olivares Aguilar, inspired and encouraged me with her strong presence and the enthusiasm she showed in contributing her thoughts to this book. She passed away in 2015 and is sorely missed by all.

I owe an enormous debt of gratitude to Margaret Greco who—without even intending to do so—has sharpened my skills as a documenter and researcher. Her example as a highly ethical ethnographer, academic, and educator has been invaluable and figures significantly into these pages. Her exceptional experiences, research, insights, and perception gave me much badly needed organization in writing this book. I thank her for her sometimes simple and always profoundly important suggestions, reminders, and photographs. In addition, her own ongoing research concerning cultural autonomy and resilience has given me insights that have found their way into these pages. It should be noted that, because her work has dealt with resilience and art in Chicano communities, our respective works have paralleled each other, and I have been able to find ways to articulate my experiences by referring to the knowledge base she has accrued in her research trajectory, which is much longer than mine.

As well, I owe a humbling debt to Dr. Megan Biesele who took time away from her profoundly important projects to read and give critical feedback on this book. She brings not only decades of anthropological research to this endeavor but also insights gleaned from continuous fieldwork in ritual dance.

Many thanks are owed to Stephanie Yearwood whose suggestions were so helpful in articulating my ideas in succinct, clearer ways than I would have otherwise. Her ideas were at once helpful and heartening because they reflected an understanding on her part of things I was trying to say yet knew better ways for me to say them. The fact that she so readily grasped my insights despite being new to the *danza de matachines* has not been lost on me.

Undoubtedly, I would be remiss to not thank Professor Joseph de León, the curator of archives for the Old Spanish Missions of San Antonio housed at Our Lady of the Lake University. With professional efficiency, he responded to my research-related requests and questions. He also patiently waited without complaint when I took longer in finishing a translation project I promised him, due to the attention that this book demanded.

I will be ever grateful to my mother Rose Botello who passed away peacefully and suddenly as this book entered its final stages. She enthusiastically supported my membership in La Danza Guadalupana de Pablo Olivares Sr. And her memory and example as a friend and scholar have been an added inspiration for me to finish this endeavor.

Por último, le debo gracias a La Virgen de Guadalupe.

We Dance for the Virgen

1

Introduction

Encountering the Dance

The *danza de matachines* is a Spanish-colonial-era dance, versions of which vary as widely as they range geographically. This dance, "can be found as far afield as Mexico, Guatemala, El Salvador, Colombia, Perú, Bolivia, Ecuador, Paraguay, Chile, Brazil, New Mexico, Puerto Rico, the Philippines, and south India" (Harris 2000, 18). As for possible pre-Spanish-colonial-era origins, Moreno (2005, 17) notes that scholarly writings about this dance emphasize what they identify as New World influences and origins as opposed to ones of the Old World. Tony Aguilar has on occasion referred to it as "Indian dance" and has referenced archaeological sites in central Mexico. One thing is clear: When Bernal Díaz del Castillo accompanied Hernán Cortés as a soldier under his command, he observed "a large amount" of dancers at the service of "the great Montezuma" and wrote that these dancers *resembled matachines* (emphasis added)" and inhabited a neighborhood in the Aztec capital dedicated to dance (Díaz del Castillo 1994, 170). This observation suggests that dancers called *matachines* did exist in the New World and that their dance occupied an important role in the realm of the Aztecs. For lack of a Spanish term describing what the Aztecs were dancing, the word *matachines* may have been used by default. But my intention here is not so much to take a definitive stand on the scholarly debate about whether the dance originated in Europe or America but to establish an idea of how old it is for the reader.

While I make sure to demonstrate appropriate rigor regarding pertinent historical and cultural authorities relevant to the *danza de matachines*,
more importantly, I establish my own cultural authority. I do this by establishing my cultural authority on the *danza de matachines* itself. Cultural
authority in the dance means coming from a place of authenticity. It also
means having grown up with experiences and associations directly related
to certain geographical and cultural phenomena (in this case, the *danza
de matachines*). Lacking authenticity precludes cultural authority. During
the thirteen years spent writing this book, I danced in a troupe that was
composed mostly of members of the Aguilar family. The Aguilar family
not only taught the me the dance steps but that they did so while continuing their *danza*'s tradition since its initiation by Pablo Olivares Sr. Equally
important is that Molly and other close relatives of the troupe's founder
shared with me what they knew about the background of the steps and
their dance's history. I became one of the troupe's core dancers, practicing
during the many times when there were only five of us dancing in temperatures well into the 90s. Molly and Tony asked me to accompany them
in representing La Danza Guadalupana de Pablo Olivares Sr. in meetings
with other *danzas*, and, because of my dedication, they entrusted me with
the high-ranking role of *monarca* (Moctezuma II). Through this process of
active participation I became one of the legitimate carriers of the dance's
lineage, traditions, and of the iterations of this family-based *danza de
matachines* troupe. Our *danza*'s lineage, traditions, and iterations, rooted
in central, Spanish colonial Mexico, have their own authority and authenticity, which do not require validation by academic study.

When I began to dance, I knew that my technical skills as a dancer would
improve over time. However, I did not realize how much my understanding of the *danza* would grow as well. In fact, I found that participation in
the dance increased my understanding of its significance, its structure, and
its origins. I also learned that there is an internal, private relationship to the
dance. From the beginning, my relationship to the dance began to mature.
That maturity caused me to place less importance on analytical thinking.
At the same time, I learned to place greater value on learning intuition and
to allow things (e.g., the dance) to act on their own accord. I learned to feel
the weight of responsibility of a leader, specifically Moctezuma II (cited
as Montezuma by some scholars) whom I represented in the *danza*. This
role was at once an incredible honor and a source of duty that was almost
too daunting for me. A series of dreams contributed significantly to my

profound sense of obligation. They began subsequent to my first seeing La Danza Guadalupana de Pablo Olivares Sr. Because of the impetus they have lent to my participation, I have included them in the chapter "Memoir of a *Monarca*."

Community and communities are an important part of understanding La Danza Guadalupana de Pablo Olivares Sr. and matachines troupes in general. This may be best illustrated when we dance outside Our Lady of Guadalupe Church in the heart of San Antonio's West Side. Its residents are mostly working-class Mexicans or of Mexican descent. Almost invariably people there demonstrate an immediate recognition and understanding of who matachines are and what our role is. Such indications could take the form of a smile, a nod, an impromptu blessing with the sign of the cross, or requests to kiss the standard we carry bearing the image of Our Lady of Guadalupe. Often, I have sensed that such devotees feel that the devotion expressed in our dancing is a vicarious expression of their own devotion. This is also the neighborhood where devotees respond in the greatest numbers to our invitation to dance before the *Virgen*. Although this is a geographic community, to me it is also a segment of the larger community of San Antonians for whom the *danza de matachines* has been a familiar part of their lives. Our troupe encounters them in working-class neighborhoods in San Antonio even though they may have grown up with the *danza* in other communities. This wider community of devotees of the *Virgen* is the one I refer to when I speak about community members.

Being Chicano and Catholic in San Antonio, I grew up exposed to and familiar with practices, traditions, and perspectives that allowed me to be comfortable as a *danzante* as well as highly respectful of this role. In addition, I was also fortunate that Molly Aguilar was so sincerely receptive to having people from outside her family join the *danza de matachines* group formed by her uncle years before. It has been a privilege to receive the amount of information and have the experience of dancing with La Danza Guadalupana de Pablo Olivares Sr. An onus of integrity accompanies this privilege. For example, I have received information about our *danza* that might prove educational to the reader but that is inappropriate for those who do not share our experiences and devotion. Such parameters are based on my concern for safeguarding the spiritual integrity of our *danza* and of those involved with it.

The catalyst for this book was simply that I felt strongly about documenting the *danza* and was quite happy when Molly and Tony welcomed the idea. However, it became the fulfillment of a *promesa* (promise). When I was much younger, my mother made and fulfilled a *promesa* to Nuestra Señora de San Juan de los Lagos. Her *promesa* inspired me to seek help from La Virgen de Guadalupe in the same way. Many years later, after I began dancing as a *matachín* and writing about it, I often reflected on the prior *promesa* I made. This reflection was inspired mostly by *danzantes* and other devotees of the *Virgen* who fulfilled *promesas* on her feast day. As a result, I eventually realized two things: (1) Although she granted the *promesa*, I had never fulfilled what I had promised to do, and (2) my intended act of gratitude was ill suited to her as it essentially involved the veneration of saints other than her. So, I began to interpret the unique position I found myself in, that is, that of a *matachín* and documentarian as an opportunity to fulfill that *promesa* made so long ago.

Scholastically minded readers may note a relative scarcity of direct quotes from "informants" in this book. There are a number of reasons for this. One of them is that I have no informants but only peers who came to accept me as family. Second, this is not an academic work.[1] Third, I entered the dance as a dancer and not a researcher. That is how the other dancers rightly viewed me. Eventually, Molly (who held the lineage), and I agreed that I should write a book about it. But even after we decided this book would be a good idea, my role as a dancer remained primary and *my priority*. My role as a documentarian was secondary to both myself and the other dancers. For this reason, I very seldom carried writing or recording implements into the field. There is one exception: The section of the book titled "Life History of the *Danza*: A Continuity" consists of a highly informative conversation between myself, Molly, her husband, and her mother.

Readers who are well read in the study of the *danza de matachines* and kindred cultural phenomena will note the lack of discussion on syncretism, that is, the argument that Indians of Mexico and their descendants have retained their belief in a pre-Spanish pantheon of entities or "gods" by disguising them with Catholic iconography. My reasons for sidestepping this discussion are simple. First, though theologians and other clerics may take this position and express concern that the *danza de matachines* is syncretic, it is a debate that I have never even heard mentioned among matachines, let alone engaged in by them. The church is concerned about it, but matachines and other devotees of the *Virgen* are not. Second, whenever significant attempts are made by the church to shift the focus or practices of the dance to be more Catholic, traditional matachines simply maneuver around these attempts objectively and seemingly out of habit, that is, virtually without giving it any conscious thought. Such discussion would distract from the reason for our organization into *danzas*: to dance for the *Virgen*. So, there is not even a need for matachines to be aware of it.

The purpose of this book is to examine the interplay between continuity and change in La Danza Guadalupana de Pablo Olivares Sr. More specifically, this book seeks to answer the question: To what extent—if any—can a family-based *danza de matachines* troupe remain resilient in the face of contemporary challenges? To find the answer, it will be crucial to see the effects of change on the *danza*'s traditions. It will be equally important for me to frequently refer to and discuss autonomy in relation to the *danza* and its traditions because resilience rests on autonomy. And, for that reason, change and continuity are determined by the extent to which autonomy can be exercised by *danza de matachines* troupes and their individual dancers. Because I found the local mass media to be a frequent contemporary challenge through its dissemination of inaccurate information about the *danza de matachines*, the latter half of this book examines the role of the dance in the realm of power structures that stood to benefit from such misinformation.

To address this book's question, I provide a historical analysis in the chapter titled "Histories Intertwined: Colonial Mexico, *La Virgen*, and San Antonio." As the title of this exploration implies, the history of the Spanish Colonial period in Mexico explains the devotion to La Virgen de Guadalupe that arose at that time in central Mexico and later spread. On this historical foundation, the reader will later be able to see the interplay between change and continuity. This chapter will clarify the social and religious origins of the *danza de matachines*. By understanding these origins, the reader can better appreciate the enduring nature of the *danza de matachines* over time and begin to grasp how a family-based *danza de matachines* troupe can continue its traditions in the face of contemporary challenges. Also, in this chapter, having established my cultural authority as a matachines dancer, I also establish it as a multigeneration San Antonian qualified to speak of the *danza de matachines* in San Antonio.

In "The Dance: What Happens and Why," I provide a detailed description of the different dancers, specifically their dress and accoutrements, and their roles in the story that the dance tells. This narrative notes departures from the commonly understood history of Mexico. It also discusses the *danza de matachines* as a form of prayer. Finally, experienced members of our *danza* share what constitutes an ideal dance for each of them. In this way, readers can better form an understanding of why we value its integrity. Through these explanations and descriptions of the dance, I explore the question of the aspects of the dance matachines most want to conserve. This section shows that such conversation contributes to the troupe's continuity amid pressure to conform to virtually unprecedented contemporary realities.

Since it is important to assess the effects of change on our traditions, I then present a life history of our *danza* using information provided by experienced members of La Danza Guadalupana de Pablo Olivares Sr. Titled "Life History of the *Danza*," this chapter is based on the verbatim transcription of a conversation with three key members of the troupe who shared some of their experiences, recollections, and family stories involving our dance. In this chapter, readers learn not only the roots of this family's *danza* but also see the different kinds of changes members of the troupe have experienced over the years and the circumstances in which they occurred. This history reveals the values, motives, and challenges of the troupe's *danzantes* after Pablo Olivares Sr. reestablished his *danza* in San Antonio, Texas, subsequent to having initiated it in Monterrey, Mexico. This chapter addresses the question of what values and conditions determine change and persistence of tradition in La Danza Guadalupana de Pablo Olivares Sr. and thus contribute to a fuller understanding of how a *danza de matachines* troupe like La Danza Guadalupana de Pablo Olivares Sr. maintains continuity despite contemporary challenges.

In "Memoir of a *Monarca*" I present my own motives, experiences, and spiritual understandings as a *matachín*. This chapter contains the type of information that usually involves a participant-observer who is almost invariably an outsider to the culture and who receives information from a native informant. However, in this book, and this chapter especially, I am in the unique position of being both writer and native to the culture. The *danza de matachines* has two major informational components that withhold information or allow it to be public. I will call them the private experience and the public expression. Formal study of the *danza de matachines* has focused on the latter. The private experience, on the other hand, deals with matachines' personal motives, personal experiences, and their relationship with the metaphysical world, the divine. My research of material—academic and not—has turned up nothing that deals with the private experience. Because of my singular position, I am able to offer private insights into the *danza*. This chapter provides real-life instances of how traditions in the *danza* are transmitted and the sources of spiritual inspiration and affirmation that contribute to continuity despite changes that have arisen since the Spanish Colonial period.

"Culmination of Authenticity" probes what factors might make our *danza de matachines* troupe authentic, assuming it can be considered so. This is important because a *danza* cannot be considered to have had continuity if it lacks authenticity. To ascertain whether or not we are authentic, I examine studies of Mesoamerican ritual practices ostensibly carried out as pro-Spanish spectacles. By doing this, I propose the possible existence of an undercurrent of persistent Mesoamerican ritual practices. In this chapter, I also assess the degrees of authenticity to be found among academics who have studied the *danza de matachines* by viewing them through the perspective of the experience I have accumulated as a *matachín*. By exploring the parameters of authenticity in these ways, I give the reader a better understanding of the characteristics that must be present in a *danza* for it to have continuity. This chapter also illustrates that there is a direct relationship between the authenticity of voice and the ability to write authentically about the *danza de matachines* tradition, including with regards to troupes' continuity into the twenty-first century.

In the chapter titled "Appropriation of the Pilgrimage: A Catholic Priest Dances around the Details," I narrate how an annual dance pilgrimage our troupe had organized became incrementally appropriated. It points out how agendas originating outside the *danza* led to concessions culminating in the pilgrimage's appropriation. Specific instances of such compromises illustrate how they undermined our traditions. This chapter clarifies the differences between changes to our dance traditions made by outside entities and those made within the troupe. I discuss the dynamics of internal change that *danza de matachines* troupes use and that contribute to their continuity as well as the continuity of regional *matachín* traditions.

In "Anatomy of an Appropriated Pilgrimage," I discuss autonomy and devotion in the dance pilgrimage. These were two elements which, by default, were targeted by the institutional systems and public figures as part of the process by which the dance pilgrimage was appropriated. This chapter also examines more closely the instances of appropriation during its sponsorship by the Old Spanish Missions of San Antonio, as its role in the appropriation relates particularly significantly to autonomy and devotion. A key part of this examination is how authentic matachines troupes responded to the appropriation in order to determine the extent to which their autonomy and devotion were affected.

Overall in this work, I present the reader with expository information about the matachines dance tradition. But, more importantly and more amply, I present views, expressions, and attitudes held by members of the Danza Guadalupana de Pablo Olivares Sr. I examine how these factors indicate that our troupe ultimately traces its spiritual and historical lineage to central and northern Mexico during the Spanish Colonial period. In fact, I assess the possibility that the very tools of continuity are themselves a legacy dating to the Spanish Colonial period.

When I refer to authenticity in the *danza de matachines*, I am referring to the characteristics of participation in dance troupe traditions that have familial lineage. Its members' associations with the dance have either arisen from such a familial lineage and/or have arisen in communities in which the *danza* is publicly and traditionally practiced as ritual. More importantly, authenticity in the dance means that its participants possess a perspective on their practice that is cyclical, metaphysical, and recognizes a transcendental aspect of the dance that occurs when dancers and community members open their hearts to the *Virgen*. There are certain characteristics that are generally shared among matachines troupes. A troupe's lack of a given characteristic does not necessarily mean a lack of authenticity, though authenticity may be weakened to the extent that such characteristics are missing. Examples of such characteristics may include dress or the representation of certain historical personages by members of the troupe. Although Mexican immigrant communities in San Antonio are too new to enjoy a trajectory of tradition as ample as their mostly northern Mexican communities-of-origin, the fact that these immigrants come from authentic experiences of the *danza de matachines* in those communities enables them to form authentic *danza de matachines* troupes in San Antonio.

2

Histories Intertwined

Colonial Mexico, *La Virgen*, and San Antonio

To begin to understand and appreciate the *danza de matachines* in general and La Danza Guadalupana de Pablo Olivares Sr., in particular, we must first consider its history: the early Spanish Colonial period in North America. At the time the Spanish arrived in present-day Mexico, the Aztecs exerted a dominant military presence in central Mexico. Consequently, initial enmity between the Spanish and the Tlaxcaltecan tribe turned into an alliance against the Aztecs. This alliance soon resulted in the military defeat of the Aztecs and the creation of New Spain. As a result, the Spanish gave elevated status to the Tlaxcaltecans (also referred to in the literature as Tlaxcalans and Tlaxcaltecas; I will be using Tlaxcaltecan). Elements of that tribe were assigned the role of furthering, in the collective mind of the Spanish, Spanish colonial rule. Subsequent to the end of significant Aztec military presence, religious phenomenon led to the conversion to Catholicism of members of the greater Indigenous population in unprecedented numbers. The postwar relationship that evolved between the Spanish and the Tlaxcaltecans, together with the spread of Catholicism throughout central Mexico, ultimately had the effect of spreading the *danza de matachines* being practiced beyond central Mexico into New Spain's northern reaches. La Danza Guadalupana de Pablo Olivares Sr. emerged centuries later as part of this tradition.

The Arrival of the Spanish

The rapid and dramatic colonization of New Spain contributed significantly to the spread of the many versions of the *danza de matachines* as it is known today, including that of La Danza Guadalupana de Pablo Olivares Sr. In 1519, Spanish soldiers under the command of Hernán Cortés landed on the coast of present-day Mexico, forming alliances with several Indian tribes, including the Tlaxcaltecans (Pohl and Robinson 2005, 12). In 1521, the Spaniards and Tlaxcaltecans attacked the Aztec Empire's capital of Tenochtitlan (Pohl and Robinson 2005, 13–14). According to Spanish records, the Aztec leader Moctezuma II (also referred to as Montezuma) was killed either by his people (according to Spanish accounts) or the Spanish (by native accounts) (Pohl and Robinson 2005, 132–36) and was then replaced by his successor Cuauhtémoc, who eventually surrendered to Cortés that same year (Pohl and Robinson 2005, 14).

These events, recorded by the Spanish and traditionally accepted and interpreted for significance by scholars, are, to varying degrees, contradicted, ignored, and/or narrated in the *danza de matachines*. Yet, they are also events scholars of the *danza de matachines* interpret as parts of a supposedly indisputable "conquest" in which the dance must be interpreted and otherwise understood. This perspective is a problematic one, as it gives greater importance to the presumed static condition of the "conquest" and its presumed representation in the dance rather than to ethno-historic readings of the Spanish Colonial period that resonate with the dance. The "conquest" interpretation of the dance by scholars also assumes it is shared by the dancers. In the latter half of this book, it will prove critical that the reader be aware of this dichotomy of historical perspectives as then I will describe instances of contemporary misrepresentation and exploitation of the *danza de matachines*. And, the most important event to know in relation to the *danza de matachines* is the apparitions of Our Lady of Guadalupe, known in Spanish as *La Virgen de Guadalupe*.

The Apparitions of *La Virgen de Guadalupe*

In early December 1531, a woman who came to be known throughout Mexico as *La Virgen de Guadalupe*, appeared to a Catholic Indian named Juan Diego as he traveled a wilderness path on his way to catechism. According to the chronicler Antonio Valeriano, she identified herself as "the ever perfect Holy Virgin Mary" and the one "privileged to be the mother of the most true God, of Ipalnemohuani, . . . Teyocoyani, . . . of Tloque Nahuaque, . . . of Ilhuicahua Tlaltipaque." She asked him to instruct his bishop, Fray don Juan de Zumárraga, to build a temple for her (Valeriano as cited in Guerrero 2008, 18). During the next few days, despite much difficulty, he met with the bishop, who regarded him with some suspicion. Juan Diego continued to encounter the *Virgen* during his errands, including a third apparition when he was given roses to take to the bishop. Because it was winter, and the ground of that area was rocky, the roses were meant to be a sign to the doubtful bishop of the authenticity of her apparitions (Valeriano as cited in Guerrero 2008, 46–47). Church records indicate that Juan Diego gathered the roses in his traditional cloak, called a *tilma*, and showed them to the bishop (Valeriano as cited in Guerrero 2008, 46).

At this point it was discovered that a large multicolored image of her had formed on the *tilma*, an event that was even more powerful than the presentation of the roses. Juan Diego was subsequently subjected to two days of questioning, with the archbishop as the presiding inquisition official (Guerrero 2008, 53, 56). Word of these events spread among the Indians, and in the wake of the news millions of Indians converted to Catholicism (Guerrero 2008, 62). Conflict related to the *Virgen*'s apparitions arose, though. By 1556, there existed an undeclared political schism of sorts in Mexico City. It was between clerics supporting devotion to the *Virgen* and those who viewed it as heretical, particularly the missionaries of the Franciscan order. This conflict may be best illustrated in the enmity that developed between Franciscan Fray Francisco de Bustamante and the Dominican archbishop of Mexico City Alonso de Montúfor. From the pulpit, Bustamante called on royal officials to prescribe two hundred lashes to individuals he thought conspired to have fabricated the story of the *Virgen*. Moreover, he criticized the archbishop for his more accommodating views on the matter. This public conflict fizzled out among clergy (Matovina 2005, 1–2). This theological conflict involved clerics, and devotees to the *Virgen* were not participants in it.

This series of events constitutes the historical and religious context within which the *danza de matachines* tradition formed, and the story of the *Virgen*'s apparitions are retold in the steps, regalia, and roles of all varieties of the dance, including that of La Danza Guadalupana de Pablo Olivares Sr. To understand how this dance found its way from central to northern New Spain, eventually spreading to contemporary Texas, one must consider the

Spanish government's motives for sending the Tlaxcaltecans to that region as well as how the Tlaxcaltecans viewed their religious dance.

The New Spain Settlements and the Tlaxcaltecans

Curcio-Nagy observes that subsequent to the aforementioned wave of conversion, Spanish officials in New Spain came to use "persuasion through music, dance, and public display, rather than the blasts of muskets," in an "effort to maintain control of a newly acquired empire" (as cited in Moreno 2005, 30). Clearly, the Spanish believed these arts were on par with weaponry as tools of asserting dominance. Moreover, Lea notes that dance came to be used "as a medium of instruction" for conversion to Christianity (as cited in Moreno 2005, 30). Champe found a similar practice by the Order of St. Francis, which introduced dances and fiestas (feast days) in honor of Christian saints to, "replace the worship of Aztec deities" (as cited in Moreno 2005, 30). Champe also takes the position that the purpose of dancers taking on the role of Moctezuma II was to show the population his "conversion" to Christianity and in that way, presumably, tout its superiority over the religion of the Aztecs (as cited in Moreno 2005, 30).

It is important to note certain cultural attributes possessed by the Tlaxcaltecans and gleaned from the historical record to understand the role they would ultimately play in retaining, to a significant degree, their cultural and political autonomy. These attributes are assertiveness, independence, and diplomacy. It is also important to consider their geo-cultural relationship to the Aztecs in order to ultimately understand the portrayal of Aztecs in the *danza de matachines*. Like other cultural groups in central Mexico at the time of the Spanish Colonial period, the Tlaxcaltecans were often referred to as Aztecs and in fact shared the same Nahuatl language and other cultural characteristics though they "retained a separate ethnic identity" (Martinez 2004, 30). Jones observes that in 1591:

> The Indian pueblo of San Esteban de Nueva Tlaxcala was officially established in the immediate vicinity of Santiago de Saltillo, but as an entirely separate community. This settlement was part of a plan developed by Viceroy Luis de Velasco II and don Gregorio Nanciaceno, chief of the Tlaxcalan Republic in central New Spain, to move four hundred married men and their families to the northern frontier. These Tlaxcaltecans were to settle various designated points to induce the wilder northern Indian

nations to accept the Spaniards and to establish pacified communities. King Philip II of Spain approved the *capitulación* (contract agreement) with the Tlaxcaltecans, granting them excessive privileges in return for their settlement. They were considered *caballeros* and *hidalgos* (gentlemen and noblemen), permitted to use the title of Don before their given names, authorized to ride horses, and to carry firearms. Furthermore, they were exempt from all tribute to personal services. They were given land to work and had their own council from which all Spaniards and other Indians were excluded. (Jones 1979, 22–23)

This was the group of Tlaxcaltecans with whom the danza moved north.

By December 12, 1748, "the people of Nuevo León had begun an annual celebration" in devotion to "the Virgin of Guadalupe, an occasion marked by vespers, a sermon, lighting of wax candles, processions, and public festivities (Jones 1979, 37). Such a tradition was bound to include the *danza de matachines*, as it was and continues to be public and festive as well as processional. Information provided by Juan Carlos Martínez (1996, 43) further lends support to this likelihood as he notes that, "The Tlaxcaltecans, who arrived to the region at the end of the seventeenth century . . . brought the *matachines* dances." In fact, Tlaxcaltecans of the Spanish Colonial period brought the *danza de matachines* as far north as present-day New Mexico (J. Pohl, personal communication, September 16, 2014).

The New Spain civil community of San Luis was established to later become Nuestra Señora de Monterrey in 1596 (Jones 1979, 33). It was one of a number of Tlaxcaltecan settlements in Nuevo León (Jones 1979, 20). The Spaniards' Tlaxcaltecan allies brought with them their traditional celebrations and dances including that of *la danza de matachines* (Martínez 1996, 43). At this time, it was the policy of the marquis to populate the northeastern reaches of New Spain with Tlaxcaltecan families for the purposes of defense against the "wild northern Indian nations" of that region (Jones 1979, 22–23). This was also true in New Spain's northern provinces where royal officials also wanted them to "serve as an example to the Chichimecas and other nomadic groups" (Martinez 2004, 29). So, the colonization of northern New Spain with Tlaxcaltecans in the sixteenth century led to the *danza de matachines* as it was being danced in twentieth-century Monterrey, Nuevo León, where the late Pablo Olivares Sr. started his *danza de matachines* troupe.

The Ancestry of the Dance and My Ancestry in Béxar

Eventually northern New Spain became northeastern Mexico and later Texas and the United States. By the late 1800s, Mexican immigrant communities began to join the Spanish-speaking communities that had been in Texas for over a century. Their residents were often drawn to certain industries such as coal mining in Webb County and the quarrying of limestone in San Antonio. Just as the Tlaxcaltecans brought the *danza de matachines* to northeastern New Spain during the Spanish Colonial period, their descendants now brought it farther north into south Texas. Immigrant communities multiplied and grew over the years and generated American-born residents who continued many of the cultural practices of their ancestors. Catholic churches often served as social centers for these communities. With communities as cohesive as these, it has been relatively common to introduce and sustain seasonal traditions originating in Mexico, including *la danza de matachines*. Successive generations have been able to keep the *danza* alive in Texas, mostly as parish-based troupes.

But returning to the history of the events surrounding the rise of the dance and its migration north, I should say that these are not only historical memories enfolded in La Danza Guadalupana de Pablo Olivares Sr. Rather, they are also ancestral memories that vibrate within the dance. And my own cultural authority as a seventh-generation San Antonian, with the inherited perspectives and values that come with it, has allowed me to perceive the authenticity and intuit the ancestral memory in our *danza*, a *danza* that has come to San Antonio from Mexico. Just as it is important for the reader to know the historical context of the *danza*, it will be helpful to know historical details about my ancestry to establish my cultural authority and to understand how my place-based sense of identity and my awareness of my ancestral history facilitates the intuition I have of the *danza*.

A *Testimonio de Diligencias* (or Testimony of Proceedings, my translation) dated November 13, 1730 (https://cida-sa.org/list-of-families/), shows that two of the Canary Islanders from whom I am directly descended passed through Cuautitlán, Mexico, en route to present-day San Antonio: don Francisco Joseph de Arocha and doña Juana Martínez Curbelo Umpierre. They were from the Islas Canarias (Canary Islands) of La Palma and Lanzarote. Cuautitlán was the province where Juan Diego had lived (Anderson and Chávez 2009, 5). The testimony taken that day described don Joseph as: "twenty-seven years of age, tall, long face, brown eyes, dark complexion, meeting eyebrows, thick beard, thin nose, black hair." The same document described his wife, doña Juana Martínez Curbelo Umpierre, as: "fourteen years of age, full-faced, dark complexion, brown eyes, black hair and eyebrows, flat nose." They arrived with fifteen other families from the Islas and would have eleven children after their arrival. They arrived in the Villa de San Fernando de Béxar (present-day San Antonio) on March 9, 1731 ("List of Canary Islanders" 2014). Francisco Joseph de Arocha—soon to become known as don José—became Villa's first notary public and council clerk (Cruz 1988, 74; Hinojosa and Poyo 1991, 53–54). His eldest son, Simón, held a number of administrative positions in local government, including mayor, in addition to being a lieutenant in the provincial militia he commanded (Jackson 2014, 14–15). One of don Joseph and doña Juana's grandchildren was María del Carmen Calvillo. Though born in the Villa de San Fernando de Béxar, she became the owner of an outpost called Rancho de las Cabras (or the Goat Ranch), near the present-day town of Floresville, Texas. At the outpost, she oversaw the raising of livestock for the Mission San Francisco de la Espada community (Gibson 2002).

In the same way that the Spanish Crown had granted the Tlaxcaltecans the status of *hidalgos*, or noblemen, in exchange for helping to populate the frontier in the name of Spain, so the Crown now granted that status to the Canary Islanders. They are often credited for building San Fernando Cathedral. Yet, the Bexar Archives contain an untitled 1745 municipal ordinance issued by then mayor Antonio Rodríguez Mederos requiring residents to participate in the construction of the church that is now San Fernando Cathedral every Sunday after the high mass. It was an ordinance written after a request for volunteer labor proved uninspiring. Failure to comply resulted in a fine of 25 pesos and fifteen days' jail time (Rodríguez Mederos 1745). Ten years earlier, don Joseph Arocha was in jail with three other Canary Islanders for ignoring another ordinance, this one concerning the maintenance of fences meant to keep livestock out of a common area (Juan Leal Gorás 1735). In 1778, Friar Augustín Morfi visited and in his diary bemoaned that Canary Islanders had all but completely taken over the civil government. He added, "They are indolent and given to vice, and do not deserve the blessings of the land" (Morfi 1973, 43–44). The Morfi document had been an assigned reading for me as an undergraduate. It was the first of a series of indications—I would find—that the settlers from the Canary Islands were thorns in the sides of the church, the military, and the Spanish settlers. Gilbert Cruz (1988, 80) strengthens this perception by writing, "at times the viceroy considered some of their demands impertinent." Considering that the incremental conquest of their African archipelago had been completed by the Spanish Catholic monarchs only in 1496 (Fernández-Armesto 1987, 212), it is not surprising that they did not possess any special affinity for Spanish law. In this sense, they shared the Tlaxcaltecans' ambivalent attitude about being noble Spanish subjects.

For me the vagaries of doing things like visiting San Fernando Cathedral throughout my life added to my sense of ancestry and continuity in San Antonio, especially when I became old enough to grasp that it had been built through the efforts of my Canary Islander ancestors. I attended mass with my family, lit candles, and played guitar in its youth choir with this awareness. The late afternoon sun had a way of shining into the cathedral's dim recesses and onto its roughly hewn limestone pillars bridging past centuries with the moment. I studied the wrought iron hat clasps that lined the back of each pew, reminding me of the days when men wore hats due to greater exposure to the weather but removed them inside churches. The Botellos' and the Arochas' lineages merged when my second great-grandfather Prudencio Botello married my second great-grandmother Lucinda Arocha. Lucinda's paternal second great-grandparents were Ysidra Séguin[1] and Antonio Arocha. Ysidra's mother was Paula Ortiz. Paula's biological father was a farmer named Juan Manuel Séguin, and her parents were Felipe and María Ysarabel Ortiz. Since the Ortizes lived on Mission Concepción's recently secularized agricultural lands, an ethnohistoric interpretation of these familial relationships suggests that Paula Ortiz and her parents were *Yndios* who had been assimilated into mission life.

According to church records, I am also descended from a Mexican-born soldier of French parentage named Bartolomé Séguin who garrisoned with the Spanish Army at the Plaza de Armas in downtown San Antonio (then the Presidio of San Fernando) in the 1700s. He was also an ancestor of the Alamo courier and cavalry company leader Juan Nepomuceno Séguin. As a child, I had seen sensationalistic pen and ink renderings of him and Antonio Cruz y Arocha riding from the Alamo with a Mexican patrol in pursuit, flintlock pistols blazing. (Séguin later said they actually crawled through the brush.) Cruz y Arocha, like myself, had descended from the same aforementioned Arocha couple who came to the Villa de Béxar in 1731.

Those ancestors were on my father's side of the family, but my mother's side of the family also has deep roots in San Antonio. She grew up within a stone's throw of Alazán Creek where, in June 1813, her third great-grandfather Colonel Ignacio Elizondo camped with 1,050 troops under his command. There, three leagues west of San Antonio, he ordered the surrender of the Republican Army under José Lara and the Bostonian Augustus Magee (Thonhoff 2016). The rebels refused and then routed his troops. But two months later he led a cavalry division against them while participating in the Battle of Medina, which was a victory for the Spanish loyalists (Thonhoff 2016). Two years before that, he and his troops had captured Fray Miguel Hidalgo y Costilla, known as "the father of Mexican Independence" (Almaraz 1995–96, 455).

But I was also aware of local and family *lore*, which also gave me a heightened sense of place and identity. The stories have been about things such as the old San Fernando *camposanto* (graveyard), the presence of nomadic Indians, floods, and supernatural happenings. So, I grew up with a profound awareness that I had many generations of ancestral bones lying beneath San Antonio's dark, fertile soil. It was a palpable awareness that was more than intellectual. It was akin to feeling another person's presence in a nearby room. I had a strong sense of being connected to them spiritually, a sense that our life purposes were somehow connected and part of a meaningful series. Whenever my parents or other older Chicanos spoke of the missions and the descendants of their residents, I knew that they spoke with knowledge informed by some 250 years of oral tradition. This awareness of my ancestry made me aware of and sensitive to the idea of ancestry and lineage in La Danza Guadalupana de Pablo Olivares Sr.

Partly because of geography and partly because of my ethnic-religious background, I came to the *danza de matachines* already having some familiarity with expressions of devotion to *La Virgen de Guadalupe*. I grew up in San Antonio, with the mostly Chicano and mostly nominally Catholic West Side figuring significantly into my formative years. So, I knew that devotion to the *Virgen* was especially widespread there. One of my grandfathers had a longtime next-door neighbor known as Mamá Márquez. Her family and ours were virtually melded. She had a *capilla* or shrine to the Virgen de Guadalupe at the end of her gravel driveway. Every December, in observance of the prominence the *Virgen* enjoys from her feast day on December 12 to *el Día de los Reyes Magos* (The Day of the Three Kings), her shrine was decorated with brightly colored lights. One of my sisters, inspired partly by this example and partly by a picture book about the *Virgen* that she checked out from our grade school library, enlisted my help in attempting to build such a shrine in our backyard. When the chalky limestones fell through the chain link fence that was supposed to be the shrine's main structural support, we realized we would have to settle for the framed *Virgen*'s image we had in the house. Some twenty years earlier, that picture had been clipped from a calendar, the kind that small businesses give away as a form of advertising.

About a year later, my older brother and I rode double on his bike about a mile west of our home to Oblate School of Theology. He had recently been there for the first time and wanted me to see its sprawling, peaceful grounds. At one point, he took me up some stairs that led to the back of an imitation Lourdes Grotto enshrouded in oak foliage. At the top of the stairs was a large, tile mosaic rendering of *La Virgen de Guadalupe*. We stood there for a moment staring at the *Virgen*. My brother did not attempt to explain to me the importance of this image or this isolated place, but I sensed it. This is how knowledge of the sacred among traditional cultures is conveyed; it is done indirectly. It is intuited.

Some months later I accompanied my mother on a visit to Our Lady of Guadalupe Church on the West Side. It was my first time there. The church was empty, but there were hundreds of lit votive candles that filled the sanctuary where a large picture of *La Virgen de Guadalupe* hung facing the rest of the church's interior. I had never seen so many candles. I was used to seeing them on much smaller, neatly held racks in parts of the church that were much less conspicuous. I deduced that this church was some kind of nucleus to which all the churches in San Antonio were connected. It was, I thought in my child's mind, the mother of all churches. But it was not just the candles themselves but a sense of solemnity rooted in the awareness that hundreds of people had entered the church to light them. And though my mother did not speak a word about the church, I felt an un-nameable spirit there that I had never felt in any other parish church.

Decades later, as an adult, I became a member of that parish. The candles no longer filled the sanctuary but were kept in alcoves on either side of it. During mass, it was common for men and women to enter the church, sometimes with children in tow, to light a candle. They were virtually oblivious to the mass being said or the people in the church while they lit their candles and knelt to pray. I had seen nothing like it in the other churches of north-central San Antonio. Yet, rather than dismissing those visits as the actions of people unschooled in church etiquette, I sensed that these devotees of the *Virgen* knew something I did not and that they were acting on it.

One day during mass, the pastor announced that there would be training for a parish-based *danza de matachines* troupe later that afternoon in the parking lot behind the church. I had seen matachines dancing outside the church on the night before and day of the feast day of *La Virgen de Guadalupe*. I could hear their drumming from my residence a short distance from the church. I felt somehow called to dance as a *matachín*, so I showed up for practice. When I did, I saw a single file of small boys dancing to the drumming of a *norteño* (man from northern Mexico) wearing a cowboy hat. He was apparently teaching them. I was much older and much taller than even their teacher, so I pretended that I was merely cutting across the parking lot and kept walking. I was far too embarrassed to ask to join this troupe that was obviously meant for elementary-school-aged children. Later, when I mentioned that incident to the pastor, he spoke about the vetting process he had in place for matachines teachers and organizers. Specifically, he said that without a background check, the church could wind up with a "cult" on its hands. At the time, I did not understand what he meant. If any cults were ever formed in a Catholic church, I figured I would have known about it. I did not yet understand that his statement came from the long-standing suspicion held by some clergy of matachines in which they often feel apprehensive about the autonomy of matachines. I gave it no more thought. In a few more years, though, I would be dancing in La Danza Guadalupana de Pablo Olivares Sr. My experiences in that *danza* would gradually enable me to identify with the devotees of the *Virgen* who would walk in to light votive candles to her almost as if nothing else mattered.

In this chapter I have presented the historical context in which devotion of the *Virgen* came into being. As well, I have presented some early history of my childhood devotion to her. The larger historical context is important because it allows the reader to perceive the social and religious factors that contribute to the continuation of the *danza de matachines* tradition among troupes. More specifically, it places La Danza Guadalupana de Pablo Olivares Sr. in a larger historical context and in that way enables the reader to begin to understand the cultural trajectory in which it was formed and has been sustained.

Whereas presenting a larger historical context of the dance allows the reader to understand broad forces that have contributed to the continuity of the *danza* to the point of the formation of La Danza Guadalupana de Pablo Sr., the presentation of my ancestry does two things. It illustrates the ways personal devotion to the *Virgen*—including in the realm of the *danza de matachines*—has been successively passed from one generation to the next. These ways have included the existence of stable communities that shared this devotion and served as fertile grounds for the continuity of her traditions. They have also included intuition via nonverbal cues communicated from older family and community members to the younger. In addition, by presenting my ancestral presence in present-day San Antonio, I have begun to establish the cultural authority that should be expected of one who is to answer the question I have posed in this book.

This recounting of the history of the dance shows that it was met with an array of changes that were opportunities for continuation. When the Tlaxcaltecans reached northeastern New Spain, they found that the environment was different. So, the availability of materials for making *trajes*[2] (suits), such as specific bird feathers and river reed for example, was bound to have changed. And when communities of devotees were formed in Texas, there must have been a need to deal with the misgivings of clergy unfamiliar with the *danza* and its devotion to the *Virgen*. The momentum and trajectory of the tradition was so great, though, that it even spread to San Antonio where it displaced the devotion of Nuestra Señora de la Candelaria who had been the patroness of San Fernando Cathedral since the mid-1700s, due to the influence of the Canary Islander community that brought her devotion with them. This historical transmission of *La Virgen de Guadalupe*'s devotion intertwines with my ancestral history in San Antonio. Despite having comparatively fewer ancestral roots in northern Mexico than other San Antonians, my ancestors and older members of my family grew up with devotion to the *Virgen* as a part of the spiritual landscape shared with the larger Mexican immigrant population and generations of their descendants. And despite often attending mass at San Fernando Cathedral, which was built by my Canary Islander ancestors, I did not even know who Nuestra Señora de la Candelaria was while growing up. Even though there was a life-size effigy of the Canary Islander patroness at the cathedral, I was much better acquainted with *La Virgen de Guadalupe* because of the intensity of devotion she receives among the Spanish-speaking communities in San Antonio. So, on the momentum and trajectory of her devotion, the *danza de matachines* traditions was able to continue and even spread. Pablo Olivares Sr. immigrated to San Antonio by the late 1970s, which was long after the arrival of even my more recently arrived ancestors. His reforming of his *danza de matachines* troupe in San

Antonio would ultimately lead to my experience as a *matachín* years after his untimely passing. It would also be one of a number of chapters in the history of the troupe. Each of those chapters would see both change and continuity.

3

The Dance

What Happens and Why

La Danza Guadalupana de Pablo Olivares Sr. follows a centuries-long trajectory of *danza* originating in New Spain and, quite plausibly, pre-Colonial Mexico. The family's specific lineage is rooted in the instruction of the late Pablo Olivares Sr., who formed a matachines troupe as a youth. Because this dance tells a story about Mexico in the Spanish Colonial period, its dancers assume the roles of specific historical figures of that time. I will describe those different roles played by the *danzantes* (dancers) in order for the reader to gain insight not only into how the earlier dancers might have viewed the relationships between those personages but how they viewed themselves in the context of that era. Understanding the narrative of the *danza* is also important for understanding the transcendental atmosphere that often characterizes the dance. As well, I will describe the accouterments and regalia we generally use and those specific to certain types of dances in order to illustrate the sense of tradition and continuity that contributes to this dance's authenticity. These two aspects of the dance lay further the groundwork for understanding the remarkable spiritual vitality and profound devotion found among the dancers who practice this tradition. Then, to give the reader a sense of the values that characterize the attitudes of myself and my fellow *danzantes* toward the dance, I will provide detailed statements by key *danzantes* describing the ideal *danza*. That part will be especially significant in understanding the intentions and perspectives the *danzantes* have traditionally held. From those intentions and perspectives may be gleaned insights into the world-view of Indigenous people who began this tradition in present-day Mexico.

There are six basic segments of the *danza de matachines* as danced by the Danza Guadalupana de Pablo Olivares Sr. The first is the procession into the space where we will be dancing. It is led by a *matachín* carrying aloft a banner bearing the image of *La Virgen de Guadalupe* called an *estandarte* or *manta*. The dancers are in their positions with the *monarca* front and center, the two *malinches* at his sides, and two *capitanes* at the front of the columns and two others at the back. When reaching the spot where the *estandarte* will be venerated, its bearer stops and turns to face the files of dancers. Molly signals the dancers to stop with a single drumbeat. After a count of about three seconds, she strikes the drum twice more, signaling everyone to bow in a kneeling position.

At this time Molly plays a tension-building drumroll, heightened by the dancers' *sonajas*. Through this rattling and drumming, one of the front *capitanes* gives the order for the dancers to spin clockwise by shouting, "*¡Vuelta a la derecha!*" In response, everyone spins to the right in a crouching position. Then the other front *capitán* shouts "*¡Vuelta pa' la macueca!*" to which everyone responds by spinning to the left in a crouching position. The same *capitán* then shouts for us to take steps backward by shouting, "*¡Pa'trás! ¡Pa'trás! ¡Pa'trás!*" until Molly's drumroll switches to the beat of the quasi-skipping step called *el corridito*. This change in beat signals the dancers to begin moving forward in procession and enter the space in which they will be dancing. During this time, *el corridito* may be danced at intervals with other steps or by itself, depending on the distance over which we must dance. If the distance is far enough, we will dance the *corridito* at intervals.

I will call the second segment the pre-*adoración* (adoration). During this time, the two files of *danzantes* move toward the banner bearing an image of the *Virgen*, the *estandarte*. Upon reaching the *estandarte* during the *corridito*, the *monarca* and *malinches* stop and slowly turn around while still dancing. At the same time, the two *capitanes*, while still leading their respective files, pass each other going briefly in opposite directions and then in a straight path away from the *estandarte*, with the two files having switched sides of the columns. Upon reaching a designated distance away from the *estandarte*, the drumbeat changes, and the dancers move in the direction of the *estandarte* again, now dancing to a step traditionally ordered by the *monarca*. This time, instead of passing each other in opposite directions, upon reaching the *estandarte,* the two front *capitanes* turn the two files inward before the *monarca* leads the dancing away from the *estandarte*, going in the direction from which they came. Each time the columns reaches the *estandarte* and the designated turning point, the *monarca* and *malinches* must take care to turn slowly before dancing away from it. The completion of their turning is meant to be timed with the front *capitanes'* dancing away from the *estandarte*. This is especially true when dancing the *corridito*. Then the front *capitanes* turn at right angles to each other, dance a few yards, and then dance to either the *estandarte* or the designated turning spot, depending on which one they are at. This takes time, so the *monarca* and *malinches* cannot turn around too quickly. The *malinches*, front *capitanes*, and the *monarca* form a row at the head of the columns; they should be aligned evenly in both their approach and departure from the *estandarte*. They should also be facing the same direction at the same time.

The third part is the *adoración* itself (also referred to as the *veneración* [veneration] and the *devoción* [devotion]). It begins when a drumroll signals the two files to face each other in a parallel manner with two to three meters of space in between. Then the *capitanes* dance one of fourteen steps other than the *corridito* from the far end of the files to the *estandarte* where they kneel or bow while crossing themselves or kissing the *Virgen* on the *estandarte*. These actions, while personal acts of devotion, also represent their historic recognition of *La Virgen de Guadalupe* and, therefore, conversion to Catholicism. When the *capitanes* bow, Molly's drumming suddenly stops while all the *danzantes* rattle their *sonajas* vigorously to underscore the importance of the moment. When Molly resumes her drumming, she plays the *corridito*, and beginning with dancers on the ends of the files farthest from the *estandarte*, the *capitanes* begin to escort matachines one by one to the *Virgen* for their individual veneration. After the *danzantes* venerate the *Virgen*, they take a position at the head of one of the files, and that file moves down a few feet until everyone has venerated. The *matachín* being escorted by the *capitanes* tells Molly which step they want to dance before advancing between the two files toward the *estandarte*. It is the step that the escorting *capitanes* dance as well. The dancers in the two files dance and play their *sonajas* and *arcos* while dancing that step in place.

During the *adoración* certain steps correspond to the decades (that is, series of ten Hail Marys) of the rosary. According to Molly, there are five specific steps that represent the prayer called The Our Father, which is prayed at the beginning of each decade of the rosary. The *corridito*, which is danced at intervals with other steps, traditionally represents the decades of the rosary. She notes that because the *adoración* is a danced version of the rosary, its duration is also approximately the same as that of a rosary. In total, there are eleven steps that represent eleven corresponding parts of the rosary. Basic steps such as *El borrachito, La hinca,* and *El dos* represent the beginning prayers of the rosary.

The fourth segment is the veneration by the *viejo*. This is when the *capitanes* chase *el viejo de la danza* (the old man of the dance) who, up to this point in the dance, has been taunting and intimidating the other matachines and anyone else present in order to distract them from the *Virgen*. He does his best to evade capture and persists in his outrageous behavior even while being pursued. Ultimately, the *capitanes* force him to bow in veneration before the *estandarte*. Then comes the fifth segment, the veneration by *la gente*. It begins with *el viejo de la danza* shouting, "*¡Toda la gente!*" It is a call for the devotees of the *Virgen* to venerate her. It consists of two of the *capitanes* escorting devotees, usually two by two, from one end of the columns to the *estandarte* to venerate the *Virgen* in the same way that the matachines did.

The sixth segment takes place after all the devotees of the *Virgen* have venerated her. That is when the columns unite before the *estandarte* as in the beginning of the *veneración* with Molly playing the same drumroll and series of signals, commands, and the dancers responding. If we are in a church, we then dance backward all the way out of the church. During my first year of dancing with the troupe, the conclusion involved the files facing the *manta* with the tension-building drumroll and rattling *sonajas*, stepping backward in stooped position, then advancing while dancers slowly straightened and raised their hands in the air, shouting staccato, coyote-like cries. Eventually, however, the conclusion came to consist of the two files dancing backward and away from the *estandarte*.

Roles

La Danza de Pablo Olivares Sr. consists of five types of dancers or *danzantes*: the *malinches, capitanes* (literally: captains), the *monarca* (the monarch or Moctezuma II), *el viejo de la danza* (the old man of the dance), and the line matachines, whom Molly and Tony call in English "the line dancers." Each dancer occupies a role within the *danza*, that is, each represents and dances as a personage in a narrative telling the story of *La Virgen de Guadalupe*. All *danzantes* have responsibilities that correspond to their role. These roles and responsibilities contribute to the telling of a history that departs from textbook versions of the period in Mexico known as "the conquest." That term assumes that the Indigenous peoples who militarily engaged the Spanish were humiliated, subjugated, and socially dominated and viewed themselves as such. Yet, the story told by the *danza de matachines*, as I have experienced it during my tenure as a *monarca*, is a history in its own right. It is also in this way that many Spanish-speaking devotees of the *Virgen* make palpable our awareness of a different reality, our reality.

The *Malinches*

The two *malinches* represent an Indian woman, also known as la Malinche. She was originally Malintzin. After being offered as one of twenty enslaved women to Hernán Cortés by a Mayan Lord (Díaz del Castillo 1994, 59), she was baptized as doña Marina (58). This "excellent woman," served as a translator for Hernán Cortés who understood only Spanish (58). She had a powerful presence and "absolutely ruled among the Indians in New Spain," (62). Lea writes that, since Mexican matachines contained no Malinche figure, she was introduced to the dance "as a symbol of Christianity" since she was one of the first converts (Lea 1963–64, 9).

In popular history, she has been ascribed the status of traitor of the Mexican Indians. And there has been a movement within academia driven by politically minded scholars who view la Malinche as being maligned by the historical record and, therefore, being in need of vindication through scholarship. In our *danza*, though, there is no questioning her honor. In the *adoración* (adoration) segment and in procession of La Danza Guadalupana de Pablo Olivares Sr., the *malinches* flank the *monarca* and often carry bouquets of roses to later place before the *Virgen* on her *estandarte*.

With their free hands, they play their *sonajas* (rattles). During my time as *monarca* of the group, almost all the *malinches*—if not all—have been from the family. They have included Molly, Carmen, who is married to Manuel (Molly's brother and *el viejo de la danza*), and Eunice, their daughter. Monique, one of Molly's nieces, has also danced as a Malinche.

The *malinches* wear sequined red skirts with green trim. A Mexican eagle, snake in its clutches as on the Mexican flag, adorns the front of the skirt. They also wear white, billowy blouses with wide bands of green and

A *Malinche* wearing the typical blouse and headwear of the *malinches* in our *danza* while dancing and playing a *sonaja* in our 2008 pilgrimage.

red lace that encircle the upper part of their blouses. In addition, they wear straw cowboy hats with the brims pinned to the crowns and decorated with red, white, and green ribbons, silver-dollar-sized pieces of mirrors, flowers, and red and green beads. On the *Virgen*'s feast day, they carry a bouquet of roses in one hand and play a *sonaja* (rattle) in the other. The rattling part of the *sonaja* is held below the fist, as this gives greater rhythmic control of the *sonaja*'s contents.

Because there was only one Malinche in the colonial history of Mexico, I was intrigued that there would be two of them in the dance. I inquired about this with Molly and Tony who referred me to Molly's mother. She responded saying, *"Es la tradición"* (That is the tradition). She then kindly referred me to her sister Juanita who had also been an original member of La Danza Guadalupana de Pablo Olivares Sr. She gave the same answer. While discussing this matter with a colleague who is Native American, she reminded me that this was in keeping with the seemingly contradictory nature that often characterizes how Indigenous people in North America view their environments, other peoples, and the unseen world. She was right. The pantheon of Aztec deities, for example, is replete with ones who possess dual characters. Two *malinches*, therefore, represent the dual nature of the historical Malinche: Indian leader and betrayer of Indians. Even the nobility associated with the "-zin" suffix of her birth name contradicts her status as a slave. Interestingly, she was also called by her Spanish name doña Marina by Bernal Díaz del Castillo in his firsthand narrative titled *Historia de la Conquista de Nueva España* (*History of the Conquest of New Spain*). And, although she begins her association with Cortés as a slave, she is revered widely by other Indians as a person of great importance, as a "*cacica*" (Indian leader) (Díaz del Castillo 1994, 62), the latter fact possibly accounting for the *malinches'* placement at the front of the line with the *monarca* in the Danza Guadalupana de Pablo Olivares Sr. Similarly, Max Harris (2000) photographed her being depicted by two girls in Teotitlán del Valle, Mexico. One was dressed as a Spanish doña Marina and the other as an Indian Malintzin (244). She is the same person with dual identities. Although these are dual identities, they are not in opposition to each other. Nor are they characterized by loyalty-based tension in that tradition or in our own troupe.

Interestingly, Tony once mentioned in passing—in response to someone's asking—that the *malinches* did not carry *arcos (bows and arrows)* when dancing because they are "neutral." Molly indicated that having two *malinches* brings balance to the two lines. She seemed to suggest that the rhythmic vibration of the dance, its energy, requires this balance. I find it of interest that they are located at the head of the files with the *monarca* and two of the *capitanes*, suggesting that they are leaders too and that, in their leadership capacity, they bring balance. In any case, I obviously cannot claim that the notion of dual-natured *malinches* is anything the Aguilar family thinks about. The suggestion from my informal experience, though, deserves to be further researched, perhaps by future scholars.

The Line Matachines

The line matachines make up the majority of the group. When the group is dancing in procession, it is in two files or "lines" that form a pair of columns. Often when we are lining up, a *danzante* of authority, like the *viejo* or a *capitán*, will arrange the dancers by assigning partners with whom the line matachines can mutually orient themselves by staying even with each other. However, it is the exclusive role and responsibility of the *viejo de la danza* to maintain order in the line from the time the dancing begins until

One of our line matachines dancing in the typical vest and *penacho* (headwear) of his rank. 2008.

it ends. This role is especially important during the *adoración* since it is the culminating ritual. But it is also important when dancing long distances because fatigue can threaten the orderliness of the lines.

These dancers wear a type of woven leather sandal from northern Mexico called a *huarache* and bright red flannel vests adorned with a sequined image of *La Virgen de Guadalupe* on the back and over a forest green shirt. Two ankle-length, apron-like flannel garments called *naguas* are worn, one on the front, and the other on the back. Their color matches that of the vests, and they feature the horizontal rows of short lengths of bamboo and/or river reed called *carrizo*. The lengths of reed and bamboo dangle with trade bells attached to them so that, as the *danzantes* move, so do they produce sound. These garments could be considered musical instruments. Depending on factors such as space and the collective level of training, the line dancers may also carry and play a percussive instru- ment called an *arco* or bow, resembling a bow and arrow. The headwear for the line matachines is the *penacho* (literally "crest"). It is a red, miter-like hat that has an arrangement of vertical red, white, and green dyed turkey feathers standing vertically along its top part. An image of the *Virgen* is on the front, and lengths of beads may dangle from the front, that is, against the dancer's brow. They have gold- and silver-colored trim and bits of mirror in circular and square shapes. The mirrors, Tony tells me, deflect the type of *mal de ojo* (evil eye) that can occur as a consequence of admiration.

El Viejo de la danza ("The Old Man of the Dance")

Manuel Aguilar has generally been the *viejo de la danza* during my participation. While not in his role, he is taciturn like me. But, when he does speak, his words and their meanings are clear as a trumpet blast. During practice, his suggestions to the dancers about the dance are always concise and compelling. In that sense, he reminds me of Francisca Aguilar, his late mother. Whenever he has come to practice to check on our dancing, he has worn faded blue jeans tucked into his brown work boots, a baseball cap, and sunglasses. His is a no-nonsense personality.

El viejo, as he is also known, attempts to distract the *danzantes* and prevent them from converting to the Catholicism of the *Virgen*. He carries a baby doll which dangles from the short length of a noose. It is smeared with fake blood and is wrapped in what appears to be a rabbit pelt, with the exception of its head. In his other hand, he brandishes a coiled bullwhip. During our *danzas*, he uses both to menace the devotees of the *Virgen* who have gathered. I once saw a *viejo* take a small, mischievous and playful boy from the crowd and throw him over his shoulder, ogre-like, and begin to stride away, evoking much laughter from those gathered. On another occasion, I saw another *viejo*, Manuel, gingerly helping an elderly woman step forward to participate in the *devoción*. When she stumbled and fell against him, he caught her then pretended to be dancing a polka with her, producing laughter from the woman and those standing nearby.

Manuel's *traje* is a button-up coverall, which is hard to tell because it is covered with hundreds of tattered strips of cloth about four inches in length of various colors. They seem to flow behind him as he darts about. His mother, Francisca O. Aguilar, made his *traje*. When Molly's father danced as a *viejo de la danza* in the 1970s, her paternal grandmother sewed each strip onto it individually. And she did so while following the tradition of saying a specific prayer as she sewed each one. She did this in one sitting. So, by the time she finished, I am told, she was exhausted.

Manuel Aguilar, *el viejo de la danza* (the old man of the dance), wearing his *traje* (suit) and carrying his menacing implements in the pilgrimage recognizing San Juan Diego. 2008.

Manuel also wears a ghoulish rubber mask. Yet, despite his menacing appearance, a beautiful image of the *Virgen* is sewn to the back of his *traje*. He also has the responsibility of correcting dancers who are dancing too far apart, too close together, or incorrectly. It is a responsibility that the *monarca* cannot fulfill because his position at the front of the columns prevents him from seeing that the line matachines are dancing. *El viejo de la danza* is the highest-ranking member of the *danza*. His antics come to an end during the *adoración* when the *capitanes* give him lively chase and eventually force him to surrender to the *Virgen*, though not before startling bystanders and ululating loudly. *El viejo*'s twin aspects define each other; he brings an element of chaos into the solemn space created by the stately presence of the matachines, the kingly countenance of the *monarca*, and the devotion exuded by the *malinches*. He acts randomly and unpredictably yet intervenes when order in the line begins to lag. Through this duality, he brings balance.

Francisca Aguilar spoke emphatically of how much stricter the *viejo de la danza* had been in the early days. Her husband Crecensio would crack the whip at the feet of the dancers, just short of striking their feet. She added that in more recent years her nephew used the coiled whip to space an elderly dancer named doña Juanita and herself in the line, which caused awkward moments for her. Doña Juanita was in her seventies. She also said a stick was being used at one point by the *viejo* to space dancers in the line. I observed this apparently revived practice in the latter part of 2011 when Pablo Olivares Jr. danced as *el viejo* at a *posadas* (dramatization of Mary's and Joseph's search for lodging) *danza* and brandished a stick about the length of a baseball bat.

Molly once introduced me to her Uncle Joe who, she told me, had been a "woman *viejo*." I thought this was an exciting bit of information because I had, until then, only known of such a role in the New Mexican matachines traditions with their *abuelo* and *abuela* (grandfather and grandmother) counterparts (Rodríguez 1996, 26). When more than one *viejo* is present, they will often clown about with each other, dancing, miming, and such, in addition to alternately frightening and engaging in hijinks with off-guard bystanders. He can also be compassionate. Molly notes that when small children become nervous about dancing for the first time, *el viejo* may approach them and, having caught their attention, will distract them by dancing backward while holding their gaze. *El viejo de la danza* requires specialized, lineage-based training. Pablo Olivares Sr. trained Molly's Uncle Luís and Crecensio, her father. They in turn trained Manuel and a number of other dancers with the expectation that they would continue in those roles when the older *viejos* withdrew from the dance.

The *Capitanes*

There were traditionally four *capitanes* in the Danza Guadalupana de Pablo Olivares Sr., one positioned at the head of each of the two lines of dancers, and another pair positioned at the very ends of those lines. However, during my years as a dancer in the troupe, there have been, for the most part, only two *capitanes*, and they have danced with the *monarca* at the head of the two columns. Molly and Tony have tended to assign these roles to their two sons Antonio and Ernesto, though Tony almost always dances as a *capitán*. They represent military leaders under Moctezuma II and are more or less comparable to generals. They help to maintain order in the columns.

The *capitanes* have the same *traje* as the line matachines, except that they wear a red flannel tunic-like top sometimes referred to as a *capa* or cape. It is

Two *capitanes* at the front of the two columns. Our Lady of Guadalupe Church. San Antonio, Texas. December 12, 2005.

worn like a poncho and comes down just a few inches past the waistline of the wearer. It has an image of the *Virgen* on the back and a sequined image of a Mexican eagle devouring a snake on a cactus on the front. They are bordered by the same green *barbilla* (fringe) that hangs from the bottom of the *naguas* and they happen to be much warmer than the vests worn by the line matachines. Like the *malinches*, the *capitanes* play *sonajas* but with their left hands. This is because the right hand is needed to draw the bowstring of the *arco* (bow), which is also held in the left hand. The *arco* is held with the left hand at the left hip (as opposed to pressed against the back as is quite common among other matachines groups). The arrow points downward and away at about a 90-degree angle. When the time comes in a measure for the *arco* to be played, it is swung upward quickly until the right hand can grasp the bowstring in front of the navel area. The beats are played with the arrow still pointing downward at the same angle. The index and middle fingers of the right hand release their grip on the *sonaja* and come across the abdominal region as the *arco* is brought to about the area of the navel. The string is pulled on and released rapidly one to four times, depending on the step. The release of the bowstring causes the arrow to strike the rim of a hole in the bow that it cannot pass through, producing a clave-like sound. Then the *arco* is returned to its original position at the hip until the beats are repeated in the next measure. The five steps in which the *arcos* are used are: *El dos, El cuatro, La hinca, and Ay amá,* and *El conejito.*

Interestingly, there is a portion of the *danza* in which the *capitanes*, despite having lower military status than the *monarca*, recognize and pay homage to *La Virgen de Guadalupe* by bowing to her image on the *estandarte*. They are followed by the *monarca* and then the other dancers. After all the dancers have converted to the devotion of the *Virgen* in this way, the *capitanes* then engage in the aforementioned lively, mock chase of *el viejo de la danza*. When he is finally captured by the *capitanes*, he, with resignation, allows himself to be brought before the *Virgen*'s image on the *estandarte* where he genuflects before her. The *capitanes* are the ones who, working in pairs, then escort individuals and pairs of the devotees of the *Virgen* from one end of the columns to the other where the *Virgen* on the *estandarte* awaits gestures of devotion in the form of a kiss, genuflection, or half genuflection.

El Monarca (Moctezuma II)

A kind of duality very similar to that of the *malinches* is noted by Sklar (2001, 61–62) in Tortugas, New Mexico, whereby the *monarca* represents both Juan Diego and Bishop Zumárraga. (I think I see this in the headwear worn by all the *danzantes* of La Danza Guadalupana de Pablo Olivares Sr., except for the headwear of the *malinches* and the *viejo de la danza*. It has both feathers, which presumably represent the Indian Juan Diego, and the roughly miter-shaped headwear that alludes to Bishop Zumárraga.) Though the *monarca* represents Moctezuma II, a figure who would be associated with defeat, his role in the *danza* is not a tragic one. He could easily be seen to possess the same dual nature as the *malinches*. His name has variations, depending on the historical record being accessed. They include Moctezuma, Montezuma, Moteczoma, Motecuhzoma, and Moteuczomah. It is a compound word made up of a noun meaning "lord" and a verb denoting "to frown in anger." Hence the interpretation of "He is one who frowns like a lord" (Andrews 2003, 599) or "he who is angry in a noble way" (Brinton 1890, 174). This dualistic nature would appear to be a contradiction of terms, at least in modern, Western thinking. It suggests compassion and wrath being simultaneously manifested.

As Moctezuma II led his people, so does the *monarca* lead the mata-chines from his position at the head of the two files. Therefore, it is import-ant for him to be continually aware of the immediate physical environment where the troupe is dancing. Wherever the *monarca* goes, so follow the matachines. They rely on him to lead them in such a way that the *danza* is in balance with the setting, be it the inside of a church hall or a plaza. It is also important and traditional that the *monarca* make decisions, including with regard to what steps are danced and when. The *monarca* has to be decisive. Manuel put it succinctly when he told me, "You're the *monarca*. You're the one who leads. You tell the people where you want to go."

La Danza Guadalupana de Pablo Olivares Sr. has a general protocol of passing through a progression of ranks, upward from matachines with the *monarca* being second only to the *viejo de la danza*. Such movement through the ranks depends on factors including, but not limited to, willingness and necessity for roles to be filled, and, most importantly, experience. I began as a standard bearer. During the 2006 season I danced as a line dancer only once. After that I began training as a *monarca* during our practices, and that con-tinued weekly from the spring until the beginning of the series of *danzas* extending from December 12, the Feast Day of Our Lady of Guadalupe, to January 6. That was the year I began to dance as *monarca*.

In later dances, I worried that I was appearing immodest by accepting the role of *monarca*, which I considered to be a role of honor in our *danza*. It also concerned me as *monarca*, paradoxically, that I was departing from the tradition of spending more time working one's way up the ranks before becoming a *monarca*. For those reasons, I occasionally danced as one of the *capitanes* instead. Soon, Molly assuaged these concerns with reassuring encouragement, including her report that one of her relatives reportedly spoke highly of my dancing. And as mentioned before, my many hours of practice, often in temperatures in the nineties, were seen as an indication of serious commitment to the *danza* noticed by Molly and Tony. Granted: It took me still more time to acquire the knowledge and familiarity with the *danza* that came with experience.

Francisca Aguilar, Molly's mother, designed my *traje de monarca* in the same way she did those worn by the *capitanes*. The only difference is that the *penacho* might be referred to as a *corona* (crown) in the context of use by the *monarca* because it means crown. *Penacho*, on the other hand, means crest. Like the *capitanes*, I also simultaneously play a *sonaja* and an *arco* to the rhythm of the drum.

The author as the *monarca*, wearing the *traje* (suit) typical of the *monarca* and *capitanes* in our troupe and carrying an *arco* (bow) while waiting to dance. 2015. Photo: Margaret Greco.

The Steps

La Danza Guadalupana de Pablo Olivares Sr. has many more dance steps than those listed below, but these are the ones used the most. This is partly because they are relatively less demanding and therefore can be danced by matachines in a wider range of ages and physical conditions.

1. *El corridito*. It is danced before and after each of the steps below.
2. *El oso* (The Bear) imitates a bear walking on its hind legs.
3. *El cuatro* (The Four) counts four beats per measure while bouncing lightly on one leg and tapping beats with the foot of a leg in front.
4. *La hinca* (The Genuflection) involves bowing at the end of a three-count measure then rising quickly enough for the next measure.

5. The Side-to-Side (also called *"Línea de la iglesia"* or "Church Line"). These steps involve the repeated merging and separation of the two columns of dancers.
6. *El dos* (The Two) is a two-count version of *el cuatro*.
7. *La ventura* (The Good Fortune) is a simple, stately, step whose high steps give the *carrizos* a chance to fly about and make extra music.
8. *El conejito* (The Bunny) imitates the steps of a rabbit.
9. *El borrachito* (The Little Drunk) imitates the steps of a drunk, with the head tipping from one side to the other.
10. *La fe* (The Faith) is *El borrachito* danced backward. We use it to end the *veneración* whenever we dance it in a church.
11. *El Pablito* (Pablito's Step) involves bowing at 45-degree angles to the line while counting the final beat of each measure by slapping the ball of the front foot on the ground.
12. *¡Ay amá!* (Oh, ma'!) Involves taking large steps at three beats per measure and leaping on the third to land facing one side of the line. At the end of the next measure, the dancers land facing the opposite direction from the last time.
13. *El brinquito* (The Hop) is a faster, more dramatic version of *La ventura*.
14. *El tornado* (The Tornado, also called "The Turn Around") involves dancers dramatically turning 180 degrees, with the *naguas*.
15. *La cruz* (The Cross) is similar to the Side-to-Side.
16. *La vuelta de paso* (The Return Step) involves stepping forward then back.

I will describe *el corridito* here because we use this step many times in every *danza*. When Molly taught me this step, I could tell it was very important to her that I dance it correctly. Two steps are made with the leading foot pointing diagonally outward at 45 degrees and the other one pointing straight ahead as the body follows the direction of the lead foot. Then the opposite foot leads, now taking the body forward and at 45 degrees toward the other side. Molly stressed the importance of my getting the diagonal part right because "we want the body to go diagonally." And this movement, she said, is accentuated by the *penachos* as the body turns, as long as the dancer keeps the head pointed in the same direction as the body is moving. She said that everyone needs to be stepping in the right direction at just the right time.

When she taught me the importance of this visual aspect, I remembered seeing the *corridito* danced many times by our group and could appreciate all the more Molly's firmly expressed concern that the body move in the right direction at the right time. When this happens, what you see are the two lines in their entireties virtually and simultaneously pivoting 45 degrees to the left of our direction and then 45 degrees to the right. It is very impressive to behold, and the sight of the feathers of the *penachos* pivoting in unison is very striking. The *penachos* point the way, as it were. And, by rhythmically dipping your head at the beginning of each measure, the momentum is created that allows you to press sideways from the back leg in such a way that there is no effort made by the front leg to move in that direction. This is because you're pushing your whole body with the back leg. And, because the soles of the feet rise no more than an inch above the ground, it's a fairly low impact dance step. It has to be because it is danced at intervals throughout the entire dance.

The *Danza* as Prayer

Very often devotees of the *Virgen* have asked us to dance for the alleviation of adversities besetting them. They ask that we do this in the same way that other Christians ask each other to pray for them. One reason for this is because to request something *of* the *Virgen* through dance is as much a form of prayer as dancing *for* the *Virgen*. Perhaps stationary prayer and danced prayer ultimately have communication with the sacred as a common factor. The only difference here would be that in the case of pre-Christian religions, divinity would be an aspect or aspects of nature. Another reason is that the time beginning with feast day of *La Virgen* through the Feast Day of the Epiphany is both an opportune time to fulfill *promesas* made to her and to request her aid. This is because the *Virgen* is especially powerful at this time, and dancing for her is a powerful form of prayer.

I feel presences in the dance that I could only describe as that of the *Virgen* and of ancestors. So, to me, praying through dance on behalf of someone else or for a personal petition is to place those prayers in that transcendental space and time created by the *danza*. I couldn't think of a better place for them. But in my experience, this form of prayer has no words. It's all in the intention. And, the intention is present even in practices. I think I can feel it building among the other *danzantes* while everyone is in the parking lot putting on their *trajes* before a *danza*. When Molly begins drumming before the lines, the intention truly begins for me, and it doesn't end until after the echoes of the final drumbeats have dissipated.

Views on What Makes a Good *Danza*

By asking fellow *danzantes* what they consider to be the elements of a good *danza*, and by reflecting on this as a *monarca*, I can approximate the essence of the dance for our group. Outside the *danza* I have perceived dance as entertainment and a folkloric tradition requiring technical and emotional execution. I anticipated that answers to "What makes a good *danza*?" would elicit a different type of answer for a different type of dance. I have not asked as many *danzantes* this question as I would have liked to, but the responses seem consistent and typical.

What Makes a Good *Danza* to Me (*Monarca*)

Gradually, perhaps as I gained more confidence in my ability to execute the dance steps, I became concerned with the integrity of the *danza* in two respects: the form and appropriate attitude among non-*matachín* attendees. Although my immediate concern was to dance the right steps at the right times and to lead correctly and with a haughty, kingly presence, I was also attentive to the order being maintained in the files, including our adherence to the instruction Molly, Manuel, and Tony had given us. I paid close attention to each detail and made every effort to dance each step exactly as it had been shown to me. Likewise, I was very aware when factors such as fatigue took their toll on the quality of the form, that is, attention to detail. However, since I was not a *viejo de la danza* whose responsibilities include actively correcting dancers, I would only make mental notes in case Tony or Molly asked for my opinion in this regard. (Reticence here may actually had been wise, since I began to learn the steps much later in life than the older dancers and might have been blind to my own shortcomings.) My concern for this aspect of the *danza* came from a desire to remain faithful to the steps as they were taught by Pablo Olivares Sr. By doing this, I hoped to respect his legacy. And I felt I should do so, given the privilege it is to dance in the group he formed so long ago. Moreover, and more importantly, I felt that by doing so I was participating in devotion to the *Virgen* in a way that was put into motion hundreds of years ago and that is still taking place over space and time.

With regard to the integrity of the group in front of its attendees, I expect the usual respect and recognition from the attendees for what is taking place when we are dancing. The vast majority of the times that we dance at a *posadas*, mass, or in a pilgrimage, the devotees of the *Virgen* who gather to participate with or otherwise pray with us are reverent, respectful, and appropriately joyful. Their appreciation of the *danza* has its basis in what it represents for them. However, on occasion I have been aware of individuals who, out of either ignorance or insolence, fail to regard our procession or our *adoración* with the right attention. On the other hand, it is expected and understandable that small children may pull loose from a parent's hand and run about the dance space or for the people whom *"el viejo"* accosts to laugh with surprise. That type of random activity is an integral part of the *danza*. But, when, for example, I have the sense that someone is excessively photographing or recording us for reasons that preclude respect for the moment, it is disappointing. That is because their inattentiveness to that moment subtracts from the collective attentiveness of the *gente* (people), that is, the devotees who are in attendance and who dance and kneel before the *manta* during the *adoración* because they understand what is taking place on a visceral level. So, to me the best *danzas* are when the best technical aspect is in order and when the attendees, who gather for the *danza*, have the right attentiveness.

When I dance, I feel as if I have been charged with preserving the integrity of our *danza*, its lineage. I feel I am actively serving as one of the many *danzantes*, spanning centuries, who sustain the lineage of this dance. To me, time and space, past and present, are merged into a single event that at once *is* happening and has happened and continues even when we stop. Ideally, what happens in the best *danzas* is the summoning of the transcendental and ethereal sense of the past not being the past. At those times *La Virgen de Guadalupe* is most present, and I feel the most humbled, excited, and honored to have my turn to be escorted by Tony and Antonio to the *estandarte* to bow before her.

What Makes a Good *Danza*: Molly (Drummer/Malinche)

She is physically diminutive but possesses a charisma that often makes her seem taller. She speaks with wide, guileless but powerful eyes that are set in her round face. Other features, such as her straight, dark hair, allude to indigenous ancestry rooted in central Mexico. Her ability to maintain straight posture while dancing and drumming may have been a by-product of her experience as a folkloric dancer.

When asked what made a good *danza* to her, Molly said that it was very hard to put into words but that it was an awareness of a spirit that occurs when all the *danzantes* in the group are synchronized spiritually and technically. She said it is a kind of spiritual feeling that spreads to all those in attendance. "It doesn't always happen," she said, "but, when it does, you know it." One instance of it being felt was at a *posadas* in which a daughter of the home-owner invited our group. There were many people present, including many evangelical Christians. Despite the differences of religions and potential for tension or discord, a considerable number of members of both religions were enthusiastically willing to participate in it. "Certain people got it, and others did not. So, it doesn't have to be that everyone gets it. . . . You can feel it from those people." She described it as feeling "like a bloom, something lifting up inside you." During such *danzas*, all the dancers are "in tune."

Molly also shared an anecdote: a woman approached her after one of our rituals and told her that she could feel the vibrations of the drumming and of the coordinated stomping of the dancers vibrating throughout her body. The woman said this was the way that the spirit of the dance was being communicated to her.

What Makes a Good *Danza*: Tony Aguilar (*Capitán*)

Tony has a voice and gaze that communicate almost constant optimism and groundedness. His speech is animated, but he is measured in his words and gestures. His eyes are piercing but bright and warm. They calmly assess situations—both immediate and abstract—and they look up at me over the rims of his glasses as he speaks and attentively listens. Like Molly, he possesses physical features that hint at central Mexican indigenous ancestry. He is dark, stout, and his bristling hair is black as is his stylish goatee. I consider him a master of improvisation in times of minor crises.

When I queried him about how a good *danza* might be defined, he more than agreed with Molly. To simply say that he agreed would seem a little dubious only in that it implies the convergence of two separate perspectives whereas, in reality, their perspectives were seamless. So, it's enough to say that they *share* the same view. It is a given for both of them that what Molly describes in the above paragraph is the best thing that can take place. Tony adds that he becomes especially glad when the group's dancing draws crowds of people who even stand in long lines as they wait their turn to dance with us in pairs during the *adoración*. He gave the example of the time the group danced in Our Lady of Guadalupe Church in 2005, and students who had been walking home from nearby Whitney Lanier High School came in, danced in the *adoración*, then went to tell their parents, who followed suit.

Good *Danzas*, Continuity, and Change

What is interesting to note in Tony's anecdote is the virtual reversal of roles between parents and children with regard to the dance. It is generally assumed that older generations pass on their traditions to younger people and otherwise encourage them to practice them. In this case youth were facilitating the continuity of the dance among their parents. Despite the increasing demands placed on youth in contemporary times, these students' actions demonstrated their investment in the devotion of the *Virgen*.

It is significant that there are no formally set expectations about how a given *danzante* should experience the dance on an individual level. Yet, although Molly, Tony, and I had never spoken to one another at such length about our experiences in the *danza*, Tony's and Molly's experiences sounded very much like my mine. We all sensed a unifying kind of spirit in our midst. And, judging from my experiences in the dance, these experiences are shared by all, and everyone senses that they are essentially sharing the same experience.

For *danzantes* in formal and informal leadership roles, such as Molly, the ability to perceive the presence or absence of this spirit of the dance among *danzantes* can serve as a kind of informal gauge of the vitality of the troupe. For example, as long this type of experience can be recognized during the majority of our *danzas*, then we know the troupe's overall vitality is strong.

4

Life History of the *Danza*

A Continuity

As the *danza* moved into the United States and became established in Chicano communities in parts of the American Southwest, it maintained many of its distinctive features: a focus on the *Virgen*, a narrative that tells the story of her appearances to Juan Diego, its *trajes*, the liveliness of its steps, and its communal nature. Yet, each autonomous troupe has its own history, and, in keeping with this book's stated purpose, I will be focusing on the history of La Danza Guadalupana de Pablo Olivares Sr. This remarkably long-lasting troupe has maintained its identity and consistency of practice from its founding in Monterrey in the 1960s into the present day in San Antonio. The family ties, which have carried the troupe from generation to generation and place to place account for much of its continuity. So, this chapter will draw from a conversation that took place among Molly, Tony, Molly's late mother Francisca Olivares Aguilar, and me.

Some weeks after agreeing that I would use the notes I was writing to form this book, Tony asked me when I was going to "interview" members of the family to include their voices in this endeavor. The idea of meeting with the family to ask questions about the dance was an excellent idea. However, the idea of an interview seemed too clinical to me. I preferred the idea of informally recording a conversation with but a few questions and letting things go wherever the family took it. And, as it turned out, that is pretty much what Tony had in mind as well. Tony's suggestion was import-ant because the conversation summarized in this chapter gives the reader insights I never could have communicated as succinctly. And, of course, information arose that I had been unaware of. This is especially true of Molly and her late mother's contributions to this talk, which took place in their living room in March 2009. Tony was also present and contributed to this history. Several years later, Molly clarified some points for me.

Beginnings

According to Molly, her Uncle Pablo Olivares Sr. began his *danza de mata-chines* troupe when he was fifteen or sixteen. He did this by organizing some children in his neighborhood in Monterrey, Mexico. His troupe would usu-ally take off on their procession from someone's home in his neighborhood called Colonia las Américas. It continued, with pilgrims joining along the way, until reaching the plaza in front of a church dedicated to *La Virgen de Guadalupe*. His troupe was one of many converging from their respective neighborhoods to arrive at the plaza and dance their *veneraciones*.

Molly recalls that he had made a *promesa* for their grandfather who had been ill, which he fulfilled in the formation of his troupe. By the late 1960s, Pablo immigrated to San Antonio, Texas, joining his three Texan siblings. There he started his *danza* again, this time using his children, nieces, and nephews as dancers. At that time, Molly's mother, whose involvement had previously been limited to making the *trajes*, began to dance as one of the rearguard *capitanes*. Molly's oldest brother was at the front of one of the *danza*'s two processional columns. Her younger brother danced behind him, and Molly danced behind them. Molly's father, Crecensio Ernesto Aguilar, was dancing as *el viejo de la danza* in addition to helping to make the *sonajas* and *arcos* (bows). Molly's siblings in the dance included her brothers, Antonio, Ernesto C. Aguilar, and, later, Ernesto's wife Esperanza. Their pictures hang in the living room among other family members.

Molly was born in San Antonio in 1964. A picture of her in one of the family photo albums shows her at the 1968 World's Fair (marketed as "Hemisfair") when troupe members danced there. Prior to dancing, she had seen matachines dance and attended *mañanitas* (early morning singing for the *Virgen*). She had also participated in dramatic reenactments of the story of Our Lady of Guadalupe and Juan Diego that were organized by mem-bers of her family. The decision to organize and perform the reenactment

Pablo Olivares Sr. wearing his *traje* (suit) in San
Antonio, Texas. 1979. Photo courtesy of Amalia
Aguilar.

was the idea of her uncle and grandmother who wanted to help people see
the relationship between the *danza* and the story of the *Virgen* and Juan
Diego. Molly played the part of the *Virgen*, her brother Manuel played the
part of Juan Diego, and four of her cousins alternated the role of Bishop
Zumárraga. The troupe was independent of any particular home church,
and the children performed their reenactment for San Martín de Porres
Church one year, and then for Our Lady of Guadalupe Church for a couple
of years. In addition, they performed at a private home. Playing the *Virgen*
became second nature for Molly. So, by the time she began dancing, she
recognized that the story of Juan Diego and *La Virgen de Guadalupe* was
taking place in the *danza*. She says, "Our reaction was 'Oh! We're doing
the Juan Diego thing! We're the Indians!' I knew we were Indian, but, till
then, I never had made the connection that 'Oh! The Indians were the ones
dancing for her. *That's* why we're doing this.' That's when I really put the
connection together."

     She began dancing in 1971 at the age of seven. One of her memories
about the *danza* back then was the weight of the *penachos*:

> The *penachos* were made out of *lámina* (sheet metal), covered with flannel, and the feathers had *varillas* (metal bands) holding them in place. We used to have really small feathers because those were the only kind we could get here in San Antonio. My mom and my aunts would tie them with thread all the way to the top, tie each feather into the thing, and from this little feather, you would have this big old *penacho*. Each would have three *varillas*, three or four. Whenever we would do this [inclines her head as if bowing], we would be dancing. It would look like we were going all the way down on purpose, but we weren't! [*laughs*]. We were doing the step going forward, but, you know, having to come back [up] was a strain.

The feathers, she says, were not the attached turkey feathers used now. They were short plumes. She also recalls being "afraid" of her father and uncle who felt the *danza* was so important that they were taskmasters. However, having practices and *danzas* meant that she and her siblings would get to see their cousins. Throughout the year, she and her cousins' families would have parties together, and this included when they gathered for practices and *danzas*. Her parents impressed on her and her siblings that they wanted their children to dance for them but allowed them to decide for themselves. Some of her cousins, she says, resented the responsibility of dancing, but overall there was no major opposition on the part of the children. She adds, "I think Our Lady of Guadalupe had been such a big part of my family because of the grandmothers." In fact, the troupe danced exclusively for *La Virgen de Guadalupe*, as is indicated in its name: La Danza Guadalupana de Pablo Olivares Sr. Molly began dancing "in the line," that is, as a rank-and-file *matachín*. By the time she had her first son, Antonio Ernesto, she was dancing at the front of the columns. Once he was born, however, she carried him as she danced, and her position moved toward the back of the file. Though her primary role now is drumming, on occasion she has had to "double" as one of the *capitanes* (captains) and as a drum-playing Malinche.

First Accoutrements

Molly's mother sees La Danza Guadalupana de Pablo Olivares as having started in San Antonio. She and two of her siblings were Texans residing in San Antonio. The *trajes* at that time, she says, were the same as now. That is, the *capitanes* and *monarca* wore red *capas* (literally cloaks) and *naguas*, the rank-and-file matachines wore red *naguas* and vests with forest green shirts, and the *malinches* wore white blouses with tricolor skirts adorned

Molly Aguilar drumming in front of Our Lady of Guadalupe Church on the feast day of Our Lady of Guadalupe. San Antonio, Texas. December 12, 2005.

by an eagle devouring a snake on a cactus. (These are the colors and image of the Mexican coat of arms.) But some changes evolved over time. The headwear, she said, initially consisted of the heavy *penachos* she describes in this chapter. However, there was a scarcity of materials in San Antonio for making and maintaining them, including feathers, tin, and colored fabric. This scarcity of materials eventually resulted in a temporary substitution of straw cowboy hats (or *sombreros vaqueros de paja*) for *penachos*. Because straw cowboy hats are associated with the countryside, they represent Juan Diego who is frequently depicted as a *ranchero* (rural person). But, three years into dancing in San Antonio, Pablo Olivares replaced the troupe's hats with *penachos*. Elaborating on her description of the *penachos*, Molly says, "They were of sheet metal. And later they had longer *varillas*." She said the *varillas* were about ten inches long. The *malinches* continued to wear the straw cowboy hats. They decorated them with red, white, and green ribbons.

At this point I am shown photo albums going back several years. One is from 1968, when Molly was four. Some of the *capas* have silver-colored thunderbird emblems on them instead of the *Virgen*. I had seen these worn by a few of her cousins at the *danzas*. When I ask about them, Molly's mother says, "Well, we started with that because it was easy to make." She added that images of the *Virgen* were available on small pieces of cloth, and that these could be used for the children's *trajes* because they were in proportion to those smaller *trajes*.

By the mid-1970s, the number of participating family members had grown significantly, giving rise to the need for more *viejos de la danza*. Her *tío* (uncle) Luis had nine participating children, and her father had eight. To remedy this crisis, her Uncle Pablo trained her father Crecensio and her Uncle Luís to maintain order in the lines as *viejos de la danza*. In the late 1970s, the group experienced one of its hiatuses. Of Pablo Olivares Sr., Molly says, "My uncle stopped because he was tired, and that was for several years, and then Junior got married, and he had his boys. [Her uncle] decided to stop because he felt like he just couldn't. At that time, his older kids were teenagers, and there was less participation. All the older ones were teenagers, and kind of on their own." Junior, his oldest son, began to dance with other troupes. Molly recalls that "Junior was [dancing] off and on with other groups like [I am] with different parishes, but he would go stay in that parish." One of those groups was called La Fe. I ask Molly about its formation; she says, "La Fe formed during one of our lapses. Junior joined them at the time when he was dancing with different churches like St. Mary Magdalene's and ICC [Immaculate Conception Church]. He was in ICC International with [the members of La Fe], and that's when they began dancing with him, and they formed from there." Molly adds that they were cousins on her mother's side of the family, her mother's uncle

La Danza Guadalupana de Pablo Olivares Sr. in San Antonio. Pablo Olivares Sr. plays a drum at the front and center of the two columns. Our Lady of Guadalupe Church. San Antonio, Texas. Ca. 1979. Photo courtesy Amalia Aguilar.

to be exact. "They started with us. Some had started with our group, but that's when Junior was helping them. Junior was with the group, but he was helping them. And he was using our colors. And, then he stopped teaching. They knew some of our steps."

Eventually, the *danza* resumed with Junior heading the group because of the passing of his father in the late 1980s. By 1996, Molly and Tony were married, and Molly gave birth to Antonio and Ramón in 1997 and 1999, respectively. In 1997, she danced for the *Virgen* while holding Antonio. Soon after Ramón was born, Junior summarily recruited Tony into the troupe as a *capitán*. "I was going to stay in the truck with Ramón," Tony tells me. "And, all of the sudden I'm told, 'No, you're in the front [of the line].' I said, 'What do you mean? I don't even know the steps!'" to which Junior replied, "'Well, I need you as *capitán*,' because the deal was that there were no females allowed to be a *capitán* or *monarca*. [*laughing*]. That has changed!" Molly adds, "The *Virgen* changed that, didn't she?" laughing. So, Tony essentially apprenticed into his role, dancing in the same line with Molly's brother Ernest, who was a *capitán* at the time.

Tony adds that in 1997, the troupe gave up the series of graduations of ranks to make Molly's brother Manuel and her cousin Roger *los viejos de la danza*. Because it takes time and experience to rise through the ranks to become a *viejo*, the *viejos* tend to be the oldest in the troupe. Those would previously have been Ernest and his cousin Luís, but they now felt they were too old for their roles. That is how Roger and Manuel became *viejos*. Molly says, "Manuel took it from my father, and my cousin Roger took it from my uncle Luis Robles. In other words, they inherited their positions." Although Roger became a *viejo* before Manuel, he had previously been a *danzante* with him. The two cousins did extraordinarily well as "*viejos*" by imitating their fathers. Manuel especially did a remarkable job of imitating his father's skill as a *viejo de la danza*. So they were in a position to follow the *viejo de la danza* lineage of their fathers, and they also embodied their roles exceptionally well.

The Troupe Opens Up to Nonfamily Members

By 2004, the troupe was experiencing another hiatus. Nonetheless, Molly took Tony and their children to Guadalupe Plaza on the feast day of the *Virgen* where, on their own initiative, they danced before a large, public image of the *Virgen*. It was then that Molly decided that she would assume leadership of La Danza Guadalupana de Pablo Olivares Sr. if Junior did not reconvene it. By 2005 the troupe had still not been reconvened, so Molly announced to her family that she not only would be taking its reins but that she would also open up its ranks to people outside the family. In addition, she would be continuing the tradition of dancing under the name of her uncle's troupe and using the *estandarte* (standard) bearing his name, which her mother had kept. This announcement met with the disapproval of some of her cousins, but other relatives, especially the older family members, gave her their wholehearted blessings. According to Molly's mother, Junior was among those of Molly's cousins who initially opposed the idea of her reviving the family *danza*. However, he did occasionally play drums with them during the first two years of her leadership and was a *viejo de la danza* for them on occasion.

I first saw the troupe dance in 2005; they had received some support from Holy Family Parish. Though the family was not registered at that parish, it allowed Molly to put out the invitation to its parishioners that they could join the troupe. So, at that time, the majority of the dancers were from Holy Family Church, which had also given them a practice space. The rest of the members were family by blood or marriage. With

The author holding the *estandarte* of La Danza Guadalupana de Pablo Olivares Sr. Also called a *manta*, it was made by Amalia Aguilar's mother, Francisca Olivares Aguilar. Photos of Pablo Olivares Sr. appear on both sides of the *Virgen's* image. Antonio, one of Molly and Tony's two sons, is standing by. San Antonio, Texas. 2006. From author's collection.

membership numbering over thirty dancers, it was a large troupe by their standards. By the time Molly was preparing for the next dancing season, though, the church was no longer willing to provide a practice space or otherwise collaborate with the troupe.

During the same year, Manuel's wife Carmen had a momentous conversation with a priest whose hair she was cutting at her work. His name was Father Francisco, and he had recently been assigned to St. Alphonsus Parish Church on the West Side. Because the feast day of Our Lady of Guadalupe was approaching, he asked her if she celebrated it. Her answer was yes and that she in fact danced in a matachines troupe. As it turned out, he was in need of matachines for the *Virgen's* feast day and that of the Epiphany. Carmen put Father Francisco in contact with Molly, and she offered him La Danza Guadalupana de Pablo Olivares Sr. This happened at a time when an increasing number of priests from Mexico were being assigned to the barrio parishes. They were familiar with the *danza de matachines* and understood and respected it as a popular tradition, encouraging its practice in their parishes. For that reason, the troupe's commitment to dance at St. Alphonsus led to invitations to dance at other churches during the next few years. In fact, it was during that phase when I first photographed La Danza Guadalupana de Pablo Olivares Sr. Molly emphasizes that before then, things had been different. "For a while there really weren't many priests who knew anything about matachines. It was like we were just presenting a show. And, then we started again—our group. We came to Holy Family [Catholic Church], the woman who actually asked us to go there explained to the priest that we were coming and the story we did [so he would know] what we were doing." She says he was, "a little reluctant to have us," but the parishioner who invited the troupe reassured him. His response, Molly summed up as, "Okay, yeah, you can dance, okay." As a result, parishioners who understood the *danza* and who had made *promesas* they needed to fulfill came out of the parish woodwork. Later, as she has recounted, Mexican parish priests serving San Antonio parishes welcomed the troupe.

Thoughts on the Past and Future

Over the years, Molly has seen a number of troupes form and then dissolve after a season. She says it's because "they didn't place the same emphasis on their families as we did with our families. Our parents took us and let us know that is what we're going to do because this is what we're doing with our faith. They taught us everything to understand the *danza*." She contrasts this with other groups that "didn't go down into the second generation because it was like, 'Uh, that's okay. We're dancing once; that's enough.'" She says those troupes do not place "emphasis" on passing the tradition to the succeeding generation. The ones that do last longer.

Traditionally, Molly says, dancers have had different motivations:

Some have a devotion to Our Lady of Guadalupe. Others have a devotion to San Juan Diego, and then there's those who are fulfilling a *promesa*, and maybe they told us the year before, Well, I'm going to come dance with you because I still have to make a *promesa*. I'm going to dance for Our Lady for a promise that I had. And, so far some people have not come back. We had people from Holy Family. . . . Some woman had the shingles. I don't know if she's better or not, but she fulfilled her promise, then that was it. And, another woman had another promise, and that was it. And, like, [one of our dancers]—I don't know if he's going to like for me to say this—[he] had his dancing in thanksgiving, and [his wife] dancing with him. I don't know if he told you, but he was in a fire. So, it's a big thing for him. They didn't know that we were here until they saw an older woman who was dancing with us named doña María.

Doña María, who danced with La Danza Guadalupana de Pablo Olivares Sr. for two years and who had also danced in La Fe, turned out to be related to the couple. According to Molly, she, "was dancing to get her kids back to the religion."

Today, Molly sees the *danza* as a prayer, as matachines have for centuries. "You're dancing for a people. It's a prayer that you can use to tell a story." She and Tony see their sons and their cousins as the third generation of *danzantes* in the family. Molly and Tony encourage them to continue dancing by reminding them of the prospect of becoming *viejos de la danza* when they are older. They tell them that if they ever want to be *viejos*, they need to know the steps correctly.

At one point, Molly mentions that each of the dance steps has a special meaning and a Nahuatl prayer. She makes the analogy of a rosary having different meanings (that is, beads representing different prayers according to their spacing). She says also, in the context of that information, that her paternal grandmother, that is, Pablo Olivares Sr.'s mother, was a speaker of Nahuatl. It was the language of the Aztecs and Tlaxcaltecans, in addition to other central Mexican peoples. It is still spoken in parts of Mexico today, though its speakers are fewer in number. And, according to Tony, Pablo Olivares Sr. knew the prayers associated with the steps but he died before they could be taught to anyone else. Fragments of this knowledge remain, though. Molly, while training children who were the same age as she when she began dancing, suddenly remembered the relationship of the rosary prayers to the dance.

I think that the fact that those traditional prayers were once part of our *danza* is remarkable. It speaks to the resilience of the tradition in our troupe's lineage. Also, the linkage of Nahuatl prayer to our *danza* ties us directly to the Spanish Colonial period, if not longer ago than that. Finally, this revelation confirms for me in a tangible way that the matachines dance tradition in contemporary Texas by way of Monterrey is in fact from its Tlaxcaltecan past. In other words: This reality does not only exist in some obscure books and published research. Rather, La Danza Guadalupana de Pablo Olivares Sr. is collectively a living descendant of the broader *danza de matachines* lineage of the region of northern Mexico that the founder brought with him.

I relate Molly's words on Nahuatl prayer in the danza to a lecture titled "Across Seas: Cultural Interchange and Social Transformation between Mesoamerica and the American Southwest" (delivered at Trinity

University on September 16, 2014). In that lecture, John Pohl included a Spanish Colonial graphic image of a Tlaxcaltecan being instructed in praying with a rosary whose beads are adorned by Tlaxcaltecan iconography from tombs, among other places. This graphic associates the rosary and the Tlaxcaltecan worldview. It was made in an effort to convert Tlaxcaltecans to the Catholic faith (J. Pohl, personal communication, September 16, 2014). I believe this image also indicates the importance the Tlaxcaltecans placed on prayer and the importance that they came to place on the rosary. As well, the importance of the rosary may be manifest in the physical configuration and choreography of the *danzantes* in our troupe during the *adoración*. In this respect, I find it potentially significant to note that, like a rosary that is actually composed of a series of prayers, so is our *danza's adoración* a series of dancers who approach the *Virgen's* image on the *estandarte*, also in prayer. The resemblance of the *adoración* to the praying of a rosary is further strengthened by the position of the stationary *estandarte* as the focal point that each *danzante* approaches and then departs from, like the beginning of a rosary that is visually made distinct by the presence of a small crucifix and the placement of four beads in a pattern different from those on the rest of the rosary. For these reasons, I believe it all the more relevant that Carmen, one of the *malinches*, has called the *adoración* the "heart" of the *danza*. And it is significant that, despite the loss of the dance steps' meanings with the passing of Pablo Olivares Sr., continuity of tradition can occur as matachines like me perceive aspects of the dance as prayer. In my case, I have seen the *veneración* as a danced form of the rosary.

The casual observer may assume that this use of the rosary is an indication of Indigenous assimilation to conventional devotion. But the situation is actually the reverse. It is not an assimilation of Indigenous people. Rather, it is an assimilation of prayer by Indigenous people. This follows a pattern of Indigenous cultures assimilating clothing, language, and spiritual practices for as long as there has been a historical record of it.

5

Memoir of a *Monarca*

I was perplexed when a man in his late fifties casually approached our *danza* as we practiced in a park and casually asked, cigarette in hand, "What's the meaning of this?" He gave me the impression that he expected a clean-cut, pocket-sized but accurate explanation of the *danza*. Whether he realized it or not, he was asking what the *danza de matachines* was. An outsider observing the *danza* cannot fully know the experience of the *danza de matachines*.

When most people think of the *danza de matachines*, they think of the sensory experience: People dancing in formation, bedecked in bright, uniformly colored *trajes* and feathers. They see us dancing to one or more drums that are loud and mostly rapid in their cadence. Even our decorative *sonajas* rattle plangently, and the *carrizos* with their bells contribute to the sensory aspect of the *danza* as they sway in unison. Some observers might notice more subtle aspects of form such as differences among the steps, patterns in the drumming, types of *trajes*. Some onlookers may even perceive the *danza*'s form, that is, its structure from beginning to end. These outward manifestations of our dance are all parts of its *public expression*. It is what writers on this topic have addressed because they have not danced as *matachines* and lack the private experiences of the *danza*.

Private experiences of the *danza* are inaccessible to public observation. The private experiences include a sense of serendipity, dreams, and traditional bonds with community members who also have spiritual ties to the *danza de matachines*. They also include dancers' individual motivations for dancing for the *Virgen*. So the private experiences of the *danza de matachines* may not even be shared with other dancers in the same troupe. In this memoir, I hope to bridge the distance between lived experience of a *matachines* dancer and those who may even be reading about the *danza* for the first time.

My memoir as a *monarca* is a series of recollections of my experiences as a *matachín*. Written with the benefit of hindsight and increased knowledge, I introspectively relate and reflect in the voice of my personal experience. With retrospection now on my side, I am able to process these events for meanings that I often could not readily perceive when they occurred. Having already given the reader a sufficient sense of my chronology in terms of my relationship to the *danza*, I seek to reveal the emotional and experiential realities. So, I suspend analytics and facts in favor of subjectivity, which is important because the private experiences of the *danza* seldom conform to the linear and objective assumptions that characterize western thought and language.

During my first ten years of dancing, I saw emerge four salient and recurring reflections. The first reflection, *authenticity*, was best evidenced in demonstrations of autonomy on our part, intrusions into the dance, and conflicts with the city government and clergy. I cite the hallmark quality of autonomy as a characteristic of our authenticity because of the historical record of the Tlaxcaltecans and their interactions with the Spanish. My notes on the second reflection, the *metaphysics of accoutrements*, concern my experiences and the often highly personal practices in the relationships between dancers and the accoutrements we used. The third reflection, the *community of devotees*, deals largely with a kind of "floating community" of nondancers devoted to the *Virgen* who play invaluable roles in the *danza*. The final matter I reflect on is the *dreams* I have had related to the *danza*. I describe those dreams and reflect on their meanings in relation to matters such as being called to dance, my presence in our troupe, and its relationship to ancestry. I follow each reflection with an assessment of why I find it unique to the *danza*. And I mull over the roles they play in dealing with change and fostering continuity. Then, after having completed my reflections, I examine how the private experience of the dance is critical to appreciating the dance in its entirety.

In this chapter I give the reader the unique opportunity of having access to my private experience of the dance. I share it in my triple role as *matachín*, documentarian, and interpreter of the dance. The impressions I try to articulate of my subjective impressions are rooted in the authenticity of my experience as a member of the culture. This is not always easy

7-10 mns
2tr a week

because written language is linear—at least the one I am using is—and the events I observe and experience do not always lend themselves to written communication. Still, this memoir is an expression of my experience as a *matachín*.

I follow this chapter with a dated, intermittent chronology of events affecting our *danza*, and I narrate my gradual transformation as a *matachín*. This transformation occurred not only in terms of technical skill and knowledge but also in terms of greater spiritual awareness of my relationship to the dance. The relatively casual, often introspective, and first-person nature of this section allows the reader to holistically read about my experiences as a *matachín*.

I culled the following reflections in this memoir, for the most part, from notes and journal pages penned between December 2005 and December X 2009. Our *danza* practiced twice a week and nine to ten months of each year. During those years, as well as during the years that I have continued to dance, I have been able to reflect on those experiences as a *monarca* and gain insights into the *danza*. In this chapter I reflect on a twofold question: What is the nature of change that comes from individual private experience, and does such change lead to continuity? To answer this twofold question, I describe my experiences as a *danzante* within a certain time frame to share insights that contribute to the overall understanding of the dynamic between change and continuity. With those descriptions, I hope to share my experience. Penned while dancing in the troupe, these narrative notes provide a more intimate context for the *danza*. In this way I hope to answer the question I have posed about the dynamics between change and continuity and the events I observed. It will be clear that the man who approached us in the park would have needed to sit down and listen for a long time for me to have approximated an explanation, much longer than it takes a cigarette to burn.

the media

First Reflection—Authenticity

Since the beginning of my time in the *danza*, I noticed widespread misperceptions that people entertained about the *danza de matachines*, mostly originating in the local mass media. The first instances when I noticed these misrepresentations were innocuous and few, partly because the news media seldom reported on the *danza* to begin with. After all, I thought, these occasional articles were written by people working on deadlines who probably never heard of the *danza* before. At first these articles were in the local daily and Catholic newspapers. As time went by, though, I increasingly found such articles being featured in those newspapers as well as in local online news sources that were the unofficial organs of the emerging real estate development and big business interests. At this time, I was running into people who had been misinformed by these sources. At least one local historian even cited these sources in his own work. And as these disappointing reports grew in number, so did their distance from the truth. These misrepresentations of the *danza* especially intensified after our *danza* started an annual dance pilgrimage. This stepped-up misrepresentation disturbed me deeply, and I struggled for a long time to articulate for myself the reasons why. It galled me that these news sources, which were clearly not part of the *danza*, had reporters writing about it as if they knew the *danza* quite well. Eventually, I realized that I felt this shoddy depiction of our *danza* placed our authenticity at stake. I had never given authenticity of the dance a thought before then. But I soon understood that I felt that, by misrepresenting the authenticity of the tradition, those inaccuracies were undermining that authenticity and, consequently, the continuity of the *danza*.

Today, having since reflected much on those articles and authenticity, I have come to understand that the authenticity of our traditions cannot be undermined so easily (though that poor-quality journalism would later negatively affect certain Spanish-speaking communities in San Antonio). And because of those misrepresentations of authenticity, I am now inspired to explain what authenticity in the *danza* is through the following reflections. Fortunately, I can do this because I have the private experience of the dance, without which authenticity in the *danza* cannot be understood.

The Authority of the *Estandarte* as Authenticity

I showed up at the parking lot of the Church of the Little Flower, prepared to carry and hold the *estandarte* bearing the image of *La Virgen de Guadalupe* for the troupe as I had promised Molly. Though the sky was sunny and an almost cloudless turquoise blue, it was very cold by San Antonio standards. I wore a pea coat and gloves. I waited anxiously as I considered this a serious responsibility and an honor to be offered any role in this *danza*. Tony and Molly were the first to arrive. After greeting me warmly, they opened the back of an SUV, and Tony began assembling the *estandarte*. He had designed it from a kind of rectangular stand with short metal poles. As other matachines and their families arrived, he attached an

Photos by Edward A. Ornelas / San Antonio Express-News

Cristina Cordova, a member of the Kalpulli Ameyaltonal Aztec Dancers, takes part in La Danza de Matachines Sunday at Mission Concepción. The mission celebrated its patronal feast, the Immaculate Conception, which falls on Dec. 8.

Matachines dance to honor the Virgin

700 costumed dancers perform

By Jeremy T. Gerlach
STAFF WRITER

Members of Danza Azteca, from Our Lady of Guadalupe in Helotes, perform during La Danza de Matachines on Sunday.

> "I dance ... for the faith, for the tradition, for the Virgin de Guadalupe."
>
> *Josefina Merida, matachine dancer*

More than 700 colorful matachine dancers took to the streets near Mission Concepción on Sunday to celebrate the Immaculate Conception, some garbed in bright dresses and tall, feathered plumes as music from drums swelled to a fever pitch.

The celebration is part of the mission's patronal feast — which honors the Virgin Mary — dating back to colonial times more than 280 years ago, according to Father David García.

"This is history, culture and tradition," García said.

This was the second year Mission Concepción has hosted the matachines, which came from area parishes and a variety of cultural organizations to march from the mission to the San Antonio River, performing elaborate, traditional dances along the way. In the colonial era, missionaries incorporated native indigenous music and dance into Catholic celebrations, evolving into the dancing now replicated in modern times.

"A lot of (indigenous) people didn't know how to pray (in those times), so this was a form of prayer for them," event organizer Tony Aguilar said.

Clad in red and yellow, Josefina Merida, 42, danced with the Sacred Heart Catholic Church group. At 80 dancers, it was by far the largest of all the ensembles at the Sunday event.

They've been practicing since September to get ready for the performance.

"I dance ... for the faith, for the tradition, for the Virgin de Guadalupe — that's the more important part," Merida said. "I've been doing this since I was 8."

The tradition links both young and old, Merida added. Her group has dancers ranging in age from 4 to 55.

Aguilar said the celebration's footprint is growing.

"We have groups from out of town — Pearsall, New Braunfels, Helotes — coming here now," he explained.

jgerlach@express-news.net

A newspaper article from December 8, 2014, heralds matachines but features photos of *danza azteca*. This inability to distinguish between the two traditions illustrates the lack of familiarity of local news sources with the *danza de matachines*. Accompanying photos by Edward Ornelas. This photo appears courtesy of the *San Antonio Express-News*.

American flag to one of the perpendicular poles and a Mexican flag to the other. He hung the *manta* (the fabric image of the Virgen) from a horizontal pole. He showed me how I was to carry it, holding it aloft. He added that I would be at the front of the troupe as we danced in procession. Then, during the main part of the ritual, I would allow the rack to be stationary as I continued to hold it as a focal point for the dancers. (Wednesday, December 9, 2006)

Early
primer
- a
should
moved

That I was also asked to carry the *estandarte*, the banner bearing the *Virgen*'s image, was daunting to me, given the honor the act carries with it. Your intentions need to be sincere. The *Virgen*'s image on the *estandarte* makes it a sacred object, that is, something through which she can be revered. Her image on the *estandarte* has great power to aid those who pray and dance before it, and, together with the dancers' sincerity, it helps to bring the spirit of the *Virgen* into the dance. That's why having an *estandarte* is essential to having an authentic *danza*. Carrying the *estandarte* is an internal commitment. If you are physically present but just going through the motions, no one else may know it, but the *Virgen* does. And, you know that she knows. This is why it is a great honor. So, Molly's request for me to carry the *estandarte*—as pressure free as it was—was unquestionably one I felt I had to accept.

An outsider to the dance might wonder why matachines place so much importance on carrying what seems to be a fabric bearing the image of the *Virgen*. On the one hand, the *estandarte* is a material and external thing. But the role it plays in the *danza* and in making the *danza* authentic is a thing of the *spirit*: the spirit of the dance, the spirit of the dancers, the collective sincerity of the dancers, the things we experience internally, our internal motivations and inspirations. All these things are greatly inspired by the power of *estandarte*. So, a *danza de matachines* troupe needs to have an *estandarte* to have those spiritual qualities that make it authentic.

Matachines troupes dance in front of their *estandartes*. The *estandarte* summons the presence of the *Virgen*, and her image possesses power. That is why it is so important for the troupe to be real, to be authentic. Wherever her image is—be it on a statue on a home altar or in a framed picture in a church—her presence is there also. This is the kind of sacred matter that is learned intuitively. *Gente* begin to learn this from an early age. You do not need to be a *matachín* to understand this. That is also why you do not have to be a *matachín* to carry the *estandarte* in procession or to hold it during the *veneración*. If a troupe does not have an *estandarte*, it cannot be authentic.

An instance that illustrated the authority of the *estandarte* occurred at a *posadas* in 2006. When matachines are invited to participate in *posadas*, we follow the larger body of participants in our usual column formation. On that night, the pastor, who was a robed friar from Mexico, saw me carrying the *estandarte* as we and his parishioners were preparing for the event outside the parish hall. He looked at the *estandarte* and then at me with a concerned gaze. He seemed to be assessing my approachability. Then he approached Molly and spoke to her with an expression that barely belied his apprehension. She responded by coming to me and telling me that the pastor had asked us to leave the *estandarte* in the parish hall during the *posadas*. It was something we were going to do anyway because we were going to dance there afterward, and we knew that Mary and Joseph were the focus in the *posadas*. As well, the *Virgen*'s special period of veneration that started on December 12 had not yet begun. What I was picking up on in the priest's concerned gaze was a preoccupation with competing icons. Earlier in this book, I mentioned a priest who intimated that a *matachines* troupe could easily turn into a cult. The authenticity of the *Virgen*'s authority in her image was at the heart of that concern. And the pastor was basically taking a precaution to ensure that Mary and Joseph would not have to vie with that authority.

Because I was new to the *danza*, the authority of the *estandarte* was new to me, but I understood the authority of the *Virgen*'s image that it bore. And I could see that it was underscored by its prominence in procession and the *veneración* (veneration) segment of the dance. So, when Tony finished assembling the *estandarte* and handed it to me with both of his hands, I took it, making sure that I was present in my role both internally and externally. Years later, as our troupe was beginning a *danza* at the Aguilar home, Manuel abruptly stopped the ritual's introduction by shouting and raising his hand before darting into the house to retrieve the *estandarte*, which he then placed at the head of the troupe. Somehow, the *capitanes* had forgotten it, and its authority was so great that Manuel had to immediately correct the oversight.

The authority of the *estandarte* is so great partly because of the work that goes into making it. When Molly and her cousins began to dance, her uncle used an *estandarte* made by her maternal grandmother. Much time and care went into it according to Molly, who showed me a photo if it. It was highly detailed with many embroidered roses and flowers. Some of the designs had first been hand drawn onto the fabric with colored drawing implements. Those designs were then embroidered with matching colored threads. Other designs were made with special iron-on graphics onto which the embroidery was sewn. The image of the *Virgen*, sewn onto the center, was made of multicolored sequins. Molly described seeing it for the first time. "It was beautiful! It was one of the most beautiful things we had seen. Hers was all handmade, pretty much."

Her mother Francisca also made an *estandarte*. It was the one being used by La Danza Guadalupana de Pablo Olivares Sr. when I began to dance with the troupe. The fabric was white satin and measured about two and a half by three feet. Like the *Virgen* on Molly's grandmother's *estandarte*, Francisca's was also made of sequins. In addition to three red roses that were part of her sequined image, Molly's mother sewed two large sequined red roses near the upper corners and two smaller embroidered ones slightly below the *Virgen*. The *Virgen* was tightly encircled by silver lace. The *estandarte* had gold-colored fringes running straight along its top and a type of gold lamé fabric bordering the bottom. Centered between the fringes and the encircling silver wave lace was an ornate three-inch silver cross. About two inches below it was a small red star with two slightly larger silver stars on either side. Other such dazzling decorations bordered the outside of the circle formed by the silver lace. Molly remembers her working on it when she was a child. She would only do so in quiet solitude, and the moment Molly and her siblings would arrive home, she would quickly put it out of sight.

Unlike the *estandartes* of parish-based troupes, the ones in family-based *danzas* remain in the family. And family-based *estandartes* are so powerful that members involved in the dance often make sure to be buried with them. Molly's maternal grandmother was buried with the one she had made. Her father Crecensio, who had been a *viejo de la danza*, was buried with the one his wife had made. Pablo Olivares Sr. was buried with one that he led his troupe with. And Molly's mother was buried with hers. She had told Molly that it was her wish to be buried with it and that, to help ensure her wish was fulfilled, she instructed her to display it next to her casket during her funeral and rosary. It was not only placed there; it was enshrined in an elaborate floral arrangement. As Molly observed, "Someone made a kind of altar with it next to her casket. . . . Before my mom's casket was closed, they put that one inside covering her." Molly's mother passed on to her the role of making *estandartes*. It is a responsibility that she finds daunting because, "She had a legacy of doing these *beautiful estandartes*. . . . It's a lot of work."

How One Enters the Dance as Authenticity

I called Molly to find out where and when I could photograph La Danza Guadalupana de Pablo Olivares Sr. as I had the previous year. Much to my surprise, she additionally invited me to become a *danzante* in the troupe on December 12, the feast day of the *Virgen*. Her invitations came with no pressure, yet I was almost overwhelmed by the intimidation I felt. I was not only being asked to dance with the troupe but in the presences of the *Virgen* and of ancestors, presences I had felt when I had seen the matachines dance several months prior. I was being asked to enter territory very few devotees of the *Virgen* enter. (December 4, 2006)

A big part of authenticity in the dance is how one enters into it. My entry into the tradition was marked by serendipity. By that I mean that it was the outcome of a series of unforeseen events. I did not find the dance; the dance found me. Usually, someone enters the *danza* because they're born into a family that practices it, or because it is a tradition in their *barrio*, or they're making a *promesa*. But I was responding to what the *Virgen* was asking me to do. Since being called to dance is a spiritual request, how people enter the *danza* makes their participation either authentic or an empty gesture. If someone joins because they think it looks cool, or because they want to entertain people, or their godmother thinks it would be nice, or they want to write about it, they are just going through the motions of the dance and its ritual. That does not mean they could not experience something spiritual in the dance, but it would owe to the devotion of the other dancers. Their reasons for dancing would have to change, or they would not endure the demands of training for very long. Granted: Sincere dancers are not always called. Like I said, some *danzantes* are fulfilling a *promesa*. They usually dance for only a year. And those who are born into a *matachines* family do not necessarily remain dancers beyond childhood. Work and the need to maintain a steady income, especially after having started families, compete with dancers' time. Some *danzantes* even give greater priority to playing sports in city leagues. Even in adolescence, sports competes for after-school and weekend time.

    The *danza* came to me through a series of events and dreams that were the actions of the *Virgen*. Molly invited me to the dance based on an intuition that should not be confused with whimsicalness because the *Virgen* was inviting me through her. She was a conduit for the *Virgen*. I have to say, though, that judging from my dreams around this time, ancestry also influenced strongly my entering the dance. When I say that, I'm not talking about any kind of preknowledge about my ancestry but instead a meeting of ancestors. It is my hunch that they were my Indigenous ancestors. They wore the *trajes* of our troupe, and I took that to mean that I was being called to dance for the *Virgen*.

ancestros

[handwritten marginalia: "Open recruitment brief ~ family ~ ... more important"]

The timing of my being called to dance was important. It was during a relatively brief time when Molly had just taken leadership of La Danza Guadalupana de Pablo Olivares Sr. and had broken with family tradition by recruiting dancers from outside the family. Her simultaneously taking charge of the troupe and opening it up to new *danzantes* coincided with me meeting her as an amateur photographer wanting to photograph her troupe. But, because this active open recruitment policy caused tension among some members, it ended sometime after I joined. Though Molly invited me to dance in the troupe, she never discouraged me from what I wanted to do: photograph the *danza*. But she did not suggest how I could both dance and photograph. It was a given that dancing for the *Virgen* took precedence over photography, even though we both thought the photography was meaningful. Her attitude was much like that of the *Virgen*'s in this sense. There was no pressure to do anything I did not want to do. To accept this call to dance meant accepting a heavy responsibility, but it was also a great honor. And, the weight of this book in your hands shows that I accepted that invitation, that I entered it through an appeal by the *Virgen*. I think it is safe to say the timing was the *Virgen*'s.

Because of the serendipitous timing, the dreams I had, and a clairvoyant experience Molly's mother had—to be described later—how I entered the dance was undeniably a spiritual matter. And entering the dance is a spiritual issue of great importance because the intention of the dance in terms of authenticity is connected to how one enters the dance. Authenticity in the dance and spirit are tightly intertwined. One can enter the dance with motives that are not spiritual, but such a person's dancing would be inauthentic.

The Sharing of Food as Bonding and Memory as Authenticity

Today we danced all day at a number of different churches, beginning in the coffee-black predawn hours. The first *danza* was supposed to be at 5:30 a.m. . . . . *We returned to the residence of the Church of the Little Flower that had a manta of the Virgen outside, so we could dance in front of it.* Manuel again controlled traffic in his *viejo* suit as we crossed Zarzamora Street and as we danced in the street raising his coiled whip to motorists in a gesture that asked them to stop for us. Drivers patiently sat behind their wheels and waited for us to finish, neither bewildered nor anxious about getting anywhere quickly. Afterward, we were invited to the Casa del Carmen again, a kind of church annex on the same block, where we were treated to seasonal Mexican food, e.g., tamales, coffee, pan dulce (sweet bread), and hot chocolate. (Tuesday, December 12, 2006, Feast Day of Our Lady of Guadalupe)

After dancing at *posadas*, masses, house blessings, or Epiphany celebrations, the hosting family or parish members serve us plates of hot food like the kind I have described here. It is served in parish halls, patios, carports, and yards of private homes of hosting families, where dancers are seated at folding tables. It is much more than a polite gesture made by a host to guests, and it is definitely not compensation. The food immediately nourishes us, restores our energy, and warms us, all of which we need to go to the next *danza* we have scheduled for that day or evening. In addition, the *danza* is seen as incomplete without our acceptance of this food. Rather, it bonds the *matachines* with the parish communities, while, in homes, it bonds the *danzantes* and the other devotees with their host families. In both instances, it bonds the dancers with one another and to the devotees of the *Virgen*, and that bonding transcends the food. Although being fed is not a stipulation of our dancing, the lack of food being shared weakens the overall feeling that a *danza* has taken place. It diminishes its authenticity.

Bonding through food is not unusual in the barrio. But it is almost always among close family and other relatives. When there is a *danza*, that custom changes dramatically to include the *matachines* and members of the immediate community. The better the community can bond with the *matachines*, the better the chances are that the matachines will continue to have good *danzas* with that community. Although the bonding through food is a collective experience, individual memories accompany it. At one *danza*, the seasoning in the tamales took me back to a December day in the 1980s when my mother and older sister made tamales that tasted like that. I recalled the rainy, cold days of that December, and the energy of the house as friends and family came and went, either from shopping for presents or bringing them. At another *danza*, the aroma of Spanish rice blending with the acrid scent from bits of red chiles in the tamales transported me to a second childhood home of sorts on the West Side. So did the pungent but somehow pleasant smell of slightly singed chalupa shells, whether I smelled them in a parish hall or at the home of a *posadas*. There, a relative made rice that tasted just like that, and it reminded me of her patience and kindness. I could almost hear her exuberant, sing-song voice in the kitchen, the singing of her caged canaries, the instrumental jingle of the Spanish-language radio

station. The smell of cinnamon from the *champurrado* in homes and halls
after *danzas* remind me of markets on the West Side where my mother would
shop at that time of year and of Mexican chocolate in my home, long before
I began dancing. So, the food put people and places of the past at the fore of
my world. Yet, the evocation of these things is not nostalgia but continuity
of these experiences with these seasonal foods. It is visceral, not intellectual.
And, while some of these foods are actually eaten year-round, such as refried
beans, Spanish rice, and enchiladas, others, such as *champurrado* and tamales,
tend to be eaten during the *Virgen*'s season from December 12 to the Feast
of the Epiphany. So, through personal memories evoked by the tastes, smells,
and colors of the food, we transcend time. Because this sensory and transcendental experience through food is integral to the *danza*, it contributes
to its authenticity by connecting us not only to our past but also with our
ancestors who ate the same seasonal foods.

The Endurance of Tradition as Authenticity

> As we finished our practice of dancing around the lake, the *sonajas* of the
> *capitanes* quickened their tempo as did the drum, though we had come to
> a stop. Tony, who was dancing as *capitán* on my right, called to his older
> son Antonio, who was dancing as *capitán* on my left, cuing him, appar-
> ently, with "What do you say, Antonio?" Antonio shouted to the columns
> in his young voice, "*¡Vuelta a la derecha!*" ([Make a] Turn to the right!) It
> was a command I recalled from many previous *danzas*. Upon hearing this,
> the *danzantes* crouched a bit at the waist and spun around once clockwise.
> Then Tony shouted "*¡Vuelta a la macueca!*" ([Make a] Turn to the left!).
> The columns then spun around once counterclockwise, after which Tony
> shouted the command "*¡Pa'trás! ¡Pa'trás! ¡Pa'trás!*" (Backward! Backward!
> Backward!), and the columns, still crouching, responded by stepping slowly
> a few yards backward. Then, while advancing, we rose from our crouching
> positions and raised our *sonajas* in the air, shaking them vigorously. This is
> how the *veneración*—the final stage of the *danza*—ends. And, during the
> last practice it had been agreed that we would be ending our practice laps
> around the lake this way also. (November 19, 2007)

The ending of our practice in this way is also the way that the *adoración*
(also referred to as *la reverencia* or *la veneración*) ends. This was the first
time Antonio shouted those commands, and I thought it was remarkable
to witness this one small but important aspect of his being groomed, as
Tony put it, to ultimately be a *viejo de la danza*. This was an authentic
danza moment because it demonstrated the continuation of the dance's

trajectory. When I say trajectory, I mean both the ancestral past and the present of our *danza de matachines*. Without trajectory, there can be no authenticity. And, I feel the trajectory was most strongly shown in the use of a single word, *macueca*. It is an archaic word meaning left. Our *danza* uses it synonymously with counterclockwise. I had heard this command given before by our older, more experienced dancers. But the fact that it is such an old word tells how long this aspect of the dance has been part of the tradition. Every generation of *capitanes* going back to Pablo Olivares Sr. and even centuries beyond that are links in a chain connecting all the *matachines* in our present *danza* to our ancestral past. I have always tried to be a strong link in this chain by following Molly's dance instructions faithfully because I know they were taught to her by her uncle. And, each successive generation is a glimpse into the troupe's future. That is, the younger generations in La Danza Guadalupana de Pablo Olivares Sr. know they are the future of the troupe. Their collective character, quality of devotion, and discipline as dancers will define our *danza* when they are older. So, to hear Antonio, who was so young that his voice was just beginning to change, shouting out this order just as previous generations of *capitanes* had long before, and to see the columns respond to him, was very moving. Without this kind of tradition-based trajectory, there can be no authenticity to sustain the continuity of what we experience in the dance. *authenticity to Pablo Oliuan*

Lineage as Authenticity

> Tony has told me that the name of our *danza* has been changed to Los Soldados de la Virgen de Guadalupe. This change is because Junior has resumed using the name La Danza Guadalupana de Pablo Olivares Sr. for a troupe he has once again convened, and, as before, he is drawing from family for members. Those are the names these two *danzas* would be known as in the local press as our respective members stayed the same. (December 1, 2013)

You'll remember from the life history of the dance that the troupe had become inactive when Junior stopped convening it. Now he has resumed his place as lineage holder of the *danza*, and the name of the troupe he inherited from his father was his to claim. Lineage is yet another characteristic that makes a *danza* authentic. Molly held her uncle's lineage, and that gave us authenticity in volumes. Junior's reclaiming of the name, though, was disappointing in that we had spent years establishing the name in San Antonio. What is truly important is that he is carrying on his father's tradition.

As explained in the life history of the dance, Junior was the legitimate lineage holder of the *danza*. Molly had introduced a change in the *danza* by assuming that role and opening the troupe to nonfamily members like me. She did this with the support of her mother, who held much authority as an original member of La Danza Guadalupana de Pablo Olivares Sr. But, after the passing of Molly's mother Junior resumed his leadership role and formed another family-based troupe. That's why he could take back the name we had temporarily adopted and continue his father's dance tradition. In the case of both troupes, we equally acted with authenticity and gave vitality to our continuity, even if it meant Molly would have to work to regain name recognition again.

Although authenticity among matachines troupes is not something that can be readily defined, more than ten years as a *matachín* have educated me in such a way that I can recognize it. And, it is most readily recognized by qualities and characteristics that arise in poignant moments or even by contrasting it with inauthenticity. To me, independent *danzas* such as ours can more adhere to their traditions and indirectly safeguard their authenticity than those aligned with institutions. We can do this because our independence allows us relatively more freedom to address problematic changes that arise in the dance. In that way, we can be more resilient and therefore better ensure our continuity. On the other hand, troupes that are organized by formal membership in, say, a parish church, must more frequently decide how to or if they will reconcile the authority of the *Virgen* with the authority of church leadership.

Authenticity as Autonomy from Institutions

This evening I attended a parish meeting at Our Lady of Guadalupe Church. When Molly and Tony had asked that I attend, I thought it was going to be like the several planning and organizational meetings we had there concerning the pilgrimage. The people from our *danza* who attended were the women in our group from Holy Rosary Church, Molly, Tony, and myself. It turned out to be a routine parish meeting, the kind in which events are planned and administrative concerns addressed. The women from Holy Rosary had asked for a space on the agenda to express their indignation about the pilgrimage being misdirected into the church before being redirected to the plaza. They patiently waited their turn to speak. And, when they did speak, they expressed outrage to the pastor, saying that a church volunteer misdirected participants of our dance pilgrimage into the church after we had firmly agreed differently. With measured but powerful gestures, they also expressed—with equal openness—anger at the pastor for having deferred to the volunteer's version of what had happened. Their concern was that these issues made our group look bad because they implied that we did not keep our word. The lay volunteer scrambled to defend herself. Taking the floor in an impromptu manner and looking like the proverbial deer in the headlights, she said she had acted "naively." The pastor, taken by surprise, tried to be diplomatic but could say little to quell the women from our group. And, when the meeting moved to the next point, the members of our *danza* departed, our *danzantes* from Holy Rosary Church having spoken for the record, so to speak. (Sunday, December 16, 2007)

Cordiality characterizes the relationship between clergy and matachines unless a code of respect is violated by the clergy, regardless of whether they understand this code or not. This ethic is not unique to matachines, but, rather, it is common in San Antonio barrios (Spanish-speaking neighborhoods). Because matachines in San Antonio are largely from barrios, it is not surprising that the Holy Rosary women would voice their ire with such directness and with the support of other members of the troupe who were present. This incident only illustrates the autonomous nature of the relationship between independent matachines troupes and the church. Specifically, it is an example of how we make sure that the respect for and integrity of the troupe is safeguarded. This incident demonstrated a tradition of distance and, therefore, autonomy that matachines have had from institutions. Matachines are tactful and may even be diffident. However, when codes of respect or boundaries are broken by institutions, there is no patent respect for them that replaces our indignation or assertions of needs. While I would not go so far as to say the value placed on keeping one's word is essential to a matachines troupe's authenticity, I would say that it is a mark of authenticity among its members in that it shows that they sub-scribe to barrio codes and values and are not afraid to be confrontational when these values are at stake.

Autonomy cannot be readily measured. And it is relative, including for *danza de matachines* troupes like La Danza Guadalupana de Pablo Olivares Sr. that are family-based rather than parish-based. But, because our troupe is an autonomous one, we place greater value on our autonomy, as you can see in this confrontation. The reason why we value autonomy so much is because authenticity depends on autonomy from institutions. *Danzas* like ours do not submit to institutions, not even parishes.

Integrity of the Danza as Authenticity

We danced at a *posadas* on the southwest side of town. We had danced there before on December 22, 2007. Despite this being at a private home, the priest from San Martín de Porres Parish had maneuvered the agenda in such a way that our *danza* was to take place last, while thirty to thirty-five people were sitting on a patio and finishing their traditional Mexican dinner. My guest noted that the parish priest stood by, making disrespectful comments and jokes about our *danza* to others as we danced. And there was a young mother of a small child who was speaking on a cell phone the entire time. Before we began, I overheard Molly's mother tell her, "*Están danzando, nada más.*" ("You're [going to be] dancing, nothing more.") That is, something was lacking that would prevent the dance from being what it could be. Molly's Aunt Juanita would later signal Molly to bring the dancing to a premature but appropriate close.

Afterward Tony, Molly, the guest, and I all sat down to eat and wound up discussing the priest's behavior . That particular *posadas* was organized "by the community," as Tony pointed out, that is, independently of its parish. However, the parish priest had been invited by the host to participate. (I recall him in 2007 leading the rosary that traditionally precedes the *posadas*.) He was apparently also deferred to with regard to scheduling. The matachines customarily dance after the *posadas*, immediately before participants partake in the meal of traditional food. The dancers—I was the only exception—were all related to the Aguilar family by either blood or marriage, and it was clear to the adult dancers that we would not be dancing there again.

Despite their disappointment, Molly and Tony were quick to tell me about a recent *posadas* in which there was much interactive and enthusiastic participation by those who had gathered, including non-Catholic Christians. Molly and Tony were still very happy about that event. (December 20, 2011)

 For the *danza* to be authentic, it cannot be viewed as a form of entertainment. If it is intentionally danced as entertainment, it has no authenticity. The *danza* cannot be turned into entertainment. If those who attend a social situation see the *danza* as entertainment despite the intentions of the dancers to make it a sincere prayer, its authenticity is still compromised. When it is compromised, those in attendance cannot be appropriately attentive to the *danza* or fully experience it. This attentiveness is an important part of the *danza*'s authenticity. So, if even an authentic *danza* begins to continually dance as entertainment, it can lose its authenticity.

Several years have passed since that incident, but I still vividly recall Molly's Aunt Juanita's expression after it became clear that we were "*danzando nada más*," as Molly's mother put it. Her presence had unmistakably become one of corrective authority, and she appropriately carried herself with great dignity and purpose. I remember seeing her walking diagonally across some carpet grass after giving the signal for us to end the dance and preserve our integrity. At that moment she had all the presence of a *monarca* though she has never danced as one. In a photo featured much earlier in this book, she can be seen standing next to the troupe's founder. She looks not a day over nine. And, though the angelic expression with which she gazes at the camera is quite different from the one of contained indignation she had at that *posadas*, I do notice a common factor: an awareness of what happens in the dance, of how it is supposed to be experienced. In other words, she had already formed an understanding of this at a very early age. I would venture to guess that she may have become even more keenly aware of it as she grew older, but she nonetheless understood this at a very young age. This incident further suggests that the experience of the *danza* is not based on knowledge about the dance as much as visceral awareness of what occurs in it. That is why authority in the *danza* is based on the accruement of experience. Most importantly, this incident serves as an illustration of how change not of our making can threaten continuity of the dance. Molly's older family members do well to safeguard the *danza*'s integrity with such deft understanding of the dance, as shown in this by her mother and aunt in this incident. Otherwise, the *danza*'s authenticity and, consequently, its continuity would stand to be compromised.

Authenticity vs. Associations Not of Our Making

Along the pilgrimage route, I was surprised to see in the dim morning light two people from a local political, nonprofit arts organization. As the drumming of the troupes echoed off homes and small businesses, I noticed that their clinical gazes contrasted with the knowing, elated, and smiling eyes of the devotees of the *Virgen* who lined the streets. Although I had been on cordial terms with them, I could not help but think that they looked out of place in that barrio. (Feast Day of San Juan Diego and Day of the Pilgrimage, Sunday December 9, 2007)

I had seen those individuals in settings removed from the working-class barrios of the West Side. I had seen them at political rallies or organizing for political events north of downtown. When I see something in my surroundings that is out of place, I become alert and even wary. This tendency is a part of basic street smarts that I gained over time from having to walk alone, often at night, in urban settings. It is not mainstream deduction learned in school. So, when I saw these two people, I thought something was wrong. And, though I was not in immediate bodily danger, something was not right.

I would have been unconcerned by their presence except that I sensed that they wanted to use the extraordinary visual value of the *danza* pilgrimage as political poker chips in future newsletters or press kits. They could convince San Antonio at large that they somehow represented working-class Chicano communities and justify continued grant funding. Unlike the many devotees who stood by taking pictures now and again of loved ones or of the *Virgen* on her *estandartes*, the activists were taking away images for purposes that were both public and political. But the *danza* is not political, so I felt like something was being taken out of our hands and repurposed.

They had not requested permission or explained the purpose of their photography. This behavior concerned me because I thought it possible that they would use the photos to try to advance an unrelated cause by publishing them out of context, with a political essay for example. Such an act could have only been a distorted representation of our pilgrimage because of the apolitical nature of our intentions for organizing and carrying it out. I had witnessed such co-optations of events such as the Day of the Dead to bring awareness to social causes. I felt an obligation to prevent such a possible distortion. Yet, though I was the *monarca*, Moctezuma II dancing for the *Virgen* at the head of our troupe, there was nothing I could do because this was, legally speaking, a public undertaking.

Gente from the barrio who were photographing the dance pilgrimage had not asked permission either. But they were photographing for different reasons: because they were devotees of the *Virgen*, because they had family in the pilgrimage, because they had lived in that barrio for generations, because they had neighbors in the pilgrimage who were like extended family to them. The interlopers, though, could not claim any of these things.

In this occurrence, the authenticity of the *danza* stands out in relief because of the effort by people outside to claim it as integral to or an aspect of some separate sphere of activity with which they are involved. I imagined how their images might appear in one of their future publications and its subtext: "Look at these colorfully feathered brown people dancing in *devotees can take picture or video as memories of the experience (not as capturing a cultural [external] experience*

the streets of these old communities! We know working-class Latinos who still practice old traditions. Therefore, we are as authentic as they are." It would look so exotic to outsiders that they would have to trust whatever self-serving characterization that nonprofit gave the pilgrimage. As time would go by, I would see similar opportunism among self-styled theologians, at least one new ager, and activists claiming that ancestral connections to the missions made them Indians.

In this case, individuals were attempting to use the *danza* to claim authenticity through an association with it. Paradoxically, they forfeited any such claim by committing a number of faux pas. One was failing to recognize that, though we were dancing in a public space, the action was private, that is, intended for ourselves and the community of devotees. And, as mentioned before, they made no effort to ask us for permission ahead of time. If they had an authentic association with the *danza* or the *Virgen*, they would have known to ask permission. Being photographed by these individuals in order for them to pursue cultural capital felt unmistakably invasive.

If you enter the *danza* for the wrong reasons, you come away with nothing of authenticity. This means, if you come to the dance in order to become authentic, you will forfeit any claim to authenticity. Nor can authenticity of the *danza* be destroyed by the presence of such people. Even if such people try to use the *danza* as a product or marketing prop, it cannot destroy the authenticity of the dance because their dance is not *the* dance. It is a facsimile of the dance.

Implications for Authenticity, Change, and Continuity

While exploring these thoughts on the role of authenticity in the *danza*, I found that, in addition to the moments that directly illustrated them, there were moments that *indirectly* illustrated them. They *implied* authenticity. The moments that directly illustrated authenticity were in the seemingly serendipitous way that the *Virgen* brings people to the *danza*, the bonding and experiences that come from sharing food, the adherence to traditions in the *danza* over generations, maintaining the integrity of the dance, and observing unwritten codes about the holding of lineage. The moments that illustrated authenticity through implication did so by revealing the authority of the *estandarte*, the importance of intention, and autonomy from institutions.

By organizing these thoughts on the *danza*'s authenticity into general themes and reflecting on them further, I know that authenticity stands on sources of spiritual and social authority. The sources of spiritual authority are the *estandarte*, how one enters the *danza*, the sharing of food, and endurance of the *danza*. The sources of social authority that the *danza*'s authenticity rests on are ancestral lineage, autonomy from institutions, integrity, and freedom from politics.

I did not set out to understand the *danza*'s relationship to authenticity in the ways that hindsight has unexpectedly allowed me. Nor did I interview anyone to arrive at these understandings. And I especially could not fully understand these situations and articulate my thoughts and feelings with respect to them at the time. But my long-term experience in the *danza* led to insights because my years of dancing allowed me to form frames of reference for authenticity. This lack of premeditation on my part and years of experience are actually what qualifies me as a person to write about La Danza Guadalupana de Pablo Olivares Sr., especially as far as authenticity is concerned. I entered the dance with no other aspiration than to respect its traditions. I had no preconceived idea of what authenticity in the *danza* might be, though while growing up I accrued certain related experiences that served as a foundation for dancing for the *Virgen*. And because I have been a long-term dancer, I have been able to look back on incidents like the time the priest made fun of us. Over the years that followed that night, I have been able to relate it to exchanges I have had with Molly's mother and aunt, which I would not have had if my commitment to the *danza* had been brief. I have been able to process those exchanges and others like them internally, over time, consequently gaining firmer frames of reference for what authenticity of the *danza* is. It is important to have accurate and well-rooted frames of reference for authenticity because when authenticity is lost continuity is also lost.

Second Reflection—The Metaphysics of Accoutrements

In my experience as a *monarca*, I have often had the unmistakable sense that our accoutrements have a metaphysical aspect (like other aspects of the *danza*). By that, I mean that objects we use in the *danza* can transcend their physical realities. Over time, I have noticed that objects are imbued by the intention put into making. The act of making the accoutrements can be transcendental as well. That is, when making them, you can transcend time and space. Key dancers in our troupe have told me of instances of clairvoyance happening during the act of making *naguas*. By clairvoyance,

I mean being able to tell on some level that a certain change in the dance is approaching. It was only with the passage of time that I was able to look at experiences, sometimes separated by years of dancing, and see how metaphysics connected the dots that spelled out the roles that accoutrements play in the *danza*. To understand the metaphysics of our accoutrements is to understand how this aspect of the *danza* helps us to dance for the *Virgen* and gives it continuity.

Metaphysics of Clairvoyance and *Trajes*

Tonight we danced at a *posadas* near St. Alphonsus Church. It was cold and dark by the time we finished. But I had assembled the photos I had taken of La Danza Guadalupana last year into an album and had been looking for an opportunity to give them to Molly and Tony as a Christmas present. So, as they were packing the *trajes* back into their vehicle, I rushed to present the album to them. They were delighted, and I was so glad that they liked the photos. Up until that point, the three of us had little opportunity to talk because we were concentrating on assembling the *estandarte*, getting dressed, and starting on time. So, my presenting them with the photos seemed to make us all realize that we could decompress, so to speak, and talk more socially.

It was then that Molly told me something that took me by surprise. Her mother shared with her and Tony that weeks before meeting me, she had felt compelled to sew a pair of *naguas* for someone who was tall and thin, but she did not know why. She did not know anyone that looked like that. Then, when she saw me in the parking lot at the basilica, she realized that she had made them for me. I was stunned that she had that experience and felt a kind of honor that Molly and Tony trusted me enough to share that with me. (December 17, 2006)

Fluidity of time can be accessed through the process of making accoutrements. Several years later, after Molly's mother, Francisca Aguilar, passed away, Molly and Tony told me that whenever they were contacted to dance at a last minute's notice, her mother would tell them, "Be sure to invite Roberto," referring to me. Molly once told me that shortly before either of them met me, her mother felt inexplicably compelled to make a *traje* for someone who was taller than anyone who had been in the *danza*. On that day, I had come to the *danza* to carry the *estandarte* at Molly's request. So, when her mother realized she had been making a *traje* for me, I was still iffy about dancing. There was not even an expectation that I would dance in the future.

After making my *traje*, she continued to make others in this way, even intuiting the personalities of other people who they would fit before having met them. It was as if she were transcending time and space or being told about these people in advance. The last time I saw Molly's mother was at a *danza* held at her home. It was cold and at dusk, and additional coldness came from the moisture that was rising from the ground. Shortly after I arrived, she saw me. It had been a while since we had seen each other because she had been busy caring for one of her daughters. She took both of my hands and clasped them tightly as we greeted each other on her gravel driveway in the darkness. Then, looking at me a bit puzzled, she said, "*¡Tanto he soñado contigo!*" (I have dreamt so much of you!) Because I had so much respect for her, I did not have the nerve to ask her to elaborate. The intensity with which she spoke those few words to me and the directness of her eye contact are still with me. Her facial expression was expectant, as if I might be able to explain why she had those dreams. Whenever I was in her presence, she was very measured in her words and actions. That moment was no exception, and I knew she would not have said that to me unless she felt it was important.

Starting in my early years in the *danza*, I began to hear from Molly and Tony that Francisca Aguilar was impressed with my dancing. That was, of course, great news. Just knowing that she approved would have been high praise, given her association with La Danza Guadalupana de Pablo Olivares Sr. since its beginning. And, as time went by, the news of her admiration of my skills continued (surprising me perhaps more than anyone). I think that my skills as a dancer were at least part of the reason why she made sure I went to the last-minute *danzas*. But I also think her clairvoyant experiences making my *traje* and dreams she had of me were also reasons.

The Metaphysics of Harvesting *Carrizos*

I finished the eighth and final row of my *naguas* yesterday. But before I could finish, I ran out of *carrizos* twice. That meant I had to harvest more *carrizo* stalks. Maintenance of the rows of *carrizos* is an ongoing task. A few *carrizos* fall off at each *danza* because of the vigor of the dance. So, you wind up having to repair lines of *carrizos* in between *danzas*. When I began to select and cut stalks, swinging the machete at a downward angle felt natural. It was almost as if someone else were doing it. When people feel this kind of sensation, they often say things like, "I must have done this in a previous life," with varying degrees of seriousness. I did not feel like I had done this in a previous life, but it felt familiar, as if something like genetic memory were connecting me to ancestors. (September 3, 2007)

Harvesting *carrizo* stalks is also part of the process of dancing and an activity that reminds me that I'm participating in a very old process. The *carrizos*, after all, are native to the region. And, in nearby northern Mexico they have been harvested for *naguas* for as long as the tradition has existed. When harvesting them, I have an intuitive awareness that I'm sharing this act with generations of the dance's ancestors. I feel like it would sound too grandiose to say that harvesting *carrizo* stalks is a ritual, so I will not. But it does have the kind of transcendental sense about it that traditions do, as mundane as harvesting *carrizo* stalks may seem.

I have given much thought to Francisca Aguilar's powers of intuition in relation to her decades of work as a maker of *trajes*. The repetition and intention of such work over the years can facilitate access to the fluidity of time I spoke of earlier. Perhaps this access occurs when we engage in those especially traditional aspects of the dance—including the making of accoutrements—because our ancestors in the dance have never really left. They are still here, sharing in these activities for the *Virgen*. By ancestors, I am not talking necessarily about lineal ancestors but rather those of the dance's lineage. They have gone before us in the dance and its traditions and continue to participate with us not only in the dance but even in the harvesting of *carrizos* for our *naguas*. It is, after all, an activity that is as old as the *danza*.

The Metaphysics of Heart, Flow, and Intention

Today Molly's mother accompanied Molly and Tony to practice. She brought me the vest and *naguas* she sewed for me. The vest already had a sequined image of the *Virgen* sewn on the back. I just need to add the carrizos to the *naguas*, and she has given me some along with some wooden beads and trade bells to get started. Molly and Tony told me how to cut the *carrizos*, adding to make sure each one is the length of my palm. The lowest row should meet the green fringes (called *las barbillas*), and the uppermost row should begin about ten inches from the top. Each length of *carrizo* should be aligned vertically with the one below it. I listened to all of this with the same intensity as when I was instructed in the dance steps. And for the same reason: I knew this was rooted in tradition. Tradition and spirit are related. And, the *danza* is all about spirit. Its traditions, even ones having to do with material things, are spiritual. (July 16, 2007)

As the seamstress for the troupe, Molly's mother measured, cut, and sewed the red flannel and linen interior of the *naguas*, vests, and *capas*. She would also sew four kinds of trim onto the vests. And she sewed sequined images of the *Virgen* onto both vests and *capas*. However, she left the task of sewing the *carrizos* onto the *naguas* for the individual *danzante* for whom they were made. One reason for this was that it is a *very* time-consuming task. I wound up sewing on four rows consisting of sixteen *carrizos* each, and there was room for another row. The likely prospect of having more than one new *danzante* that year would have meant hundreds of hours of work she alone would not have completed by the beginning of our dance season in mid-December.

She had only requested that I pay her $25 for the materials she purchased to make the basics. Also, she gave me a plastic bag containing some wooden beads, trade bells, *carrizos*, a spool of nylon string, and a large sewing needle that she had attached to a piece of red linen. On the linen she had written her name and phone number in large, graceful cursive, showing indirectly how much value she placed on the needle, which was on loan to me.

In the parking lot of Woodlawn Lake Park, Molly showed me how to sew the *carrizos* into the *naguas* by sewing one into the piece of red linen in the bag. When I arrived home from practice, I went to work on the *naguas*, following the instructions she gave me. First, about a yard of nylon string has to be cut. I found I could approximate this measurement by holding the spool at the center of my collar bone and, with the free end of the string in my left hand, extending my left arm as far to my left as possible. I then cut this length of string at the spool to double-thread the needle. I pushed the threaded needle through the linen side of the *naguas*, that is, the part that faces inward when worn. I had to take care not to pass the string entirely through the *naguas*. I then passed the needle through a length of *carrizo*, then through the loop of a trade bell. At this point, I passed the needle back through the length of *carrizo* and through the front part of the *naguas* about one-quarter inch to the right of the other hole, forming two pairs of strings that I tied securely together. But I had to be sure to leave enough slack for the *carrizo* and its bell to swing and make noise.

Because the trade bell is slightly bigger than the opening in the length of *carrizo*, it can be loosely held in place there. Care must be taken to return the double-threaded needle through the interior of the length of *carrizo*. If this is not done, the *carrizo* will not be able to move, and the string on its outside will be unsightly. When sewing on the first or last *carrizo* of each row, the needle and string are passed through a brown, wooden bead instead of through a trade bell. As complicated as this may sound, I noticed that from the repetition of the physical movements involved in this process, a rhythm developed after many sittings and hours of repeating these steps. By the time I finished sewing all the lengths of *carrizos*, I felt the process was starting to develop its own consciousness.

When it develops its own consciousness in this way, it imbues the item being made with intention and heart. My heartfelt intention when I was sewing on my *carrizos* was to dance for the *Virgen*. I also think that this consciousness of repetitive action may come from participating in a traditional activity initiated by ancestors. Based on my experiences in the *danza*, I think the activities of ancestors transcend time. So, it leads to reason that ancestors who sewed *carrizos* are still making them. And, on some level, we can plug into that awareness if we share the same intentions of dancing for the *Virgen*. I had a chance to share in this activity with ancestors over space and time. Ancestors, after all, connect the past with the present. The dance and even the act of making accoutrements have ancestors, and that lineage does not necessarily follow linear, genetic lines. Rather, it follows the trajectory of the activity, whether it is dancing or making accoutrements.

I have reflected much on this in relation to how Molly's paternal grandmother made the *traje* for Molly's father to wear as *el viejo de la danza*, his *traje de viejo*. In one long sitting, she sewed each of its hundreds of cloth strips individually onto coveralls. She recited a specific, traditional prayer with each strip she attached, and, by doing so, imbued the entire *traje* with intention. This is another example—probably the best I can think of—that shows how repetitive, heartfelt action imbues accoutrements with that energy of intention that contributes to the *danza*'s vitality. The prayers that went into sewing each of these strips of cloths facilitate *el viejo*'s ability to become transformed into the rowdy, raucous *viejo*. His voice changes, and he can spontaneously and effortlessly project it as he shouts at the dancers.

The Metaphysics of Aesthetic Expression and Individual Needs

A few days ago, as we rested after practice at Woodlawn Lake, Tony told me Molly's mother finished the *sonajas* that she had begun to make and even has some *carrizos* for my *traje*. I will just need to sew them into the *naguas* made for me. He mentioned, as he does from time to time, that Pablo Olivares Sr. emphasized the importance of the members of his *danza* decorating their *trajes* according to their individual tastes. An example of this is how we space our *carrizos* on our *naguas*. Some people can sew their lengths of *carrizos* tightly together, with barely any space between them. Or, they can space them farther apart, adding yellow trim between the rows, or

not, and so on. The idea is that there is a balance between the general uni-
formity of the *trajes* and individual ideas about how one's own *traje* should
look. This practice is spiritual in that it is following an aesthetic guided
by an underlying spiritual principal our founder initiated. (May 27, 2007)

Pablo Olivares Sr.'s emphasis on individual aesthetics meant members of
his *danza* could decorate their *trajes* according to their individual needs. In
other words, this ethic allows us to imbue our *trajes* with those aesthetics
that are most related to our individual motives for dancing. For example,
some dancers pin photos, handwritten notes, or scanned images of loved
ones they are praying/dancing for to their vests and *capas*. By doing so, that
loved one's image is placed in physical and metaphysical proximity to an
object imbued with sincere intention: the *traje*. It strengthens our dance by
making it metaphysically active and, consequently, strengthens the prayer
that our dance constitutes.

I first experienced this metaphysic when I danced for the first time in
a full *traje*. Francisca Aguilar lent me her son Tony's *naguas*. (This Tony
should not be confused with her son-in-law.) In addition to the profound
sense of honor the loan made me feel, two things engraved themselves into
my mind on that occasion. One was that at that *danza* she danced wearing
a photo of her son whose *naguas* I was borrowing pinned to her *traje*. In the
photo he wore a US Navy uniform, and I sensed that the photo pinned to
her *traje* was a measure for his protection by the *Virgen*. And, in hindsight,
I understand that the photo being pinned to a *traje*, that is, something
made with heart, added vitality to her dancing and the prayer contained
in it because they are one and the same. The second thing that stood out
from that *danza* was the *traje* I had been loaned. Since that was my first
time to dance, I had little experience at the time. So, I watched and imitated
the other *matachines* who were dancing. I should have felt awkward, but
instead my dancing felt full of energy, relaxed, and almost as if my legs were
not subject to gravity. One reason why I think this happened was because
of the heartfelt intention that Molly's mother put into making the *naguas*.
Another reason is because it had been worn and danced in by a *danzante*
who danced with heart. Over the years, as more members came and went,
I could see how this allowance for individuality makes the troupe more
human and, consequently, more vibrant. More homogenous troupes, on
the other hand, especially the ones with mass-produced *trajes*, seem like a
single but less organic and less vital unit.

Francisca Aguilar's son was alive and well, but he was on active duty in the navy. Judging from my own mother's habit of placing photos of her children in proximity of the *Virgen* during times of concern, I had a hunch that this was Francisca Aguilar's way of praying for her son Tony's safety. But, other than that instance, the photos I have seen pinned to *trajes* have been of our late founder. His image attached to a *traje* imbued with heart means he is dancing with us in spirit.

After I had received my *traje*, I dreamed of the image of a blue bear. I thought that if I designed a graphic based on that image and sewed it onto my vest, I might later learn why I had that dream. Before I got around to making the design, though, I became the *monarca*. This meant that I would be wearing one of the five *capas* used by the *monarca* and the *capitanes*. At the time, the *capas* belonged to Molly and Tony, so it would have been wrong for me to decorate with a permanent image. As it later happened, our dance step called *el oso* (the bear) became my favorite step, and I danced it almost consistently whenever it was my turn to venerate the *Virgen*.

Implications for the Metaphysics of Accoutrements in Relation to Change and Continuity

My experiences in the *danza* point to a relationship between our accoutrements and the metaphysical world. Accoutrements are conduits for spirit/ancestors. I learned this from Molly's mother's intuition that I would be joining La Danza Guadalupana de Pablo Olivares before she even knew I existed. As I harvested *carrizo* stalks with a machete, I felt an empathetic awareness of *matachines* before me doing the same thing. Similarly, by listening to key dancers in our troupe and by sewing my own *carrizos* onto my *naguas*, I gained insights into how the physical action of making accoutrements can have a metaphysical effect on the accoutrement and the *matachín* who uses it. These are insights that can only be known through the private, long-term experience of *matachines* who dance in a troupe that has lineage like ours does. They are happenstance insights. When I had these experiences, I did not even know enough about the *danza* to ask questions that these insights would have explained. They came to me only later through personal, private reflection. The metaphysical aspects of our accoutrements give the dance life and, in that way, help us to dance for the *Virgen*. They make me aware that I belong to a community of *danzantes* who started dancing centuries ago and who dance with our troupe. They

Molly wears photos of her uncle Pablo Olivares and of her late parents. When photos of deceased matachines are worn in this way in the *danza*, they too participate in the dance. Photo: Margaret Greco.

give me as a dancer an awareness of the importance of my role in the *danza* and of the *danza* itself.

Third Reflection—The Community of Devotees

In the ensuing years, I have come to reflect on my interactions with the many people who came to our *danzas* in the barrio churches and at *posadas*. Unlike other devotees of the *Virgen*, they are people for whom the *danza* is a familiar tradition that makes the *Virgen* spiritually present and predisposed to answer their prayers or receive their thanks for prayers answered. Their devotion to the *Virgen* and familiarity with the *danza* spans age ranges and varies in terms of places of origin and levels of acculturation. This is not simply church-directed devotion. In my experience, practices such as making requests of the *Virgen* on her feast day or praying rosaries at *danzas* are traditions devotees of the *Virgen* developed independently and have been practiced for many generations. I realized that this remarkable consistency resembles a "floating" community in that we are people whose intensity of

*at + here, the author
admits link to other
danzantes*

A member of the community of devotees of the *Virgen* holds an *estandarte* with her image during our 2008 pilgrimage in recognition of the feast day of San Juan Diego.

devotion and participation in related, ritual traditions are not necessarily limited to physical communities. As a *matachín*, I recall dancing in West Side barrios then driving to dance on the opposite side of town where I found the same emotional attachment to the dance, the same understanding of unwritten protocols, and same reverence for the *Virgen* as I did on the West Side.

These reflections are snapshots that recur in what I have come to know as the community of devotees. It is a community of non-*matachines* that has singled out the *Virgen* as the main focus of devotional practices throughout the year. These devotional practices include such things as the upkeep of a home altar, lighting votive candles before her image in church, and praying the rosary. Members of this community also pray to her for aid in their vicissitudes and those of loved ones. They feel a closeness to the *danza de matachines* and show up at our *danzas* as if wanting to dance for the *Virgen* through *us*. Before or after the *danza*, it is not unusual for such devotees to ask to touch our *estandarte* so they can make a silent petition to the *Virgen* while doing so.

The devotees of the Virgen are *gente*; they are concentrated in barrios and share the values and codes of conduct of those neighborhoods. The community of devotees is made up of people with their own individual, if similar, relationships to the *Virgen*. Such devotions are expressed mostly privately in homes, churches, and shrines. Despite the private nature that characterizes individual devotions to the *Virgen* in the community of devotees, its members have existed since her appearance in Colonial central Mexico.

The Participation of the Community of Devotees in *la Veneración*

> We were dancing *la veneración* at the Church of the Little Flower. The *capitanes* had finally captured *el viejo de la danza* and won his conversion to the *Virgen*. He knelt before her *estandarte* as the *capitanes* stood on either side of him, watching him as he crossed himself resignedly. Then a *capitán* shouted to everyone gathered, "*¡La gente!*" He and another *capitán* then began to lead parishioners to the *estandarte* two by two. Those who felt inspired tried dancing. Those who did not still seemed ecstatic to be able to revere La Virgen de Guadalupe in this way. (December 12, 2006)

When the *capitanes* escort members of the community of devotees in *la veneración* (also called *la devoción*), they do it by dancing between the two lines that form the columns, going from one end of the column to the other where she awaits on her *estandarte*. When they reach her end of the columns, they may express their devotion to her by kissing or touching the *estandarte* or by genuflecting.

Each individual who is escorted to the *Virgen*'s *estandarte* brings a personal, private message for the *Virgen*. It may be one of gratitude or urgency. And, it may involve prayers for these individuals' loved ones or for their own needs. But these individual expressions made through their participation in our *veneración* contribute to the continuity of our *danza* and, by extension, the continuity of the larger *danza de matachines* tradition. It is not unusual for *veneraciones* to last forty-five minutes, and there have been times when they have lasted much longer than that. The duration of a *veneración* depends on the size of the community of devotees in the parish or barrio where we are dancing and on how many of its members know that we are dancing that day. So, by participating directly in our *veneración*, members of the community of devotees expresses their individual needs with a solemn, celebratory devotion. These private expressions infuse our dance with a vitality that contributes to the dance's continuity and ability to deal with change.

The Devotion of Immigrants

For today's practice we danced and drummed around Woodlawn Lake again, twice. It was humid, and the sun shone brightly amid wisps of steamy white clouds. When we were finished, Tony bought snacks and refreshments from one of the concession trucks parked nearby, and we went to seat ourselves in the grass. As we sat resting, Tony, Molly, and I speculated about immigration legislation being presented in Washington and what effect it might have on the participation of matachines who are undocumented workers. Molly and I took the position that it would inhibit undocumented workers' participation in the *danza* on December 12. Tony, on the other hand, believed that because farmers are complaining about the labor loss in the wake of raids, the latest drafts of a new bill would allow for a more lenient stance by Washington and consequently make undocumented workers less inhibited about attending public feast day events. I was not as optimistic and pointed out that workers from Mexico are switching from agricultural to construction work to be less visible. (May 29, 2007)

Mexican immigrants constitute a significant part of the community of devotees in San Antonio. On the feast day of the *Virgen* the previous year, immigration and customs enforcement (ICE) conducted raids, targeting Mexican immigrants. The *Virgen*'s feast day activities tend to draw undocumented Mexican citizens into the public, making them vulnerable for possible detention and deportation, a fact that ICE took advantage of. Though we do not involve the *danza* in politics, politics—in the form of immigration legislation—affects us by undermining the community of devotees' ability to participate in and sustain our dance tradition. To that extent, strident changes in the application of immigration policy hinder the continuity of the dance.

Up to this point those of us in La Danza Guadalupana de Pablo Olivares Sr. had never talked about problems that immigration status might pose. But this was a different year because we were organizing a dance pilgrimage that was bound to bring more *mexicanos* than usual together publicly. The presence of Mexican immigrants in the community of devotees is extremely important to the continuity of the *danza de matachines* in San Antonio. Our founder, Pablo Olivares Sr. was an immigrant himself. When he immigrated to San Antonio, he brought with him knowledge and understanding of the *danza*'s traditions in addition to knowing and being able to teach dance steps to the younger generation of his family who would be born in the United States. Because of his experiences growing up in Monterrey, he knew what it was like to dance in an autonomous *danza de matachines* troupe. Similarly, Mexican-born members of the community of devotees are the lifeblood of the traditions that are both central and peripheral to our *danza* traditions. Many of them become *matachines*, and many more become those who prepare food at their homes and parish halls and host our *danzas* at *posadas*. They are among the ones who most appreciate being invited to dance in the *veneración*. Through all the direct and indirect roles that they play with confidence and dedication, they contribute to the *danza*'s continuity.

Freedom of Organization among the Community of Devotees

Today was the first day for me to dance as a *monarca*.... *The dance went well. It was a religious event (a rosary) that took place in an indoor basketball court of a West Side community center. Perhaps one reason it went so well was because it started with a rosary that* had a grounding effect on our dancing and on the community of devotees.

The event began with the actual praying of the rosary. When it started a small group of about seven people from the neighborhood formed a semi-circle to the side of a highly decorated altar beneath one of the basketball hoops. It had a three-foot statue of La Virgen de Guadalupe, fragrant roses in vases, incense cones burning, votive candles, and religious pictures. The tastefully decorated altar together with dimmed lights converted the basketball court into a place of reverence.

The rosary was being recited in such a low, almost hushed tone that most of our group did not notice. Then one of the women in our group from Holy Family Church realized it and quickly gravitated to the altar. She was followed by other dancers and by members of the community of devotees who had been seated in the chairs conversing, unaware of the praying. One of the women who had recently joined our troupe from Holy Rosary Church interrupted the rosary to ask if the woman leading it could pray "*Más recio*" (louder). These women are quite devout and did not want an understated rosary. The devotees who had been talking then joined the others in praying the rosary. (December 2, 2007)

That community center was on the West Side. Members of the community of devotees from that barrio organized that *danza*. Many more members had come to pray the rosary and, of course, to attend our *danza*. They had also prepared an *altar* to the *Virgen* on the floor of the indoor basketball court where we danced, which says much of their resourcefulness. I was impressed that these women had organized this event on their own initiative; that is, they were not acting on the directives of any organization or institution. Nor were they acting as members of an events committee for the community center. There was a sense of improvisation put forth by the devotee organizers. It was almost as palpable as the devotion, which also could be sensed during the rosary. This event illustrates the spontaneous spirit of organization that can be present when institutional participation is marginal.

It is critical to understand that this event was driven by the collective devotion of its organizers. There was no political agenda, no box on a grant application that this event's organizers checked off. It would not have been unusual for such an event in a venue under the city government to have the presence of an administrator, a security officer, signed waivers of liability, a public relations photographer, a local politician, and possibly the mass media. Yet, this event was organized free of hierarchical and bureaucratic control, having as its sole purpose the veneration of the *Virgen* with a *danza* and rosary. And though there had been no publicity other than flyers on the door and bulletin board, it was well attended by the community of devotees in that barrio. This degree of simplicity would be expected at a hosting residence but not at a public community center. What also made this event's organization free from institutional organization was that since the community center could not schedule the *danza* for December 12, the *Virgen*'s feast day, the devotees decided to settle for having it ten days earlier.

The *danzante* who told the organizers to pray louder would not have felt as free to express her individual, spiritual frustration if this had greater formal organization and obvious presence of sponsorship from an institution. (Though *danzantes* are not members of the community of devotees, I saw her as one because she was still very new to the troupe and had often showed in word, action, and prayer that she had been a member of the community of devotees for many years.) Just as importantly, she could not have asserted her (and other dancers') need for the prayer to be louder if she were not among members of the community of devotees. She spoke because she was talking to other members of the community of devotees whose presence dominated the gym. Members of the community of devotees readily understand that everyone has thanks, praise, and petitions for themselves and others that they want to put before the *Virgen*.

If there had been a secular presence in the form of politicians, tourists, and/or paid staff, it would have eroded the intimacy that our troupe and the devotees created on this day and try to create at every *danza*. Because private devotions to the *Virgen* are the motivating force behind the community of devotees' organization of *danzas*, its members keep secular factors from interfering in the *danza*'s spirit. By doing so, they contribute to the continuity of the *danza*. And, the community of devotees' freedom of organization facilitates continuity of the dance through that style of organization and its ability to improvise in the face of change.

The Community of Devotees and Sidestepping Attempts at Redirection

The feast day of Our Lady of the Angels was on August 2, but Our Lady of the Angels Church celebrated it on the seventeenth, a Sunday, by having their matachines and those from other parishes dance in procession around the block. La Danza Guadalupana de Pablo Olivares Sr. was there too. We were behind Our Lady of Angels' matachines. As is often the case, we stood in formation—this time in the street—waiting much longer than we expected. Carmen and Manuel were there as Malinche and the *viejo de la danza*.

The matachines at that church mostly have *penachos*, but some wore bandanas instead. Their bandanas had the national colors of Mexico, red, white, and green, and the Mexican coat of arms. The feathers of their *penachos* were red, white, and green too, and had a red base. They looked like short ostrich plumes but not as soft. I recognized a *viejo de la danza* from the night of the 2006 Feast Day of the Epiphany/Día de los Reyes Magos at St. Alphonsus Church. There were two children who were so frightened by him that they were almost in tears.

A pickup truck led the procession. It had a statue of Our Lady of the Angels in the bed of the truck, which was bedecked with light blue and white sheets. There were two or three drummers sitting on the open tailgate. To our surprise, the group in front of us paused as many as three times to dance in a stationary rectangle that they formed. Their *monarca*, a middle-aged woman, repeatedly danced the length of the rectangle. She was quite impressive and had the commanding presence of someone in her role. She danced as if she wielded a metaphysical power. She and her husband had actively participated in our fundraisers. They are both very unassuming. But, in her role as leader of her *danza*, she seemed to be more of a force than a *danzante*, in total command of her steps and timing. It was truly as if she were operating on a different frequency, so to speak, as

Our Lady of the Angels
vs
DLG

if the context of the dance had transformed her into a force of nature and a distinctly different person. I repeatedly tried to photograph her with the small camera I carried. But, each time the dance turned her away at the moment the shutter opened as if the force that carried her did not want that moment documented. It was something that would have been hard to explain as shyness because I was too far away to be noticed by a person of normal perception, especially one who was dancing as intensely as she was.

When we finished the dance procession, the parishioners present, numbering about three hundred, gathered in front of a limestone shrine about thirty feet high. It contained a statue of Our Lady of the Angels, the church's namesake. There Ramón stood and sang a *serenata* (literally serenade) to her in Spanish. His singing amazed me. Though he was still very young and, therefore short of stature, his voice powerfully carried the mariachi-style song without the aid of a microphone. Equally impressive was that he not only memorized all the lyrics but also seemed to fully understand their weight. I sensed that this was a prayer as much as it was a song, and he understood this profoundly in his heart. Yet, he looked unswervingly at the statue and sang with a kind of determined feeling I had never seen before in a child. (August 20, 2008)

Although this event was for the church's patroness, Our Lady of the Angels, I had the impression that the community of devotees, whose presence was strongly felt, saw *La Virgen de Guadalupe* at the center of this celebration. I do not think the church's organizers of this event understood their enlisting of matachines for the Feast Day of Our Lady of the Angels as a departure from matachines' traditions. And sometimes church-based matachines troupes dance on the feast days of their patronal personages. But there are a few things you need to keep in mind before assuming devotees of *La Virgen de Guadalupe* should be able to shift their devotion from the *Virgen* so readily. Devotion to *La Virgen de Guadalupe* is profound among the Mexican immigrant community in San Antonio. She is, after all, the patroness of Mexico. But there are many reasons why among parish-based matachines troupes like the one we danced with on this day, it made little difference that they were dancing on the feast day of Our Lady of the Angels.

One reason for this was that their matachines troupe, like ours, wore the national colors of Mexico, the Mexican coat of arms, and images of the *Virgen*. Such images are almost inextricably bound to one another. Also, it was clear that the mariachi style *serenata* was for the *Virgen*, especially since both the *serenata* and the *Virgen* are married to Mexican identity. So, the community of devotees seemed to see Our Lady of the Angels as a kind of stand-in for *La Virgen de Guadalupe*. This was coupled with the fact that there was a substantial representation of immigrants from Mexico whose devotion to the *Virgen* is especially strong. Consequently, despite the feast day being of Our Lady of the Angels, this segment of the community of devotees of the *Virgen* was especially vigorous in directing their devotion to her. As if this devotion were not palpable enough, one person shouted, "*¡Viva la Virgen de Guadalupe!*" to which members of the community of devotees answered, "*¡Viva!*" And, the custom of having drummers and a representation of the *Virgen* ride in the bed of a pickup truck is one reserved for the *La Virgen de Guadalupe* in December. She's usually accompanied by a boy dressed as Juan Diego.

Finally, the only way the parish *matachines' monarca* could have danced with such power was because she was dancing for *La Virgen de Guadalupe*. It was like she was channeling an energy that only comes from the *Virgen*. As I watched that *monarca*, I knew that the transcendental quality of her dancing directly involved the *Virgen* and that it was evoked in this *danzante* by the palpable devotion of the community of devotees that surrounded her. Her consistent evasion of my camera manifested the single-mindedness of her devotion to the *Virgen*.

Just as I do not think the organizers thought it inappropriate to use *danza de matachines* troupes in this event venerating Our Lady of the Angels, I do not think the community of devotees saw anything contentious about adhering to the associations they had with the *Virgen* and the *danza*. They were merely making associations by default to the *Virgen*. Private devotions of the community of devotees, like the ones in that parish, maintain the focus of the *danza* on *La Virgen de Guadalupe*, even when organizers were trying to redirect our devotions to someone else. In that way, private devotion contributes to the continuity of the *danza*.

There is a theological tenet whereby there are many manifestations of the Virgin Mary: Our Lady of Mount Carmel, Our lady of Fatima, and Our Lady of Czestochowa. But it is a tenet that the community of devotees, like matachines, does not consider. She is separate from that institutionally created pantheon of Virgin Marys. And because she has been a part of Mexican identity for centuries, the community of devotees associates her with many of its visual symbols, including the colors of its flag, and its coat of arms, which consists of an eagle devouring a snake as it perches on a cactus. Even the *capas* worn by the *monarca* and the *capitanes* in our troupe have this image prominently on the front and that of the *Virgen* on the back with equal prominence. I have also seen at other *danzas* as well, that mariachi music is associated with her. It is not unusual for mariachis to appear at churches on the eve of her feast day to play *serenatas* for her. These are all nuances which, when seen all at once by the community of devotees, mean that the *Virgen* is to be venerated.

Intimacy of the Community of Devotees' Barrios

After the *danza*, a woman from the church invited us to have food at a house down a street in the neighborhood. With Manuel once again motioning for traffic to stop, we crossed Zarzamora and walked to a house called Casa del Carmen that the archdiocese owned. . . . Afterward Molly told Tony and me that she had seen a house that had a picture of *La Virgen de Guadalupe* outside. She also explained to someone that her *tío* (uncle) and founder of the group, Pablo Olivares Sr., would traditionally have his troupe perform in front of houses that had statues, pictures, or miniature shrines with the *Virgen* in front. So, after eating, we danced in the street in front of that house.

After a day of dancing at a number of churches, we returned to the Church of the Little Flower at 7:00 p.m. for a mass. Despite the early hour and cold, wet weather, there was an energy and excitement as families greeted each other and people helped one another prepare for the *danza*. Families arrived often in the company of extended family and friends of the family and neighbors who had come to not only support us but because they were members of the community of devotees of the *Virgen*, just as the many nearby residents and other parishioners who come to our *danzas*. The church had invited us, Tony told me, so that the priest could bless the matachines. Just prior to the mass there was much drumming and dancing in front of the church. Rather than there being any coordination of the troupes, they all danced at the same time before their *estandartes*. I counted at least four matachines groups and one of *matlachines*. Each troupe was accompanied by a community of devotees. That there were five troupes dancing at this church tells you how intense devotion to the *Virgen* is in that parish. It also tells you how much the *danza de matachines* has been practiced there. It's a parish where my mother received catechism in the 1930s (though she really belonged to neighboring St. Agnes Parish), and she could recall the *danza de matachines* in the area going back that far.

This church is located on Zarzamora Street on the West Side. Its residents are mostly working- and middle-class Chicanos and Mexicans. It's a street lined with a combination of small and chain businesses: auto repair shops, meat markets, Mexican food eateries, and convenience stores. It is a part of town I know well because I have family there and I have lived and worked there for several years. Just a mile-and-a-half down the street from the church there was a feedstore that had been there since the 1940s that both my grandfather and I had patronized. Though the community of devotees of the *Virgen* is distributed throughout San Antonio, this West Side neighborhood is definitely representative of the barrios where devotees of the *Virgen* are concentrated. (December 9, 2006)

Now, with many years of dancing behind me, I have danced in front of private homes with icons of the *Virgen* displayed outside. They may be tapestries, statues, altars, painted tiles, or prints. And they may be permanent or temporary. What impressed me for years to come was the understanding that existed between our troupe and the residents who would often come out onto their porches to see and acknowledge our *danza*. Without having to exchange a word with us, they understood that, as matachines, we were obligated by our devotion to go out of our way to dance before any such public images of the *Virgen* we might encounter. Though their displays of the *Virgen* are private in that they are on someone's property, they are also public in that they are visible from the street. This practice would be much less likely to happen in a community where a broadly shared devotion to the *Virgen* did not exist. And, because it exists, there is an intimacy that facilitates not only the displays of the *Virgen* but also our tradition of dancing before her. This intimacy of space, created by private devotion, contributes to the continuity of the *danza*.

The description I've given of the physical community where this reflection is set is pretty much typical of the barrios where the greatest concentrations of the community of devotees lives in San Antonio. So, I have described the physical community of a spiritual community. When I worked and lived in that area, I was able to bus, bike, and walk to wherever I needed to go. I encountered the same people at my places of work as I did at church, the grocery store, and waiting for the bus. In addition, public services, commercial entities, and churches are often located in walking proximity to residents. I point this out because this layout helps create a greater sense of community than that of residential areas that have less public transportation and greater distances between commercial and public entities. This spatial relationship among residents and key community locations also characterizes their relationship to one another as they come into contact with neighbors whom they would not know in other circumstances.

The social interconnectedness among fellow community members on the West Side occurs because the physical community forms a relatively insulated intimacy among the community of devotees. It is an intimacy that becomes most visible in December with the *posadas* and the *danza de matachines*. Although I am referring to environs that are technically public and semipublic they are actually *private* and have intimacy. Barrios such as these are places where people share cultural values and attitudes. They are also where those values and attitudes are reflected and affirmed through the interactions that occur among residents in the form of codes, worldviews, and language and ritual, including those in relation to the *Virgen*. These are also the communities where individuals maintain outdoor shrines called *capillas* and home shrines called *altares caseros* (indoor altars) and *nichos* (alcoves) to *La Virgen de Guadalupe* and *Nuestra Señora de San Juan de los Lagos*. A casual observer from outside would not understand that their acceptance in such communities is not a foregone conclusion, even when those outsiders are Chicano. The privacy of these places where the community of devotees are most concentrated contributes to the continuity of the *danza*.

For instance, our *viejo de la danza* Manuel signaled the neighborhood motorists to halt as he stepped into the center of the street and raised his coiled whip. Because they were familiar with the tradition, they did not bat an eye at his fierce appearance and, instead, halted and waited patiently for us to pass. Having lived in the community for generations, as is very often the case, they "knew the drill" in a sense. They understood what we were doing. In the following years, I continued to see him hold traffic for us in the same way and with the same cooperation from motorists.

The Roles of the Community of Devotees in the Dance

In the community of devotees there are diverse perceptions, attitudes, understandings, and intensity of devotion. One devotee may be a devout Catholic, regularly receiving all the sacraments. Yet, other devotees may never set foot in a church because their home altars to the *Virgen* and their relationships to her are more meaningful. What links us all, though, is having experienced the reality of the *Virgen*, generally in the context of appealing to her for her aid in vicissitudes of our lives or the lives of others. We do not imagine or accept on blind faith that she is real. Rather, we intuit it. This intuition, perhaps, is what so quickly places devotees of differing citizenships and income brackets side by side either as matachines or as devotees. This collective devotion is one of the reasons why our *danza* traditions continue.

Even though the roles of this community may seem to be peripheral and, therefore, marginal to the dance itself, they are roles that sustain the dance. And each member of the community of devotees playing their role—whether it be serving food in a parish hall or placing a picture of the *Virgen* outside for us to venerate—is like a hand carrying a giant *estandarte* at the front of our columns. All these hands come together between the *Virgen*'s feast day and that of the Epiphany and help to sustain the traditions of our troupe and of the *danza de matachines* in general. Yet, unintended, less formal roles this community of nondancers play are equally as important. Its members who approach our *estandarte* before or after a *danza* to give thanks to the *Virgen* or to pray for her help affirm our efforts as emerging from a shared set of values that can be found in every barrio. Our troupe could dance without this community, but the *danza* would not be the same. It would lack the communal experience of being part of a collective effort to be with the *Virgen* through our dance.

Fourth Reflection–Dreams Related to the *Danza*

In the Spanish-speaking communities of San Antonio, dreams have long served as a means of guidance, protection, and reflections of circumstances that may not be obvious in waking life. Yet, rarely do dreamers in these communities share their dreams unless they carry an urgent message. Dreams are a source of private knowledge about the self and soul that aid in making one's way in the world and in maintaining balance in life and with the world of the sacred. So, to be in the habit of divulging dreams is to risk compromising valuable information used to maintain relationships with those worlds. This safeguarding of dreams is also present among members of our *danza de matachines* troupe when the dream is about the *danza*. Yet, these dreams are meaningful to the individual *matachín*.

The vivid dreams I have always had were, to me, a form of communication coming from somewhere beyond my waking reality. But the vividness and frequency of those dreams grew and centered on the dance during the months prior to my becoming a dancer. To try to understand them better, I sat up and wrote them down as they occurred. Each time I made a written description of one, I assumed it would be the last because it seemed so extraordinary. But they continued. Looking back now on my years of dancing and the notes I scrawled about those dreams helps me reflect on the *danza*.

Dream of a Call to Arms

I am in an isolated part of Brackenridge Park by River Road at night. I am practicing a traditional martial arts weapons form that I do practice in real life. Then I see matachines dressed in red *trajes* present at about thirty yards. There is a bright light with them that someone is shining in my direction. And, there is a police squad car nearby. The *trajes* the matachines in this dream wear are identical to those worn by La Danza Guadalupana de Pablo Olivares Sr., who I have recently photographed at Our Lady of Guadalupe Church. (December 20, 2005)

Brackenridge Park is a large, partly wooded city park in San Antonio. At the time, there was little to indicate that the isolated part I was in was a park other than its mowed grass. There were no tables, benches, or water fountains, and it was partly bordered by the San Antonio River and its wooded banks. Serpentine River Road roughly parallels the river. Coincidentally, an elderly Mexican-born man who lived there most of his life once told me he and his niece would sometimes see the spirit of an Indian in the form of fire dancing in that secluded spot.

A couple things about this dream remain engraved in my memory. The first of those things is that I had never been in that area at night. That it was nighttime when I was dreaming lent it the surreal illusion that it was happening "in real time" somehow. Another intriguing aspect is that even though the *trajes* were traditional, they were not as traditional as you would expect of ancestral matachines because materials and aesthetic tastes have changed since then. I think this dream shows that dreams can make you aware of what ancestors are guiding you to do in the *danza*.

In hindsight, this dream had the feeling of a kind of call to arms, though not necessarily a call to confrontation. When I had this dream, I had not yet danced to a single drumbeat. Yet, the speechless matachines, dressed in *trajes* like those of La Danza Guadalupana de Pablo Olivares Sr., stood looking at me as a light that was coming from their direction shone on me. It was as if they had come to wake me up to make me aware that I could and should dance as a *matachín*, and they had chosen that part of the park. The police car perhaps represented local authority and the city government that we would be dealing with in the future in order to have a dance pilgrimage we would later organize.

It seemed relevant to me that this was also a place where I had often practiced martial arts, making the dream more poetic, given the martial character of our dance with its four *capitanes*, regimental-style drumming, two columns, and mock bows and arrows. In trying to understand this dream, I made an effort to be as objective as possible. Molly had not yet invited me to dance, and I had not even been remotely considering the dance, which means these dreams were not coming from within me. Rather, my ancestors—spiritual or lineal—were communicating with me. They were telling me that conditions beyond my senses were conspiring in such a way that I was assured it was an important time for me to dance for the *Virgen*. I would later learn that Molly, unbeknownst to me, had recently taken leadership of the troupe and opened it to membership outside the family. She and Tony were actively seeking new dancers, and their recruitment would last a few years. I know now that if I wanted to, I could have at any time danced in a parish-based troupe without any problem but not in a family-based one, like Molly's. So, the timing of this dream was especially opportune. I do not know why I was being called to dance via this dream. I had felt inspired to photograph the *danza* but not to actively engage in it.

This dream has shown me that dreams are a way to be called to dance for the *Virgen*. When you are called to the dance in a dream, it is not a command. There is no threat, ultimatum, "guilt trip," or anything like that involved. Instead, your ancestors tell you that you are at a time in your life when, for reasons unknown to even the dancer, the time is right to dance for the *Virgen*. And when you are called to dance in a dream, ancestors use the language of your personal imagery to communicate. In this dream, that imagery included a physical area that I associated with martial physical activity and that I knew to have once been inhabited by Indians for thousands of year before the dream. I understood what was being asked of me on some level of consciousness, even if I could not articulate it at the time. It is only now, over a decade after answering that dream's call to dance, that I can recognize the significance of what I was seeing.

Dream of My Future Reflected

I see myself in a mirror wearing a red *traje*, the kind worn in La Danza Guadalupana de Pablo Olivares Sr. The frames of the mirror seemed to be disappearing. In a sense, the mirror is ceasing to be a mirror. This gradual disappearance seems to be saying that my role with La Danza Guadalupana de Pablo Olivares Sr. is gradually moving from that of standard bearer to dancer. However, in the dream I am not wearing the vest of the rank-and-file line dancers but the tunic-like top worn by the higher ranking *capitanes* and *monarca*. (December 13, 2006)

I struggle to explain how I realized what I was being told in this dream. I knew I was being shown the role I was moving toward in the *danza*, but I questioned it, found it hard to believe. The mirror was disappearing, but not the image. When I think of frames, I usually think of them as borders for paintings or photos, images of things instead of the real thing. So, when I saw myself in a mirror whose frames were disappearing, it was clear that I was being shown that my reality was changing.

The person I saw in the mirror looked like me but had a different, more serious vibe in addition to wearing a *traje* I never imagined myself wearing. I was in awe of the *capitanes* and *monarca* who wore that kind of *traje*. Yet, I was being shown that I would one day wear it. Naturally, I felt unqualified and even "unworthy" of having such a responsible role. So, I tried to unsuccessfully to dismiss it, to put it out of my head. Now, after having danced as a *monarca*, it has become clear that the dream was telling me where my role in the *danza* was headed. I cannot deny what that dream was saying because its prediction has happened. I became the *monarca* of La Danza Guadalupana de Pablo Olivares Sr. And, since I accepted that role, my sense of responsibility has obligated me to have the much more serious "vibe" I felt in my mirrored reflection.

About a year and a half after having this dream, I had one that seemed to be its continuation. I saw a *matachín* dressed in a *traje* like the one traditionally worn by our *capitanes* and *monarca*. He stood looking at me in dim light. I could not tell, as we scrutinized each other, if I was looking at myself or someone who looked like me. Our consciousnesses had fused together. Unlike the dream involving a disappearing mirror, there were no frames or sense that I was looking at a mirrored reflection. His presence was palpable and one of considerable authority. This is also how I feel when I dance.

The insight these dreams gave me was about the gradual nature of my transformation. I might have risen to *monarca* quickly in traditional terms. But I had been becoming a *monarca* internally since that day. This relatively quick rise had been gnawing at my conscience, and this dream seemed to be telling me that it was not an impropriety on my part to accept it. There were bigger forces at work, the *Virgen* and ancestors, and they understood what was best for the *danza* better than I did.

Dreaming of When the *Danza* Is Not *Danza*

I am dancing with our matachines group. We are dancing but without the *Virgen*. I am keenly aware of her absence. It is very unsettling, almost to the point of disorienting me while in the *danza*. We are dancing in the street, which is not unusual, but the *estandarte* must be missing because the dance feels empty. It is just steps and movement in time with the drum. There is no uplifting sense of transcending time, being in the presence of ancestors, and definitely not the usual presence of the *Virgen*. (December 19, 2006)

Though I did not know it at the time, there would be *danzas* when the spirit of the *danza* and the *Virgen* would be absent. An instance when our *danza* was essentially made to be dinner entertainment comes to mind. Having since experienced such *danzas* on occasion, this dream serves as a reminder of the importance of attentiveness and sincerity not just among the *danzantes* but among those gathered in the presence of the *danza*, be they devotees of the *Virgen* or not. The *Virgen* reveals and teaches qualities in dreams.

I relate this dream to one I had six months later in which I saw a black silhouette of a *danzante* on a triangular, yellow yield sign. It was outdoors and posted along a street. The *danzante*, a *matachín*, was tilted forward in mid-step. Though the image was a silhouette, it reminded me a little of Tony. Judging from the position of the *matachín*, he seemed to have his eyes fixed on something or someone "off camera" so to speak, but not so far off that it decreased the immediacy of the dancer's intention. It was surreal that there would be the image of a *matachín* on something as official as a yield sign. That dream was quite remarkable in its directness. I did not know what to make of it at the time. But, by reflecting on it, I perceived that, if anything, it likely predicted obstacles that our troupe would have to negotiate with the city government. After all, yield signs are not only produced, placed, and paid for by city funds, they also tell us to defer to someone else, to go slower against risk of civil penalty. This dream told me that we would need to yield. It also shows how dreams can give direction.

A Dream about Sickness and Health

I called Molly to say I would not be participating in a *danza* at a *posadas* scheduled for tonight at 7:00 p.m., explaining to her that I was still fighting a cold. (I was concerned that my immune system had taken an extra pummeling the night before.) Then I dreamed I saw the *Virgen's estandarte* lying at my feet as I stood in the street during the *posadas* we had been a part of the previous night. (December 23, 2006)

Before the *posadas* of the previous night, Molly would have been very considerate if I had told her I was too ill to dance. In this dream, the *Virgen* was telling me that she would have been understanding too, that she did not expect me to dance for her at the expense of my health. After all, the prayers the *Virgen* answers include those for recovery of health. Healing and the recovery of health are often the reason for *promesas* made by matachines and other members of the community of devotees. They're made by individuals for their own health as well as on behalf of loved ones who are ill or injured. Our own *danza* has often prayed in the form of dance for people we knew who were suffering from serious illnesses, including cancer and heart problems. We have done so as readily during our practices as for our feast day *danzas*. Even before the practices, we have prayed for people we've known to be ill. So, it makes all the more sense that I take care of my health.

This dream parallels another one I had a little over a year later in which I was looking at a predominantly light green *manta* of the *Virgen* with some gold glitter on the sides, and the entire image was upside down. That dream makes me reflect on the roses the *Virgen* gave Juan Diego. Her ability to give him roses that he picked out of season and on rocky, arid soil likely intensified any associations with the earth that the Mesoamerican peoples of that time had to have seen in her. Juan Diego's purpose for collecting them was to take them to Archbishop Zumárraga as proof that she had been appearing to request the building of a church. In the winter, the energy of the earth is one of stillness, repose. Leaves die and fall to the ground. Trees become brittle. Crops stop growing. It is also a time when we're more vulnerable to illness, and old injuries remind us that they're still with us. So, fresh roses gathered from rocky soil in the winter were bound to add greater awe and proof to Bishop Zumárraga in case he doubted the origins of the *Virgen's* image on Juan Diego's *tilma*. It contrasted with the reality of the earth at that time of year and with the land on and around Tepeyac. But these roses showing up under unlikely circumstances were not just a calling card. They said something about her, that her energy was the opposite of all those things associated with winter: vitality, healing, wellness. When Juan Diego said he could not help the *Virgen* because he had to care for his ill uncle, she told him his uncle was already healed.

The dream of the *manta* I saw on the *Virgen* was green, which I associate with healing, wellness, and fertility because of its association with the virtual rebirth of plant life in the spring. And, it was May when I dreamed this. What I saw was the manifestation of an awareness of the *Virgen*'s relationship to these things gleaned from the *danza*. This awareness arises because dreams can make you aware of the *Virgen*'s ongoing presence in the life of matachines throughout all the seasons of the year, even during the spring. Both of these dreams show how dreams can warn us to care for our health in order to dance for the *Virgen*, as we use the *danza* to pray for the health of others.

A Dream of Place and Trajectory

> I see older matachines—men and women—getting ready to dance in an otherwise empty street on the West Side. They are arising from sitting positions in response to distant drumming. It is nighttime. I hear the drum a few blocks away and know somehow that it is of another matachines troupe. The drumming is a signal to us they are preparing to dance to where we were, that they are going to dance with us. It is as if the unseen troupe is saying, "We are coming. Be ready to dance with us." (December 29, 2006)

This dream is a foretelling of our first dance pilgrimage, which Molly would organize the following year. Soon after this dream, Molly and Tony told me it was an idea they had been seriously discussing. This dream is like the pilgrimage in that it unites *danzas* from different West Side barrios. The fact that the *danzantes* I was with were older signifies the traditional nature of this kind of pilgrimage. The dream was also telling me by the presence of elders that the pilgrimage would need to be undertaken with the maturity and respect that I associate with elders. And, most of all because it would be for the *Virgen*. Of course, I did not know this at the time.

This dream deals with continuation of the *danza*, of ancestry. It is a conduit conveying the importance of the West Side as home to so many generations of devotees of the *Virgen* who have expressed not only great appreciation for our *danza* but also understanding of the *danza* in relation to the *Virgen*. This dream also reveals the importance of place in relation to the *danza*. My mother, who lived on the West Side for many years, mentioned the *danza de matachines* of her parish from time to time. Wherever there are communities of tradition like those on the West Side, tradition accrues over continuous generations. And, because of the accrued

A dream of this image which had hung in the author's grandparents' *tiendita* symbolized place, trajectory, and ancestry in a dream he had.

traditions, there are also experiences that do not conform to linear understandings of reality like those experienced in the *danza*. Here it is helpful to remember that the West Side barrios are places made intimate by shared values and the traditions and attitudes those in the barrios encompass. Almost three years to the date of this dream, I had another one in which I saw what looked like a framed reproduction print of the very old calendar graphic of the *Virgen* that hangs in my room. It was isolated in time and space. It had belonged to my maternal grandparents and had been clipped from a 1950s calendar that hung on the wall of a *tiendita* they owned on Rivas Street, just west of Alazán Creek. The *tiendita* where it originally hung was an anomaly in that it was in a repurposed 1920s-era garage in the middle of an area zoned for residences. My mother once told me that, after that picture of the *Virgen* hung in my grandparents' shop for a year, someone clipped the image of the *Virgen*, placed it in a frame, and hung it in my grandfather's house; it stayed there until the 1970s when my mother hung it in the house I grew up in. It came into my possession and was hanging on a wall next to my bed when I had this dream. For that reason, I now look back and see this dream as the *Virgen*'s announcement that the season of her veneration was approaching, which starts on her feast day. And she chose the image of her that has been in the family for decades to announce it. Ancestry has been a significant spiritual part of the *danza* for me, my own ancestry as well as that of the *danza*. Without being able to say exactly how, I have had experiences in which my ancestors figured into communications about the past, present, and future. And, my grandparents who owned the calendar image of the *Virgen* are now my ancestors. They connect me with the many generations that form my ancestral lineage. Here, when I speak of ancestors, I am including older persons who have died and who contributed to the continuity of *danza*-related traditions. They are connections to the past with each one being like a link in a greater chain that reaches back in time. In this way, they create the possibility for continuity of the dance.

A Dream of She Who Does Not Become Worn

> I am looking at a bright image of the Virgen de Guadalupe with some glitter on a faded black t-shirt. Of course, I was in awe of its beauty. The t-shirt is obviously old, but the image of the *Virgen* is bright, vivid, sparkling. (May 5, 2007)

The *Virgen*'s image is surrounded by the blackness of the t-shirt, and that is how she is during the all of the year except from her feast day to the feast of the Epiphany. She is in the darkness, that is, not as public in her display as during her special time, but no less vibrant in the hearts of *matachines*. Our troupe practices year-round but does not dance before lit altars or her *estandarte* when it is not her season. Yet, she is the reason for our practices, as rigorous as they can be. This dream came to me in spring, a time of year when she is still relatively in the background. Since I began to dance for the *Virgen*, my yearly calendar has revolved around the twelfth of December. And, after many such years, I have the experience of recognizing what this dream meant.

This is also a manifestation of the *Virgen*'s timeless and enduring presence among her community of devotees since her apparitions before Juan Diego in 1531. It was as if I had been wearing this t-shirt for many years but was unaware of the presence of this image being on it. And, since I have been dancing for her, the image is new because my awareness of her has been intensified through the *danza*. This is an awareness that has nourished my inspiration to dance. Without this sincerity of motivation, strengthened by dreams like these, there can be no continuity of the *danza* because its authenticity would disappear.

A Dream on the Feast Day of Our Lady of Guadalupe

> I see a huge, colorful picture of the *Virgen* hanging on one of the walls in Our Lady of Guadalupe Church. It is above a beautifully and elaborately decorated altar in a section of the church that does not exist in waking life. There is a dazzling, colorful array of candles, lights, and flowers. The picture is to the right of the sanctuary and gives the church a kind of *L*-shape. (December 12, 2007, Feast Day of *La Virgen de Guadalupe*)

Since having this dream, I have learned a bit more about the *Virgen*'s special time, lasting from her feast day to the Feast of the Epiphany. Though the beginning date on her feast day and the ending date on the Feast of the Epiphany are church-sanctioned feast days, the span of time in between and its importance comes from her and her devotees. It is a time when she expects attentiveness from her devotees, which is why we traditionally dance on her feast day and through the Epiphany.

This dream was a symbolic reminder that she expects veneration by her devotees at this time. I could especially see this expectation in that she appeared in a transept in Our Lady of Guadalupe Church. (It was a transept that created the "*L*-shape" that does not exist in real life but existed for her on that day.) It was a manifestation that this is a time of year when she expects attentiveness from her devotees. One of the ways her devotees show this attentiveness to her is by changing her physical environment, that is, her *altar* and even the room, chapel, or church where it is kept. Here she is reminding me that the larger the scale of her devotion, that is, the altering of her public environments, should be to show her reverence. And what better public environment to make such a reminder than a church dedicated to her? I have since had, on occasion, dreams in which I was shown that my seasonal altar had something wrong with it or was lacking something. When I would wake and look at the altar, I would realize why the problem with the altar needed to be corrected, and I would fix it. As I reflect on the dream of the altar in the church and the dreams I've had about my own altar, I see how dreams can serve to alert *danzantes* to problems related to the *danza* and, in that way, help with its continuity.

Dreams as Communication with Ancestors

I am in the presence of Molly's mother, Francisca O. Aguilar, who passed away almost two years earlier. She appears the same as I knew her in real life: slender, of medium height, and with gray, well-kept hair. In her hands is a kind of *corona* that I have never seen before, and she is telling me about it. She makes little eye contact with me, looking instead at the *corona* as she turns it about in her hands in a way that suggested it was new to her too. The *corona* is all a single shade of green with feathers that have the same shape as our *coronas* had when I entered the *danza*. They are positioned almost the same way except that their backward tilt is at a sharper angle. I think it resembles a helmet. It looks like it is made of faded linen that had been folded, shaped, and dipped into a kind of wheat paste then allowed to dry and harden. As she speaks, she seems to know much about this *corona*, but I am too surprised to be in her presence to ask any questions or even follow what she is saying. She says the *coronas* were once made this way and that we could still use *coronas* like that one if we wanted to. (May 18, 2017)

She has joined the ranks of those ancestors whose presence I so often have felt while dancing, the ancestors of the *danza*. Though their presence in the *danza* seemed somehow anonymous until then, there was nothing anonymous about her. In Spanish, one could say of her, "*Fue una persona de pocas palabras,*" which means she was a person of few words. Whenever someone says that of someone in English, it implies that person is a man or woman of action. In Spanish, there is a slightly different meaning. It means the person has a great, dignified presence and who, though taciturn and cordial, is willing to take a firm stand when values or principals are at stake. Consequently, such people are generally respected and deferred to. That's how I remember her: "*Una persona de pocas palabras.*" Whenever I spoke to her, I would frantically search my memory for any possible unwritten protocol that I might be forgetting because I definitely did not want to get crossways with her.

Ancestors are a part of the dance and communicate with me in dreams just as the *Virgen* does. The ancestors not only have access to the past, they are the past. I feel badly that I retained so little of what she told me in this dream, but I can understand why I would be so shocked as to be unable to retain what she said. I wonder why, though, I would have such an important dream if I was not going to be able to focus well enough on what she was telling me? I can only guess that I have understood it unconsciously, and that's what important in the larger scheme of things. That's what's important for the *Virgen.* Anyway, after I awoke, it was comforting to know that she seemed to think enough of me to visit. As always, she spoke with a dignified countenance, though now with enthusiasm about this *penacho.* In this dream as when she was alive, I felt extraordinarily privileged that she would take pains to speak to me about the *danza.* After waking from this dream, I knew I had not retained enough of what she said for me to propose that our troupe change the style of our *coronas.*

The insight I have gained from this dream over time is that ancestors can come to *danzantes* in dreams and make suggestions and provide guidance for the troupe. That did not happen in this dream. The closest Francisca came to making any suggestions or providing guidance was to say that *coronas* used to look like this one and that we could dance with ones like this if we wanted. But the potential for dreams to have this role was made clear by making me aware of that option. Ancestors know and see more than we do. And dreams are a vehicle by which they can provide guidance.

Dreams, Continuity, and Change

These reflections show how dreams can communicate to individual *danzantes* about the *danza.* The *Virgen* and ancestors communicate to *danzantes* about the *danza* through dreams. Sometime during my first weeks in the *danza*, I mentioned to Tony that I had been having dreams related to the *danza*. Without skipping a beat, he briefly said that was almost to be expected among *danzantes*. Interestingly, on only rare occasions did other *danzantes* share such dreams with other members of the troupe. This says much of the individual nature of each person's dreams and of the appropriate boundaries of privacy surrounding them. My dreams of the *Virgen*'s images and of matachines affirmed that I was engaged in a tradition that had a powerful trajectory involving ancestors. In hindsight and in general, I think these dreams showed that dreaming is a part of dancing for the *Virgen*. And, maybe they were an indication that I was connecting to her in a way that I had not prior to dancing for her.

At the beginning of this memoir, I pondered how individual dreams might contribute to the continuity of the *danza* in relation to change. Now that I have recounted the above reflections, I can grasp that for matachines dreams contribute to the continuity of the dance by encouraging, predicting, informing, aiding in the recovery of health, reminding, teaching, affirming, healing, and cautioning, including when changes arise. Dreams can make known the need for changes in one's life, such as joining a matachines troupe. And, they benefit the continuity of the *danza* by guiding us in discerning what changes are healthy as we dance for the *Virgen*.

Final Thoughts on the Private Experience of the *Danza*

The man who approached us in the park asking, "What is the meaning of this?" knew that there had to be more to the dance than dancing in two columns to the beat of a drum. He just did not know *how* much more. By asking for a meaning, he was, unbeknownst to him, asking about the private experience of the *danza de matachines*. He was asking about what outsiders to the *danza* cannot see, which is why news sources and religious pundits default to its public expression in their attempts to define it for the public. The insights I reveal in this memoir could only have been gained through the years of waking up early in the morning for physically rigorous practice and *danzas*, listening intensely to the instructions and references of veteran matachines in our troupe, dancing with single-minded intention, witnessing dynamics that took place between members of our *danza*, and being aware of what I was feeling as a *danzante*.

One of the insights into the dance I have revealed has included authenticity of the *danza*. Through my private experience of the dance, I have been able to experience what authenticity really is and what it is not. And I can tell that it rests in how one enters into the dance and the authority of the *estandarte* that summons the palpable presence of the *Virgen*. The accoutrements of my *matachines* troupe have a metaphysics rooted in intention and tradition. This metaphysic reaches over generations of *danzantes*. Members of the community of devotees give our troupe vitality through their direct, enthusiastic, and controlled participation in the *reverencia*. They also support it organizationally and through bonding with matachines through food. Dreams serve to intimately guide matachines. They are vehicles of communication with ancestors, and they even make people aware that they are being called to dance. What all these insights have in common is that they can only be known through years of dancing.

It is crucial for the public to have access to the private experience of the dance in order to truly understand the *danza*. But it is *not* important to the dance that the public understands it. Explaining the *danza* to outsiders is not part of its traditions. It does not figure into the priorities of matachines. The *danza* and its traditions emerged from communities in which explanation is not necessary. Matachines are not concerned with whether outsiders understand it or not. However, I have chosen to share my private experience in the dance because it is grossly absent in the unrequested write-ups in the local media. And, as part of the fulfillment of the *promesa* to the *Virgen* to write this book, I am compelled to show why the misinterpretations of the dance in the local mass media are wrong. Without insights into the private experience of the *danza*, people unfamiliar with its traditions cannot know the weight of its meaning or its spiritual depth. These insights into the *danza*'s meaning and spiritual depth will be especially important in chapter 8, in which I describe how a local church official, in tandem with secular entities, appropriated the previously mentioned dance pilgrimage. In chapter 9, I examine the colonial dynamics that brought that appropriation about.

The man who approached us in the park, casually asking what we were doing as we were in mid-step, annoyed me with the assumption that I could tell him what we were doing in a single breath. I wondered if he thought he was looking at a television screen instead of real people engaged in something that was highly important. But even if he had little idea as to what he was asking, he was being honest. And to be asked about the meaning of a *danza* by an outsider is a hundred times better than being *told* by an outsider what the *danza* means based on a poorly researched article they saw online. So, I am thankful that man asked his question. That was when I began to formulate answers in my mind in ways that would make sense to people who may not be matachines or even members of the community of devotees.

6

Culmination of Authenticity

Seeing the Dance through Experienced Eyes

My years of documenting our *danza* began with photographing it and subsequently keeping notes on it. I was initially uncertain as to what purpose my documenting should have. This uncertainty owed to my lack of familiarity with the dance at the time. So, I had to first learn about La Danza Guadalupana de Pablo Olivares Sr. through exchanges with long-time dancers, experiences, and intuition.

As my time as a member of our group went by, I felt less motivated to intellectualize the dance. At the beginning, I had no specific purpose for the notes I took, but I did feel the need to document the *danza*, whether it be for future archivists, anthropologists, or people like me who feel compelled to learn more about it. My decreasing concern for recording the details of our dance ritual was not based on a lack of enthusiasm. On the contrary, it was commensurate to an increasing maturity of visceral understanding of my roles as a *matachín*—and later *monarca*. I say this because it requires my total mental presence whenever I practice the *danza*. To intellectualize our tradition, to me, would have been to risk trivializing deeper things in the dance such as the devotion that it truly is and the meaning of that devotion. It would have meant having to take great care not to cross some undefined boundary or otherwise compromise my role. In a word, I came to see occupying my role as a *danzante* as more important than writing about it. Perhaps it could be said that to intellectualize the *danza* is to compromise energy owed to the *Virgen*, and our dance is for her and not for quasi-academic research.

Nevertheless, I continued to write about my experiences in the *danza*. It became more difficult in that so many aspects of it had become obvious to me, and my tendency is to think information that is obvious to me is obvious to everyone and consequently does not require explanation. However, whenever I could sit and get past that block, I found I could write with heightened sensitivity because I recognized that the detailed commentaries, interpersonal exchanges, and narrative in my notes present the reader with information about our *danza* as a whole. From this information, readers could also glean the values and beliefs that characterize the dance. Much more unexpectedly, I found that my notes could form the basis of a critique of the standard "conquest" reading of the *danza*. Most importantly, I learned about *resilience* in La Danza Guadalupana de Pablo Olivares Sr. by speaking with the late Pablo Olivares's kin about the *danza* in the years before I joined. As well, I saw and experienced it firsthand in how we dealt with external challenges that arose before our particular *danza*, especially as a family-based troupe. Because these challenges varied in nature, their resolutions could not rely on a single attitude or tactic. Rather, meeting such challenges involved a combination of skillful diplomacy with institutions and flexibility within the troupe.

Colonial Dynamics

The *danza de matachines* has existed in northern Mexico since the Spanish Colonial period. It was brought to the region by the Tlaxcaltecans from central Mexico (Martínez 1996, 43; J. Pohl, personal communication, September 16, 2014). Its primary purpose has been to express adoration and devotion to *La Virgen de Guadalupe* on December 12, her feast day. Many troupes of this type have existed in that region, each sharing this common history in New Spain while varying in aesthetics. Pablo Olivares Sr. formed his *danza de matachines* troupe in the 1970s, drawing from the trajectory of the traditions rooted in this development of the dance.

Rather than being associated with churches, troupes were based in families and/or barrios. After immigrating to San Antonio, Texas, Pablo Olivares Sr. eventually reassembled his *danza*, drawing again from his immediate and extended family for *danzantes*. To recognize the troupe's relationship to the church in terms of colonial dynamics, it is important for me to underscore that during his leadership of the troupe in San Antonio and for at least the first two years after his death, the troupe would dance *outside* Our Lady of Guadalupe Church on December 12. The troupe's boundaries were characterized by relative autonomy from institutions. Therefore, there was no need to communicate with the church's administration, or its laity, or even to be registered members of that parish. In the 1970s, the family would develop private plays based directly on the appearances of *La Virgen de Guadalupe* to Juan Diego. The plays were performed in the backyards of family members. And, the *danzas* were unannounced, that is, not necessarily intended for any members of the public apart from whoever might happen to be present. This autonomy is not a mere indication of continuing a trajectory of independence rooted in the autonomously minded Tlaxcaltecans. But rather, given that La Danza Guadalupana de Pablo Olivares Sr. originated in northern Mexico, it reveals that this independence from churches is more common in Mexico.

My reading of academic research of the *danza* (for example, Champe as cited in Moreno 2005, 30) confirmed that the Spanish either encouraged or tolerated the *danza* in the northern reaches of New Spain, believing, however presumptuously, that the *danza* could serve to convert the Indigenous peoples to Catholicism, which was valued by the Spanish as being an integral part of a sedentary lifestyle. Those Indigenous peoples were martially engaging the Spanish or otherwise could not be considered ideal Spanish colonial subjects (Martínez 2004, 29–30).

To clarify these dynamics, I have been careful to avoid the term *neocolonial*. Although there has been a wealth of scholarly discussion in the form of articles and books on neocolonialism, my concern is that the term implies an end to colonialism followed by its renewal. As has been discussed earlier, San Antonio experienced a period of classic colonialism under the Spanish. Yet, its colonizing institutions have been replaced with newer versions, despite the secularization of its missions and succession of governments since independence from Spain. Resilience in the face of colonization has also been continuous, including in the *danza de matachines* in general and La Danza Guadalupana de Pablo Olivares Sr., in particular.

The reasons why *danza de matachines* troupes, including ours, have continued into the twenty-first century are many. Not the least of these is because this ritual summons a time-transcendent spiritual presence of *La*

Virgen de Guadalupe that is palpable and corporeally felt. I have not experienced this phenomenon in any other context. Other variables contributing to the *danza's* continuation may well include traditions of intrafamily cooperation in which the lines between immediate and extended family are relatively blurred in comparison to Euro-American families. However, Hill's (1992) observations regarding Highland Maya nonviolent resistance to Spanish Colonial rule holds significant insights related to our *danza's* continuation. It does not matter that these insights are not based on Maya dance, because they nonetheless illustrate a Mesoamerican strategy of maneuvering, including through dance—around colonial impediments to tradition.

These include how colonized communities can secretly exercise forbidden ceremony through public performances whose ostensible purpose differs from the essential one. They also include the sophistication that can characterize such undertakings. As well, Hill illustrates how colonizers' Eurocentric assumptions about conquest can serve to delude themselves with the notion of having subjugated communities. Such delusion benefits resilience to the extent that such complacency creates the conditions for authentic traditions to continue.

I have often thought about Molly's reference to the more esoteric part of the matachines tradition. Specifically, I have ruminated on what her second great-grandmother told her about the *danza* being similar to praying the rosary. As well, I have wondered about the meanings that each step holds. Her second great-grandmother, she said, still spoke Nahuatl. It is an indigenous language spoken throughout much of central Mexico. During the Spanish Colonial period its speakers included the Tlaxcaltecans who brought the *danza de matachines* to northern New Spain (J. Pohl, personal communication, September 16, 2014). I have tended to see first languages as markers of how well people keep the traditions integral to a given language's cultural context. To the extent that such a tendency may be valid, I think it is an indication of how traditional our *danza* is.

As mentioned in chapter 4, Molly's mother had said that when making the *traje* for the *viejo de la danza*, a separate prayer is said as the maker sews each one of the hundreds of strips of cloth onto it. She said it was very exhausting for her. This practice tells me that Molly's mother's role as a maker of *trajes* in the troupe was not merely one of physical effort but also of a profoundly spiritual nature. To me it lends possible insight into her ability to have prescience of my joining the *danza* before anyone in the *danza* had met me. The fact that such spiritual components to the dance exist behind the scenes reinforces that the *danza* is not simply a spectacle. Tony has repeatedly said so in the context of saying it was his preferred form of prayer. Other *danzantes* have, in passing conversation, negated the outsider perception of the mere spectacle as well. Some of them have included members from *danza conchera* troupes. Moreover, we pray before practicing. I had dreams of the *Virgen* that placed me, and kept me, in the *danza*. So, there is much more to the *danza* than simply learning and executing steps while wearing colorful *trajes*. Otherwise, I would not be as concerned for its integrity as I have been. Whereas audiences are a liability to the essence of the ritual, members of the community of devotees are not.

Molly's shared anecdotal glimpses into our *danza*'s past, in the form of its esoteric aspects, have been few. Their relatively obscure nature may owe to the colonial context in which the *danza de matachines* came into being. In view of the role the Tlaxcaltecans had in the *danza*'s formation and in spreading it throughout New Spain, it is plausible that its traditional origins were indigenous. And it is quite plausible that they were veiled in the aesthetics of Catholic practices and spirituality in order to maintain them.

Hill's work shows how it was a common practice among Indigenous cultures in colonial contexts to present public displays of what seemed to be affirmations of and conformity to their perceived subjugation as presumably conquered peoples. Below the surface, however, their public displays were active continuations of pre-European rituals, a fact that only other Indigenous people would recognize. Documented by Fuentes y Guzmán (1680), this case study may be best interpreted ethnohistorically by Hill (1992) with regard to how the seventeenth-century Cakchiquel Maya observed their Fiesta del Volcán (Festival of the Volcano). I believe that Hill's ethnohistoric interpretation of Fuentes y Guzmán's narrative of this fiesta can provide insights into our *danza*'s continuation.

According to Fuentes y Guzmán's narrative record of that time, the festival was a performance of dance, music, and mock combat by Cakchiquel Maya Indians to commemorate their own defeat by the Spanish during an attempted uprising in 1526 (Hill 1992, 3). The event was a yearly reenactment forced on the Cakchiquel Maya but undertaken with much enthusiasm. Preparations included the construction of a volcano from timber. For both the Spanish and Indians, it represented the land. However, unbeknownst to the Spanish, the volcano represented other things to the Cakchiquel Maya. They began the volcano's construction the day prior to the event. Its construction and preparation included the creation of grottos in which they placed native animals and birds. As well, they planted and maintained live plants. These actions were carried out on the pretext of symbolically recreating the land that they would lose in combat. After much preparation, all strata of colonial society would gather as an audience to see the reenactment. It would begin with the separate entries of Cakchiquel Maya and Spanish forces. The latter, coincidentally, was played by Tlaxcaltecan allies brought from central Mexico by the Spanish.

Sinacam, the revolt leader, is referred to as the "King." Among the Cakchiquel Maya population, it was considered a high honor to play this role. When the Cakchiquel Maya made their entry, they did so in an enthusiastic yet dignified manner. Fuentes y Guzmán described the scene: "They come as warriors but their weapons have been rendered relatively harmless by prudent Spanish officials" (as cited in Hill 1992, 3). The drama consisted of a series of attacks and counterattacks between the opposing forces, with the Cakchiquel Maya holding the top of the volcano. Finally, Spanish capture the "King." Rather than being killed, he is publicly taken away in chains, which the Spanish consider to be the ultimate form of defeat for him and his people. His capture is followed by the exiting of the military forces from the plaza, with the Cakchiquel Maya leaving "with the same order as which they entered" (Hill 1992, 4).

A Congruency of Incongruencies

The dignified posture I have described previously compares to a pattern of incongruencies in the Fiesta del Volcán that seem to parallel similar incongruencies in La Danza Guadalupana de Pablo Olivares Sr. Similarly, the Cakchiquel Maya leave the battle with heads held high despite their presumed defeat. They did so with their dignity intact because the Spanish did not sacrifice Sinacam, the Cakchiquel Mayas' leader. Nor did they desecrate the Cakchiquel Mayas' temple; these acts otherwise would have constituted defeat for the Cakchiquel Maya (Hill 1992, 6–7). "Thence, for the Cakchiquel Maya, the conquest remained incomplete" (7). As can be gleaned from the descriptions of the dance I give in the preface and chapters 2 and 4, when we dance there is no sense of defeat despite playing the role of Aztecs led by Moctezuma II. Our stateliness and dignity, like those of the Cakchiquel Maya, contradict the notion of having been conquered. Moreover, we have Moctezuma II and his *capitanes* present, but neither Cortés nor any of his military personnel are to be found. The very fact that

Moctezuma II is present for the appearance of *La Virgen de Guadalupe* rejects the Eurocentric historical record that views this reality as anachronistic. In short: Our dance narrative, upon closer examination, challenges the idea of conquest. Moreover, just as Sinacam was never militarily defeated in the collective mind of the Cakchiquel Maya, neither could Moctezuma II be perceived as defeated. His death did not occur in combat or on the battlefield but at the hands of other Aztecs (Díaz de Castillo 1994, 253). Our *danza* is a chapter of Aztec history appropriated by the Tlaxcaltecans.

In both the Fiesta del Volcán and in our *danza*, participants use Spanish terms that denote royalty to refer to the leader of the Indians. For the Cakchiquel Maya, Sinacam is "the King" (Hill 1992, 7). For us, Moctezuma II is the *monarca*, which is synonymous with king. It is as though the Spanish terms were used to heighten outsider misunderstanding of these ritualistic realities. The use of these terms also suggests possible insight into the headwear in our *danza*. I had heard Molly and her mother use the words *penacho* (crest) and *corona* (crown) to refer to our headdresses. Although they were used interchangeably, the fact that one term is synonymous with crown suggests to me that the *monarca*'s headwear was once distinct from that worn by the *matachines* in the line. Though this tradition apparently fell away, the use of the term *corona* continues, albeit meaning the same thing as *penacho*.

Another parallel between the two traditions involves colonial perceptions of these traditions. In San Antonio, Catholic institutions and the mass media tend to rely on long-standing, simplistic scholarship to explain the *danza de matachines*. This scholarship interprets the *danza* as a celebration by Indians, or their descendants, of their presumed conquest by the Spanish. It also interprets it as tacit resolution to conform to colonial values. Similarly, Spanish colonial society ignorantly interpreted the Fiesta del Volcán as an acknowledgment of Spanish colonial superiority over them (Hill 1992, 5). Hill explains in his preface that the Fiesta del Volcán was described, "by people . . . who did not have a *participant's understanding* [emphasis added] of the customs, beliefs, institutions, and rituals they described" (ix). Therefore, they did not object to the pre-Spanish ritualistic practice that the Fiesta del Volcán truly was. It is plausible that generations of matachines, for similar reasons, have not objected to dancing in what seems to be a capitulation to Catholicism. As Hill notes, "The Cakchiquel, and their situation were not unique. The same range of Spanish-introduced and pressures for change were present to some degree throughout Mesoamerica, and indeed, all of Spanish America" (1992, ix).

The final aspect of parallel divergent worldviews involves the Cakchiquels' volcano and the *Virgen* of the Tlaxcaltecans, who brought the *danza de matachines* to northern New Spain. I find uncannily similar colonial dynamics between the two Indigenous groups and their respective public practices in Hill's observations when he states:

> In Maya cosmology the volcano or mountain is the Earth Lord, the super-natural being who provides, among other things, the rains essential for agriculture. The volcano/mountain is also the place where the *tonas*, the animal-spirit companions of each individual, are kept. The security of the tonas was of great concern to each individual, for if one's own tona escaped or was set free onto the surface of the world, both shared the same fate. In particular, if the tona were killed by a hunter or some other animal, its human counterpart would also die. Thus, to the Cakchiquel, the construc-tion of caves or grottoes containing wild animals in the timber-volcano was much more than a merely ingenious decoration. It was a portrayal of a fundamental component of their traditional worldview. . . . They were able to present it publicly to the Spaniards, who were too ignorant of the symbolism to object . . . The volcano/mountain was also the home of the Cakchiquels' ancestors' spirits. These beings kept watch over their living descendants who believed quite strongly that their ancestors would one day return to reclaim the land. (Hill 1992, 6)

In the Fiesta del Volcán and its preparation, the Cakchiquels renewed their relationships with their *tonas* and ancestors to successfully insure their con-tinuation as a people. It was a demonstration of resilience. Their central Mexican neighbors to the north, the Tlaxcaltecans, similarly had a cosmic relationship to earth elements whereby they were understood to be sentient. Their relationships to them were crucial in regard to farming (León-Portilla 1963, 21), fertility, and healing (Austin, 1988, 3).

I also see a similarity of colonial dynamics between the Fiesta del Volcán and Andrés Ribas de Pérez's 1645 description of "the dance of the emperor Motecuzoma" in Mexico (as cited in Harris 2000, 105–6). The dance of the emperor Motecuzoma, according to Ribas de Pérez, was a Christian dance that had formerly been indigenous. And, it is quite plausible that, as in the Fiesta del Volcán, Indians were undertaking pre-Christian ritual in Christian guise in full view of the Spanish. This dance, like La Danza Guadalupana de Pablo Olivares Sr., consisted of two lines, the use of rattles, two children at the front of the lines with an unbowed Moctezuma II, and a collective dignified countenance. (The children, in our case, are traditionally two young women who are the *malinches*.) I believe that our particular *danza* comes either from this lineage or from a very similar one and that it has morphed over time. To be sure, there are differences between the dance Ribas de Pérez describes and our *danza*, the most obvious being a lack of song involved in our troupe and every matachines troupe I've seen in San Antonio. Nonetheless, it is exciting to see this plausible historical validation of our dance.

Hill's interpretation of the Fiesta del Volcán and mine of the Dance of Motecuzoma have also indirectly led me to entertain possibilities concerning the appropriation of European cultural artifacts by Indigenous people to strengthen their smoke-and-mirror dissimulation as a "conquered people." Specifically, the words *corona* and *monarca* come to mind. But also our drum and drumming style may be such cultural artifacts. While we have used a number of drums, none have been the pre-Spanish hide-covered drums like the ones used in *danza conchera* and *danza azteca*. Rather, they have either been snare drums or have otherwise resembled and lent themselves to drumming in regimental style. The general timbre of such drums is distinct from indigenous drums. Further, the drumbeats and patterns that Molly learned from her uncle have always sounded European and military to me. I once played a video of one or our *danzas* for a friend who was a member of a North American Indian tribe. Her response to it was initially negative because it seemed to harken to a time of military oppression by Europeans. My friend's reaction strengthens what I have come to consider an important aspect of the dance: that the regimental drumming style imitated Spanish regiments to give the appearance of acknowledging Spanish military domination. In other words: our regimental drumming was an aspect of obfuscating traditional ritual like the Maya Cakchiquel who hid pre-Spanish practices in their reenactment of a Maya defeat.

Mesoamerican Time as Cyclical

My previously described internal response to the drumming and dance, that is, one of transcending time, may underscore a phenomenon I experienced in the *danza* and which Hill (1992, 6–7) coincidentally addresses. He observes that "all Mesoamerican peoples have (or traditionally had) a cyclical view of time" (7). In other words, "events which had occurred in the past would occur in the future" (8) because they were part of "recurring cycles" (8). I have often wondered if the incongruently dignified and even jubilant manner of our *danza* had to do with a view of Moctezuma II and pre-Spanish Mexico as revenant. To the extent that this speculation involves the return of a pre-Spanish state of affairs, I tend to relate my sense of transcending time and history to the traditional Mesoamerican concept of time. Here it is helpful to recall that the Tlaxcaltecans brought the *danza* from their ancestral home in central Mexico, which is part of Mesoamerica (Martínez 1996, 43; J. Pohl, personal communication, September 16, 2014).

Dancing Makes a Difference

Overall, the trajectory of thought about the *danza de matachines* has provided me with a frame of reference for writing about that *danza* and the people who traditionally dance it. I admire the rigor and sincerity of this trajectory's scholars as they generally build on a knowledge base that has been amassed with painstaking care over generations. Yet, scholarly research exists largely because of an unavailability of experienced matachines who are willing to write about their experiences as dancers. That is why it is important to have an experienced dancer write rather than an unexperienced scholar. And, while there may be different *danza de matachines* traditions, those differences do not matter in this respect. Whether a dancer's tradition is northern New Mexican, south Texan, or Philippine, experience is experience. In this section, I critique the works of these researchers, but my intention is not to be critical. Rather, it is my hope that the tension that often exists between academics in the social sciences and "subjects" writing about their experiences may spark conditions for a dialogue that would allow scholars of the dance to expand their insights beyond those rendered by limitations of their methodologies.

When our *danza* agreed that I would write about my experience in La Danza Guadalupana de Pablo Olivares Sr., I did not know what to write about, what to pay attention to. To me, everything was significant. Everything was important. I made as many mental notes as possible, at times memorizing verbal exchanges verbatim to write them down later. I wrote about my experiences as a *matachines dancer*. I found neither my master's in social work nor my undergraduate degree in Spanish could have significantly prepared me for this. Most of all, I was regretful because I believed the end product would be a book that was lacking in scholarship and, consequently, would not contribute as much to scholarship involving the dance as a trained anthropologist's would. Nonetheless, I held out the humble hope that I could write something meaningful that would reach everyday people who wanted to know about the *danza*. I also hoped to contribute a documentation of experiences that would be of value to researchers.

Diedre Sklar's book, *Dancing with the Virgin: Body and Faith in the Fiesta of Tortugas, New Mexico* (2001), influenced me by expanding my concept of what a book about the *danza de matachines* tradition could be like. That concept includes that a book on this subject could be narrative in form and subjective. The fact that she speaks of her experiences and observations in a dance community in terms of corporal and emotional memory has especially been significant to me. This approach has given me permission, so to speak, to write about my experiences in a way that is not limited to the six senses of perception as we commonly think of them. The fact that she at times acknowledges her status as an outsider is also important to me in that it made me realize how much I take for granted the familiarity I have with certain relevant cultural knowledge and experiences. This realization has caused me to take care not to erroneously assume the reader shares my familiarity with information, such as fundamental understanding of the *danza*, its history, and relationship to Catholicism in the southwestern United States.

Sylvia Rodriguez's in-depth and intellectually rigorous *The Matachines Dance: Ritual, Symbolism, and Interethnic Relations in the Upper Rio Grande Valley* (1996) served as an important reminder to me of the value of careful research. Her keen eye and insights, moreover, have been very encouraging. Max Harris's book, *Aztecs, Moors, and Christians: Festivals of Reconquest in Mexico and Spain* (2000) was especially helpful and encouraging. His research gave me a sense of being on the right track with regard to La Malinche and her apparent duality in my troupe. The research he conducted also let me see parallels between the configuration of our *danza* and that of the *danzantes* in his chapter titled "The Dance of the Emperor Motecuzoma," (105). His characterization of the *danza* comes the closest to describing what I have experienced.

Joseph Moreno's thesis *The Tradition Continues: The Matachines Dance of Bernalillo, New Mexico* (2005) provides a helpful and impressive background of the *danza de matachines* concerning the history of its study. The background he provides is succinct, bringing together a number of key scholars who have advanced insights and theories, spanning many decades.

Moreno's work has helped me to provide the readers of this book a foundation of knowledge. His dedication to advancing the possible origins of this dance is impressive.

I found value in a work by English professor Norma Cantú by critically juxtaposing it to my experiences as a *matachín* and in that way examining its lack of authenticity. In a book of collected works that she contributes to and coedits, Cantú makes a clinical effort to explain geographic aspects of the *danza de matachines* through a semiotic perspective in a chapter titled "The Semiotics of Land and Place: Matachines Dancing in Laredo Texas" (2009, 97–115). As a *matachín*, I find that this kind of social scientific analysis takes the reader away from what the *danza de matachines* means for *matachines*. In addition, Cantú cites a third party from outside the *danza*, anthropologist Sylvia Rodríguez, to define the *danza de matachines* (97). Rodríguez's rigor notwithstanding, that definition includes an erroneous characterization of the *danza* as a "drama." While I understand that drama here is used somewhat synonymously with narrative, there are elements of a *drama* that nonetheless cannot be associated with the *danza*. These include conflicts, audiences, and the use of linear time. Drawing from my thirteen years as a *monarca*, I feel confident in stating that the *danza* is the summoning of the *Virgen*. In the course of doing this, a story is told, but it is a story that does not begin and end like a drama does, and it is not danced for an audience. That story tells how devotion to the *Virgen* began, but the *Virgen*'s presence and the overall spirit that arises from the dance do not end. Rather, they remain as living entities and need only to be accessed again.[1]

In the same collected work, I found another pertinent chapter, this one by Cantú's coeditor Brenda Romero, titled, "The *Matachines Danza* as Intercultural Discourse" (185). Again, I can only find value in it by critically juxtaposing its lack of authenticity to my experiences. It relies on ethnographic fieldwork rather than lived experience in the dance. And, the importance she places on historic events overlooks the more important implications of cyclical time and other nonlinear and ahistorical understandings of it that appear in the *danza de matachines* such as the triumphant air with which the *monarca* dances, the proud presence of two *malinches* and the *capitanes*' and Moctezuma II's veneration of the *Virgen*. These are things that I have witnessed and experienced in the dance. By not considering these perceptions of time, conventional Eurocentric history becomes by default the only reality by which to understand the dance.[2]

The research presented in David Frye's book, titled *Indians into Mexicans: History and Identity in a Mexican Town*, pieces together, from primary documents and interviews, Spanish Colonial–era dynamics and their persistence in contemporary forms. I found in it uncanny parallels between priests' "meddling" in community feast days ("*fiestas*") (1996, 114) and the previously mentioned appropriation of a St. Juan Diego dance pilgrimage. In fact, Frye's research, together with my historical reading of the *danza de matachines* and experiences in it, indicate that there has been an ongoing trajectory of clergy in Spanish-speaking communities who create friction with parishioners. Such friction tends to involve priests acting in nonspiritual capacities that are ostensibly to benefit others but instead are for the aggrandizement of self, influential friends, and/or secular entities. My experience as a *matachín* supports Frye's identification of this pattern of behavior.

Robert M. Hill's book titled *Colonial Cakchiquels: Highland Maya Adaptation to Spanish Rule, 1600–1700* offered me an insightful interpretation of the Fiesta del Volcán. That annual fiesta, chronicled by Francisco A. Fuentes y Guzmán in 1680, serves as an illustration of how Mesoamerican Indigenous peoples used spectacle and Spanish Colonial assumptions and imagery to serve as a stratagem by which to continue their pre-Spanish ritual practices.

Despite being initially intimidated by those authors who had contributed to written material on the *danza de matachines*, I eventually realized that, just as these authors had contributed to the study of the *danza*, I, too, had something to contribute: my perspective as a *matachín*. By writing from the perspective of a *matachín*, without any training in any of the disciplines that study the *danza de matachines*, I was actually in a position to help researchers in those disciplines. I was able to do so, I realized, by seeing the dance with the benefit of unfiltered insight into the experience of the dance. If I saw something that didn't conform to one of the tenets of those disciplines, I would know it. And, by doing so, I could find nuances and departures from previous understandings of the dance that could lead to new insights. Moreover, writing about my experiences as a *matachín* gives my words greater weight than if I were solely writing about matachines as a researcher. Firsthand and long-term experiences in this realm are things that academics have not had access to. For that reason, I anticipate that they will benefit from this book.

Historians and readers of Spanish Colonial history can gain insights through my experiences of the dance that suggest a cyclical nature of time.

More specifically, the idea of time as cyclical, that is, that events, conditions, and people return, can help historians understand departures from linear history that are often found to be integral in the *danza de matachines*. Anthropologists and those who study the dance can benefit from my contribution by gleaning from it an understanding of the role that lineage and ancestry play in the dance's resilience. Scholars of religion can gain from this the understanding that, although their discipline holds that *La Virgen de Guadalupe* is part of a widespread Marian devotion, it is an erroneous perspective. She is a distinctly different person and is not one of many manifestations of the Virgin Mary. Finally, all who study the *danza de matachines* can benefit from this book by my *demonstrating* that public ritual can have a script that outsiders, including colonial institutions, are oblivious to. This is something I demonstrate in a way that only a native who possesses an intimate sense of place and ancestry in relation to the dance can.

7

Autonomy and Devotion

Twin Pillars Supporting Continuity

Autonomy and devotion play a crucial, dual role in the continuity of the *danza de matachines*. Without one, the other cannot exist. In this chapter, I explain how these two qualities support each other.

Autonomy and Matachines

Autonomy has been an important aspect of our *danza* for the same reason that autonomy is important to any time-honored tradition. It is at once a safeguard and marker of authenticity. Autonomy, for a *danza de matachines* troupe, is strengthened by its direct lineage to a founder, for example, Pablo Olivares Sr. Conversely, the extent to which a tradition is manipulated, altered, or otherwise influenced by extraneous entities, especially institutions, is a measure of the degree to which its authenticity has been compromised. I am aware of these realities as a *matachín* and have processed a number of instances in which I believe I observed La Danza Guadalupana de Pablo Olivares Sr. exercise autonomy.

Autonomy among the Tlaxcaltecans

It is clear and has been established in this book that the Spanish believed they had afforded their Tlaxcaltecan allies the privileges of nobles. Yet, in her dissertation, "'Noble' Tlaxcalans: Race and Ethnicity in Northeastern New Spain, 1770–1810," Patricia Martínez observes that "Charles Gibson's seminal study of Tlaxcala in the 16th century addressed this northern venture as part of the ongoing relationship between Tlaxcala and Spanish colonial authorities. Gibson concludes that the privileges given to the Tlaxcaltecans when they offered the Spanish military aid had to be "continuously negotiated" (Martínez 2004, 2). Gibson's conclusion indicates to me that the Tlaxcaltecans had already perceived themselves as worthy of privileges corresponding to an autonomous group and exercised that autonomy through continued negotiation of their role and relationship with the Spaniards. In my view, the autonomy evidenced in the Danza Guadalupana de Pablo Olivares Sr.'s relationship to various churches and priests resembles the colonial Tlaxcaltecans' diplomacy as they retained and exercised their sense of pre-Spanish autonomy. In addition, the family-based nature of our troupe and other independent troupes serves as a means to preserve that autonomy. I base this on a number of experiences as a member of our *danza* as well as from informal exchanges made with Molly and Tony that have included decisions not to deal with churches that compromise the integrity of the dance.

Frye (1996) notes a number of points of contention in the Tlaxcaltecan population of the parish of Mexquitic in central Mexico. This tension can be glimpsed in the form of a petition sent to the *alcalde mayor* of San Luís in 1776 criticizing, among other things, political collusion between the governor of the village and a priest because of that priest's departures from local customs (Frye 1996, 89). Conflicts with clergy, however, increased with the departure of the Franciscans, who had been laissez faire in their ministry in contrast to the parish priests who replaced them in 1764 with that parish's secularization. Whereas the Franciscans' priorities generally were compatible with those of the Tlaxcaltecans of the village, the post-friary priests:

> came and went with their own retinues of family and servants, and their own personalities and connections and fortunes. Their ties to the parish's past was minimal, and their investment in its future was tenuous and never institutionalized. The goals of priests tended to be personal, to secure a large parish with greater income from ecclesiastical fees, for example, or a sinecure in a large city. (Frye 1996, 89)

Frye also notes that this shift brought about bitter divisions between priests and parishioners and that there has been, according to the residents he has spoken with, a contention that has endured into contemporary times. He states, "the priest's proper place, as I hear their stories, is in the church. In the religious realm, he should not meddle in fiestas and other aspects of traditional religion, as some recent priests are criticized for doing" (Frye 1996, 114). These observations bear a subtle, uncanny resemblance to certain moments I will describe in this book between clergy and devotees of the *Virgen* in the context of dancing for the *Virgen*.

Autonomy from the Church

Members of family-based, autonomous *danza de matachines* troupes function within the Catholic Church. Members are quite often sincerely and devotedly practicing Catholics, and they are respectful of its authority. Yet, the purpose of the *danza de matachines* has always been to dance for the *Virgen*.

Autonomy among traditional, family-based troupes refers to their tendency to dance according to regional as well as family-specific lineages and traditions. As well, they look to internal, experience-earned leadership for direction. They do not dance according to liturgical cycles, and, while friendly with religious institutions, generally do not put the *danza* at the disposal of the institutions for purposes that are not in keeping with the *danza*'s traditions. And, though these troupes are diplomatic in their dealings with churches and church institutions, they ultimately keep their own counsel.

The association with and sponsorship by Catholic churches in San Antonio arose from the need for Mexican immigrant populations to form new communities after having left theirs in Mexico. Because the Mexican communities provided the continuity of the *danza* prior to immigration, parish churches by default provided the community and resources to continue *danza* traditions. In fact, parish clergy made a special effort to occupy this role after the Second Vatican Council. Ironically, our independent *danza* wound up teaching the *danza de matachines* to members of parish churches (D. García, personal communication, December 23, 2015).

La Danza Guadalupana de Pablo Olivares Sr. was created at a time prior to efforts or invitations to have it practiced inside a church. I am reminded of this fact each time we have found ourselves in the tight quarters of a church, having to improvise in order to keep the steps and not bump into pews at certain points in the *adoración*. Similarly, the *danza* does not formally fit into church teaching, apart from The Second Vatican Council's embracing of other cultures to the extent that they converge with Catholicism. It is neither sacrament nor sacramental, but it carries an equal if not greater importance to those things for Spanish-speaking people who have grown up with *La Virgen de Guadalupe* as an integral part of their spiritual spheres. Priests' attitudes toward the dance range between two poles: a genuine respect for the *danza* and one of derision. In between there are attitudes of mere tolerance, paternalism, and awkward uncertainty as to how to regard it.

Close ties between family-based, autonomous *danzas* and the church exist, but these associations are not seamless. The *danza* is our way of assessing the presence of the *Virgen*. She is the ultimate purpose of the *danza*. This owes to the fact that family-based *danzas* also have aspects that make them particular to the family, such as its lineage. These aspects and purpose carry with them the expectation that respect will be shown to the troupe and its *danza* by those close to the dance as well as those outside of it, including the church. The autonomous nature of family-based troupes acts as a kind of protective measure safeguarding the integrity of the dance should any element of the church compromise it.

One such instance of autonomy was the result of a *danza* we had after a *posadas* on the evening of December 20, 2011. Having danced there before, I knew the homeowners customarily started with the praying of the rosary, followed by the *posadas*, our *danza*, and then food. In this 2011 *danza*, however, we learned that a parish priest in attendance had arranged for us to dance after dinner had been served, with the effect that we appeared to be dancing as entertainment. Moreover, that priest stood by making disparaging comments and jokes about our dancing to parishioners, distracting those immediately near him.

Molly and Tony had a sense that the dance might be disrespected at this event, which would explain why the *estandarte* with its image of the *Virgen* was absent. Because of our being scheduled during dinner, most of the *posadas* participants were seated at tables in a patio, with their attention divided between the food and the *danza*. In the middle of the dancing, Molly's Aunt Janie gave the order to bring the *danza* to a premature end. Standing nearby, she made a diagonal cutting gesture below her chin to Molly, bringing the dance to a formal but abrupt close. That night I cautiously broached the subject with Molly and Tony while eating and drinking coffee. I did not want to appear antagonistic toward the priest. However, none of this seemed to come as a particular surprise to my *danza* teachers. They were very aware of the attitude of the priest and simply said they would not be dancing there again. Molly mentioned that her mother, who was also present, told her "*Están danzando nomás.*" (You're only dancing). In other words: Conditions were such that they reduced our usual *danza* to a going-through of motions, void of qualitative substance. I had overheard her mother when she had said that but not understood what she meant until Molly explained.

What is important to note here is that our troupe asserted its autonomy *without being confrontational*. This indicates that, although its presence is welcome, ultimately, the church is not necessary for the dance. Acting autonomously while bypassing confrontation was a de facto strategy that served to ensure continuity of the dance. A confrontation would have invited an exchange that would have alerted the priest that his authority had just been undermined. There was much greater power in nonconfrontational assertion of autonomy than in openly reacting.

On the rare occasions when Molly and Tony informed me that the group would no longer be dancing at a given church or *posadas* location, it was always communicated with much calmness and lacked the slightest malice or anger. In hindsight, I can see that such decisions were not only void of spite or ego-orientation but that they were being made in order to ensure the integrity of the dance. Nor was there any sign of ideological reasoning, all of which one might expect to find in such a situation at first glance.

This autonomy was also clear during the parish meeting concerning a *danza* pilgrimage that I reflect on in "Memoir of a *Monarca*." In that meeting, relatively new *matachines* from Holy Rosary Parish maintained our troupe's integrity and, therefore, its autonomy. They did this by putting themselves on the agenda to deliver a terse and unmistakably confrontational narration of how a number of *danzantes* had come to be misdirected into the church toward the end of the pilgrimage.

Political Autonomy

Yet another way in which I believe I saw autonomy displayed by the troupe was in politics. I characterize this realm as being composed of professional, local activists, developers, local mass media, and the people and entities who collaborate with them (including clergy, journalists, Hispanics seeking official recognition as Native Americans, and activist organizations). Fairly early on in my training, Tony mentioned to me that a priest had once approached the troupe about becoming involved in an unnamed political cause. Without even hinting at any cause or ideological orientation, he expressed annoyance at the idea of using the dance in that way. On numerous occasions since then, he has been approached by other political groups who offered to provide material assistance in exchange for using the pilgrimage to advance their agendas, but he declined in the interest of keeping the pilgrimage apolitical.

During the months prior to the first of a series of *danza* pilgrimages, the city government of San Antonio put into place an ordinance further regulating use of the streets for public demonstrations or celebrations, adding high fees for doing so. In response to the city council's actions, a coalition of activist groups was formed to litigate the issue. I attended one of the coalition's regular meetings, albeit not as a representative of our dance group and saying very little. Nonetheless, I mentioned in the meeting that our group was having fundraisers to pay the fees. The attorney for the coalition, on hearing this, gave me her card and asked me to have Molly and Tony call her despite my dubiousness about the idea. I emailed Molly and Tony about the exchange with the attorney.

When I eventually spoke with them about the matter, I learned they declined contacting the attorney. Rather, Tony told me to convey to the coalition that we essentially were not going to involve ourselves with the coalition's campaign. This was not said with any degree of spite, chagrin, or polarized sense of "us and them." Rather, it was a strategic decision to remain distanced from politics, in this case, from political activism. And, it was apparently based on an assessment that the coalition and our *danza* had different foci. Ours was to dance for the *Virgen*, and she could help us to dance for her better than a coalition or its attorney.

Years later, Tony informed participants in the *danza* pilgrimage that he had been approached by members of the local mass media wanting to know if we would be connecting it thematically with a new high-profile shift in immigration policy that stood to affect the immigrant community. Tony had told them that was not the case and cautioned that there was a chance that *matachines* could be approached individually by such journalists in an effort to get us to say that our pilgrimage had immigration as a theme. It seems the media saw the pilgrimage as a potential metaphor for immigration and an attractive news story.

In the commodification process of a *danza* pilgrimage, political and therefore secular elements that were not part of the *danza* for us prior to our formation of the pilgrimage came to constitute and dilute part of the collective motives held by troupes in that pilgrimage. This observation is noteworthy because it reveals a dynamic between larger economic forces, namely, the local mass media in San Antonio and its attendant symbiotic relationship to corporate business entities (for example, the chamber of commerce, the business community, and developers). Together these entities publicly produce shallow and, more frequently than not, inaccurate interpretations of the spiritual nature of the *danza*, with a tendency to focus on standard references to Christianity's "conquest" over Mexican Indians. And, the treatment of the *danza* as a form of entertainment at the hands of these entities not only belies their perspective as outsiders but trivializes the *danza*'s complex nature. The segment of observers responsible for such treatment is constituted by individuals who are culturally disconnected from communities where such devotion to the *Virgen* is part of daily life. That devotion may be manifested by prayer to the *Virgen* and, possibly, home altars devoted to her. Consequently, participants in these larger economic forces tend to conveniently default to inaccurate sources because those sources are more readily available than the experience. Deery-Stanton (1998) observes that:

> Scholars developing colonial and postcolonial discourse theory have attempted to analyze the impact of colonization by looking at the written texts of both colonizer and colonized. Gayatri Spivak, an important theorist in this field, uses the term *epistemic violence* to describe the colonizer's effective erasure of the indigenous history. . . . This term points to missing or destroyed documentation of indigenous voices that would have provided a more complete understanding of the impact and influence of colonial contact on the original peoples of the so-called New World, Dark Continent, and Orient. (291)

This phenomenon finds application in the economic and historic context in which the annual dance pilgrimages came to be appropriated beginning in 2013 by the director of San Antonio's Spanish colonial missions and the mass media. This context was one in which San Antonio's mission barrio residents, many of whom are descended from mission residents, were being displaced in the wake of the city's efforts to gentrify the area encompassing San Antonio's four southernmost missions in the name of economic growth. So, the commercial institutions (for example, the mass media) and at least one clerical figure were acting in tandem to achieve ends that would adversely affect people who were not consulted about the changes that would affect them, just as in the times of New Spain. And, although a local reporter attempted to make the event an annual tourist attraction that would occur in the *contemporary* downtown Main Plaza (Rivard 2013), his efforts nonetheless were in keeping with *colonial* dynamics. Those colonial dynamics exist among military, religious, and economic institutions except that the military role is not as necessary in this advanced colonial stage as it would have been in the past.

Individual Autonomy

In addition to the political and religious autonomy I have described as sources of continuity for the Danza Guadalupana de Pablo Olivares Sr., the *danza* also possesses autonomy among individuals. This individual autonomy is equally if not more important in terms of the group's continued existence despite newer, competing spheres of activity, especially work and sports among younger members. Autonomy at the individual level can be identified in at least two aspects: (1) the late Pablo Olivares Sr.'s encouragement of individual differences among the way the *trajes* are decorated, and (2) individual motivations for dancing. Members of the group may permanently sew or temporarily attach adornments they find meaningful and pertinent to the dance. A number of the *danzantes* pin color images of Pablo Olivares Sr. to their vests and *capas*. When *danzantes* pin the images of deceased *danzantes* to their *trajes*, it is so that the deceased can be dancing with us. On one occasion, others pinned small pink ribbons to their *trajes* (albeit, at the request of one of the new dancers), symbolizing a movement to bring awareness to breast cancer. While this was highly unusual, it was in keeping with the idea that individual adornment of the *trajes* can at times be temporary. And, though the basic designs and colors of the *trajes* remained the same, some members chose to decorate theirs more elaborately than others, including with gold-glittered and yellow embroidered borders.

The individual motivations among *matachines* and their views of the purpose of the *danza* are noted in the informal criteria regarding what constitutes an ideal *danza*. The majority of dancers in autonomous troupes dance because they have needs to express to the *Virgen* as they request her intercession and to fulfill *promesas*. And every *matachín*'s relationship to the *Virgen* is as different as the vicissitudes that she attends to in our lives. *Promesas* and other prayer requests may include requests for physical recovery from major injuries and help with legal and financial problems. They may be made for either a loved one or for oneself.

The presence of the *Virgen* is particularly palpable when we have an *estandarte* made by someone in the family. I relate this qualitative difference to the importance that Pablo Olivares Sr. attached to the group hand-making its own *trajes* and all the *danzantes* decorating each one according to their respective personal needs and aesthetic tastes. I also relate it to the experiences in which I perceive that certain accoutrements become imbued with metaphysical energies through contact with the individuals who make them. There are, of course, other important factors that make the presence of the *Virgen* palpable, such as spirit, the animating effect of the drum, and the participation of members of the community of devotees.

Autonomy for family-based troupes like ours, La Danza Guadalupana de Pablo Olivares Sr., has been essential for continuity. Specifically, it is clear that healthy attitudes toward autonomy have been responsible for maintaining the integrity of the dance in the context of relations with the church, whose clergy may want to antagonize or control our dance tradition. As well, autonomy from economic forces is a defense against commercial forces that, given the chance, would exploit the dance tradition and consequently impede its continuity. Finally, individual autonomy is intrinsically a part of collective autonomy. Consequently, the collective autonomy of the troupe depends on the autonomy among individual matachines. Autonomy in the realms of our relation to the church, politics, and individuals in the troupe are rooted in the forty years of our troupe's existence. While the tradition of the *danza de matachines*, and of our troupe specifically, has encountered challenges in the form of change, autonomy has been the key variable to being able to maintain integrity and, therefore, enjoy continuity.

Devotion

Devotion is the vehicle for summoning the *Virgen*. It is essential to the dance. Without devotion, her presence cannot be made palpable. And, without her presence, the dance ceases to become authentic. If the dance is inauthentic, then it cannot be said to have continuity. Devotion among the community of devotees and *matachines* tends to occur generationally. It is inspired by understanding of the *Virgen*'s presence and role in aiding in the vicissitudes of life and, just as importantly, perceiving her power on a visceral level. During the dance itself, this visceral perception can and does occur under the right conditions.

Devotion and the Community of Devotees

The community of devotees consists of those people who attend our *danzas* and share a very similar relationship with the *Virgen*, despite not being matachines themselves. They differ from individuals drawn to her because of her story or an association in that their devotion tends to be personal and learned generationally in barrio communities that affirm it. Moreover, personal, metaphysical occurrences often characterize relationships with the *Virgen* in relation to her answering requests concerning vicissitudes.

Members of the community of devotees demonstrate their devotion in different ways on her feast day. Some may traverse the length of a church on their knees in order to place a bouquet of roses at the foot of her image. Others may simply come to the church to light a candle of gratitude. This type of devotion is the substratum of the matachines' devotion. Although this community is not composed of dancers, it is one that is integral to the continuity of the dance. From this community emerge new dancers. As well, the community of devotees support us by purchasing and preparing the food they share with us after the *danzas*. I should underscore that the act of sharing food serves to bond dancers with the hosting devotees. Hosting devotees affirm the dance by acknowledging what takes place in the dance, which is something only devotees of the *Virgen* can perceive besides the matachines ourselves. They are people for whose vicissitudes we dance and at whose behest we dance at *posadas*. With our troupe in particular, they occupy a place of such importance that, unlike other troupes, we invite them to actively participate in our *adoración* when the *capitanes* escort them two by two to the *estandarte*. Therefore, the devotion of this community is essential to the continuity of *danza de matachines* troupes and our traditions.

Differentiation between the Community of Devotees and Audience

Outsiders to the *danza*, including American priests and journalists, have indicated they see the relationship between matachines and the community of devotees as analogous to one of performers to audience. One of the problems with this assumption is that performers necessarily need an audience, whereas matachines do not. Another is that it implies that our purpose is to entertain. Our *danza* is a prayer, and prayer does not require an audience. There were a significant number of occasions when we set out to dance in front of public images of the *Virgen* (for example, tapestries of her displayed on porches) as soon as we learned of residents who had them. Often those residents and/or neighbors would come outside and wordlessly smile and wave when we finished. They were happy to have us there, and we were happy that it was meaningful to their devotion.

However, they understood that we were not there to entertain. If we were to dance to entertain, we would cease to be authentic and, therefore forfeit our continuity.

A more accurate simile of the traditional relationship between *danzantes* and the community of devotees is the one that exists between a priest celebrating mass and the faithful who attend. Both the priest and the faithful understand their roles with regard to one another. The priest undertakes certain prayers in the mass, and the faithful pray with him at times and, at others, without him. But neither is a performer nor an audience to the other. Tertiary observers, that is, observers who are neither devotees nor dancers, introduce a different intention into the collective presence of those gathered for the *danza*.

Devotion and Matachines

The devotion of the matachines, like that of the community of devotees, involves daily, personal devotion to the *Virgen*. However, we are different in that our main differentiating activity, that is, dancing, is timed and has a collective aspect. We train rigorously almost all year to start dancing December 12 and dancing until the *Día de los Reyes* (the Epiphany), a span of twenty-five days.

My experience and observation as a *danzante* has been that, through the collectively experienced physical rigors of training and dancing, the *Virgen* ceases to be a remote historical, religious figure and becomes a conscious, sentient entity whose presence is palpable to the *danzantes*. Devotion to the *Virgen* is central. It is little wonder that the Spanish would propose the use of such a dance as a tool to convert Indians from central Mexico. The presence I feel of the *Virgen* is both the result of and motive for the *danza*. This is something that the community of devotees does not experience to the same extent, especially concerning the training. So, the devotion of the *matachines* is essential to the continuity of our *danza*.

The local media, academics, and church pundits often say matachines have "devotion." Because they see that the dance involves physical rigor, they assume that it requires discipline motivated by faith and that the devotion comes from that faith in "the Virgin Mary." This deduction is misleading because devotion to the *Virgen* comes from an awareness of her presence and a desire to dance for her. In other words, faith comes from the dance and not the other way around. The same presumed experts also use the word *devotion* to imply submission of Indians to Christianity, even though there are no Native American tribal communities in San Antonio that practice this dance. This explanation of the *danza de matachines* is safe and palatable. The public has generally viewed Indians as either hostile or docile. We are not Indians, but our phenotype and regalia often remind sectors of the San Antonio community of Indians. Consequently, the religious pundits and local media feel the need to feed them the stereotype for commercial reasons that have nothing to do with the *Virgen*. Yet, if what these sources said were true, we could not have had the continuity we have enjoyed so far.

For autonomous troupes, devotion is especially different from what these pundits and media types assume. It is born of experiencing the presence of a palpable spirit in the dance. Devotion is an awareness of this spirit. For autonomous matachines, devotion is also inspired through the *Virgen* responding to prayers and *promesas* made and fulfilled in the dance. The power of the dance resides in our summoning that spirit that is intrinsically part of the *Virgen*. The experience of this presence is characteristic of the dance and comes with the lineage of the dance. When a dance has a lineage, it is imbued with the power to bring about this transcendental energy, this spirit. Plus, the subscript involved when members of the media and clergy describe us as having "devotion," is to create a pleasant image that will attract an audience. Church-based matachines are sincere. For them the dance is a prayer to please the *Virgen*. Yet, autonomous matachines troupes that have lineage additionally dance because we have a visceral awareness that the *Virgen* is participating in the power of the dance with the presence she creates in it. Making this happen is at the forefront of our intentions. A given *danza de matachines* troupe that is organized under the auspices of a parish church may share the Catholic perspective on devotion that religious pundits and the journalists who claim to speak for them do. But that is because it has no family lineage. And, whereas Molly's mother told us we were "only dancing" when a priest maneuvered for us to dance as dinner entertainment, a parish priest would not know the qualitative difference between that and dancing in the presence of the *Virgen*. Because we are devoted to bringing about her presence through the *danza*, our troupe and our tradition have experienced continuity into the twenty-first century.

Devotion in autonomous *danza de matachines* troupes also plays a unique role in relation to prayer. With each one of the hundreds of ribbons that Molly's mother sewed onto Manuel's *viejo* suit, she imbued the entire *traje* with intention. Prayer occupied in years past an even more significant role in La Danza Guadalupana de Pablo Olivares Sr. Molly speaks of Nahuatl prayers that had repetitive steps paralleling the prayers of the rosary. The dance itself is a prayer, even though it consists of many steps. And certain steps traditionally used in the *adoración* have a structured order representing the prayers of the rosary. This is the kind of thing that the larger public does not see and therefore cannot understand on those occasions when nondevotees watch us and try to make statements about us. Yet, it is this kind of devotion that contributes profoundly to our continuity.

Here it is worth restating that the *Virgen* of the *danza* and the community of devotees is a different personage from the Virgin Mary of the Bible and theological orthodoxy. I have heard devotees of the *Virgen* speak of her in contexts that suggest that she has divine powers that Christianity only ascribes to the Holy Trinity. Moreover, instructional pamphlets for praying the rosary, in my experience, invariably include a series of illustrations of mysteries to be meditated on while praying, with each one corresponding to a different liturgical season. These images are all from the gospels, that is, the New Testament of the Bible, and several are of the Virgin Mary. Popular images of *La Virgen de Guadalupe*, however, are often accompanied by a marginal pictorial narrative of four frames telling the story of her apparition to Juan Diego and his encounters with Bishop Zumárraga. Such popular images never depict imagery from the gospels. This is the *Virgen* to whom both matachines and the community of devotees are devoted. Otherwise, it is obvious that both our *danza de matachines* troupe and the larger *danza de matachines* tradition would cease in their continuity because the devotion, which has been its essence since the Spanish Colonial period in Mexico, would cease to exist.

The Power of Devotion in Autonomous Context

Matachines would not be able to express devotion through dance, and members of the community of devotees would not be able to attend, contribute to, or participate in it, thus expressing their devotion, without autonomous conditions. They are two sides of the same coin. Matachines—as troupes and individuals—can only arise where there is a community of devotees. Conversely, the community of devotees could not participate in the *veneración* or ask people to dance for them on the feast day of the *Virgen*. Nor could the presence of the *Virgen* be summoned at the homes of those who hold *posadas*. However, these roles of mutual support can only take place in a context of autonomy because systems external to them engage in colonial dynamics that compromise them with changes and, consequently, stand to compromise our continuity.

8

Appropriation of the Pilgrimage

A Catholic Priest Dances around the Details

The following is a chronology of events surrounding efforts to appropriate an annual *danza* pilgrimage that was initiated by La Danza Guadalupana de Pablo Olivares Sr. The pilgrimage was begun several years before these efforts came about. As will be seen, though, larger political and commercial forces beyond our scope came into play. These forces created circumstances in which it became favorable for local entities and persons from outside the dance to make our pilgrimage tradition conform to their desires, especially regarding involvement of the archdiocese's Old Spanish Missions of San Antonio. As will be seen and would have been expected in the Spanish Colonial period, a modern-day prelate figures significantly into this series of events.

Pilgrimage as *Danza* Tradition

A pilgrimage, in its broadest meaning, constitutes movement of the physical body of pilgrims from a point A to a point B while consisting also of spiritual movement. For us, the physical movement is motivated by devotion, and the spiritual movement is an intensified closeness to the *Virgen*. The pilgrimage bonds us more strongly to the *Virgen*. In San Antonio, matachines frequently are immigrants from communities in northern Mexico where matachines undertake dance pilgrimages, usually from one church to another. As in other aspects of the *danza*, their traditions form the expectations they have about dance pilgrimages. Pablo Olivares Sr. himself participated in morning dance pilgrimages in Monterrey. Though dance pilgrimages undertaken by matachines may take a public form, they are ultimately an internal communication between the *danzante* and the *Virgen*, and, like the *danza* itself, they are not for show.

There is an important difference between our dance pilgrimage tradition and dancing in procession. Technically, a procession can be secular and, therefore, take the form of a march, cavalcade, or parade. For matachines troupes such as ours, though, the procession consists of the columns dancing a short distance—one block at the most—to a destination where the matachines will dance the *adoración*. In a procession, in addition to having the characteristics described above, the *danzantes* stop periodically to dance the patterns of the pre-*adoración* segment of the *adoración*. Matachines consistently do this whenever our route brings us into the presence of the image of the *Virgen*. The image may be a permanent fixture such as a mural or *capilla* or a tapestry someone has placed on their porch to show their devotion to her on her feast day. Molly and Tony have told me that Pablo Olivares created a number of the steps we use for the purpose of dancing long distances through the mountainous terrain of his native Monterrey, Nuevo León. The family story is that his founding of the troupe arose out of a wish to seek the *Virgen*'s help on behalf of an ill relative.

In 2007, my second year of dancing with the troupe, Molly and Tony planned, organized, and coordinated a dance pilgrimage on the West Side. It went from St. Theresa's Church to Our Lady of Guadalupe Church. The 2007 pilgrimage was the first of what would become an annual series of pilgrimages. Its purpose was to honor the newly canonized San Juan Diego on his feast day of December 9. At Tony's and Molly's request, I attended organizational meetings with representatives of participating troupes. The pilgrimage consisted of mostly church-based troupes, as those are the norm in San Antonio. Our Lady of Guadalupe Parish Church provided a space where we could meet with the representatives of participating troupes. Later, when the city began to charge us fees and insurance, the same church let us have small fundraisers on its premises to meet those expenses. Molly had anticipated that there would be red tape involved because Junior naively attempted a similar pilgrimage and was consequently fined by police.

We changed our route every year in order to benefit as many barrio parishes as possible. The pilgrimages would begin at one church and end at another, ranging in distance from approximately two-and-a-half to three miles, going from one barrio's parish church to another's. Though the first year was a difficult one in terms of getting parish representatives to communicate with us in a fluid way, participating parishes otherwise gave us considerable autonomy once our contacts were established. In keeping with tradition, these pilgrimages took place in the mornings. They were underway by 7:00 a.m. Starting before sunrise gave the experience a profound sense of intimacy among the matachines and the community of devotees who came out of their residences to see us and the devotees who had come to follow us. For me it heightened the presence of the *Virgen* each time we stopped to venerate a public image of her. At this hour, there is an energy that arises from the ground and that invigorates even older dancers, giving our dancing greater vibrancy than can be felt by dancing at any other time of the day.

Each pilgrimage culminated with troupes dancing their *veneraciones*, and, as usual, La Danza Guadalupana de Pablo Olivares Sr. continued its unique traditional inclusion of members of the community of devotees as the *capitanes* escorted them to our *estandarte*. And, despite our pilgrimages being technically for the Feast Day of San Juan Diego, there was a blurred line—if any—between his feast day and that of *La Virgen de Guadalupe*, which is on December 12. It was blurred in the hearts of the many participants and members of the community of devotees who shouted, "*¡Viva la Virgen de Guadalupe!*" and those who answered with, "*¡Viva!*" It really made little difference because the two personages are so closely linked. And, after all, San Juan Diego was the first devotee of *La Virgen de Guadalupe*.

Those pilgrimages were joyous, solemn, transcendental, and all of these things seemed to be heightened by the stillness and quietude of the morning. The intimacy of space afforded by the darkness meant that we danced with no hesitating but only immediate responses to Molly's drumming and single-hearted intention that made our dancing a deftly timed expression of devotion we had waited almost all year to express. It seemed anything could happen. The *viejos de la danza* became otherworldly in their eccentric antics. One year, a young man dressed like Juan Diego swayed rhythmically as he walked, holding a tapestry with the *Virgen*'s image for all to see, as if for the first time. Another year, a jet-black pony, spirit-like, emerged from the shadows and cautiously approached the throng with equine curiosity. It watched us from behind the fence of its property until, apparently

Barrio residents (background) watch the 2008 dance pilgrimage from their porch. The familiarity of such residents with the *danza* creates the intimacy of space in which our *danza* has traditionally taken place. This intimacy of space could not exist if the *danza* were viewed as exotic or foreign.

wanting to pet it, a girl scared away the skittish animal, which then slowly returned to the fence as the teen withdrew. I thought of the interaction as a metaphor for Juan Diego's paradoxical efforts to convince Bishop Zumárraga that he was telling the truth about the *Virgen*.

In Pursuit of World Heritage Site Status

By 2012, the economic agendas of the local, colonial power structure began seeking UNESCO's consideration of the missions as a cultural World Heritage Site. Consequently, it was in the political interests of an archdiocesan institution called The Old Spanish Missions of San Antonio[1] to claim cultural continuity. It could do this by associating itself with our *danza* pilgrimages, especially since one of our participating pilgrimage troupes included a political organization that claimed a recently rediscovered Native American identity through ancestral association with the missions. Coincidentally, it was at this time that Molly and Tony began to research how they could have the annual pilgrimage go from Mission

San José to Mission Concepción. The idea of a mission-to-mission pilgrimage was important to Molly because, for two years during the late 1960s, Pablo Olivares Sr. included one of the missions among the churches where they would dance. She said they danced there twice. Since she was very young, she does not remember which of the five missions it was. However, she remembers that dancers included her oldest brother Ernest, her other brother Tony, her cousin Louie, and herself. As she spoke of that time, it appeared to me that the experience of dancing at the mission was a meaningful touchstone for her by which she remembers her family's greatest unity because they were all dancing in a single troupe. Tony, her spouse, inspired by the story of Pablo Olivares Sr.'s pilgrimages in Monterrey, encouraged the idea of beginning one in San Antonio.

We were unaware that UNESCO's process of consideration of World Heritage status was underway for the missions. I introduced Molly and Tony to one of Mission Concepción's parishioners in order to begin communication with Father David García, the director of the Old Spanish Missions of San Antonio and pastor and administrator of Mission Concepción. It was a coincidence of timing. Father García, in what seemed to be marked contrast to the troupe's previous dealings with the archdiocese, was relatively forthcoming. He offered to sponsor the December 2013 pilgrimage observing the feast day of San Juan Diego, stipulating that the pilgrimage begin and end at his church, Mission Concepción. It was not the pilgrimage from Mission San José to Mission Concepción that had been requested, but the troupe had never been in a financial position to bargain. So, we agreed.

However, status as a World Heritage Site was not only in the interest of the Old Spanish Missions but also in the interests of a number of commercial entities, especially developers who stood to profit from the gentrification of the mission barrios. These interests were made evident by the purchase of major properties around the missions. The purchases included one adjacent to Mission Concepción and another across the street from Mission San José. Both purchases were made subsequent to World Heritage Site designation. Paradoxically, that development signaled the ultimate displacement of the people who have provided cultural continuity to the missions: descendants of mission residents. In keeping with the same colonization dynamics in place during Spanish rule, entities of power were acting with the colonial assumption that Indigenous people or, in this case, the descendants of Indigenous people, were to serve their social and political agendas. In Spanish Colonial times, friars worked to make Indigenous peoples adopt mission life, and, by so doing, made them Spanish subjects amenable to Spanish governance and, most of all, the taking of native resources. The same practices have continued into the present day as colonial agents use matachines as props and pair us with manufactured histories to facilitate growth and strengthen the presence of commercial entities. The historical and cultural manufacturing of history by these San Antonio entities is an exact parallel to Eric Hobsbawm's (2005) observations concerning Swiss augmentation and subsequent institutionalization of authentic folk practices in the twentieth century:

> It is clear that plenty of political institutions, ideological movements and groups—not in the least in nationalism—were so unprecedented that *even historic continuity had to be invented, for example by creating an ancient past beyond effective historical continuity, either by semi-fiction . . . or by forgery* [emphasis added]. (2005, 7)

The 2013 Pilgrimage: Missionization and Misinformation Begin

Like many San Antonians my age, I was familiar with Father García. A man approaching retirement age, he had a history of being publicly visible, telegenic, and of a gregarious charisma. But on occasion I had wondered about how in touch he was with San Antonio's Spanish-speaking community. For instance, the last time I had seen him, he referenced National Public Radio in a homily before working-class southside families. Theirs was a very different demographic than the kind associated with that listenership. The rote, polite distance among those families, who were more likely to tune in to a local Spanish station, was palpable.

As mentioned earlier, our troupe accepted his offer because we were short on funds for the fees that we usually paid to the city to have our pilgrimage and were left with no other option if we were to have it. His church, originally named Nuestra Señora de la Purísima Concepción de Acuña when it was founded in 1731 (http://oldspanishmissions.org/mission-concepcion), was one of five Spanish missions established in present-day San Antonio during the Spanish Colonial period to convert the numerous indigenous peoples of the region. Coincidentally, I had recently begun translating mission correspondence from this era, and I also trace my ancestry to residents of mission landholdings.

I became concerned when a local reporter announced the event one day prior, providing considerable misinformation, including that it was "the

Dance of the Moors and Christians" and that it "represents one of the earliest cultural expressions of *conquering Spaniards dominating indigenous people* (emphasis added) in the New World" (Rivard 2013). The reporter also referred to the event as a "march" and "parade," which are distinctly different activities from a pilgrimage. Firstly, the dance of the Moors and Christians is a drama set in Zaragoza, Spain, involving men engaged in mock battle in which Santiago (Saint James) miraculously comes to the rescue of the Christians (Harris 2000, 142). Although set in Zaragoza, the play has traditionally been performed in various places in Spain (Harris 2000, 211–12) and the American continent (Champe 1981, 38; Weigle and White 1988, 409). It includes mock battle in which "riders wield painted wooden swords and scimitars and bear shields painted with a crescent or a cross" (Harris 2000, 165). An observation by Rodríguez (1996) begins to explain the erroneous association of the *danza de matachines* with the Moors and Christians drama. She states that, "Some scholars (e.g., Dozier 1958, 33) have conflated the Matachines dance with *Los Moros y Cristianos*, but the latter is a separate religious drama about the expulsion of the Moors from Spain" (7). These scholars firmly establish that the dance of the Moors and Christians/*Moros y Cristianos* has nothing to do with Mexico, Juan Diego, Bishop Zumárraga, or *La Virgen de Guadalupe* in either form or content. Secondly, to state that our *danza* is an expression of "conquering" and "domination" is to make the colonial and paternalistic assumption that we matachines perceive it as such and, more egregiously, that Indigenous peoples of Mexico view themselves as having been conquered. And, to the extent that the *danza de matachines* is danced among Indigenous and formerly Indigenous populations and that the dance that was handed down to the Olivares family expresses stateliness and triumph rather than defeat, such commentary can only be considered irresponsible.

On the day of the 2013 pilgrimage, the participating *danza* groups assembled in the parking lot of the Mission Concepción at 7:00 a.m. I learned then that the pilgrimage was not one in the true sense of the word, that is, traveling from a starting point and ending at a destination. Rather, our route would initiate at the mission, follow a sidewalk along a few acres of undeveloped land and a city park, and return to the mission, creating an oblong loop. At less than a mile, the route was a much shorter distance than we had ever danced in any of our pilgrimages. The aforementioned local reporter appeared and approached Tony, asking him something akin to what future he planned for the pilgrimage. I could not hear Tony's answer, but the reporter reacted to his answer by emphatically asserting that Tony was not thinking in terms that were sufficiently grandiose. "You have to think big!" he said as he held his hands in front of him as if describing the size of a large fish. He then attempted to regale Tony with how wonderful he thought it would be for the matachines Molly had organized for the pilgrimage to dance downtown in the newly reconstructed plaza in front of San Fernando Cathedral (another landmark to which I have ancestral ties). The journalist then gravitated to Father García. Video taken during the "pilgrimage" shows him and Father García conversing as they trailed behind the dance procession, virtually oblivious to it. Afterward, García announced proudly that he had accompanied the dancers the entire way. Subsequently, I learned from the reporter's website that he was calling for all the groups of participating *danzantes* to dance in the Main Plaza to "showcase" the city's cultural diversity. He posted a link to a video of one of our previous pilgrimages. Coincidentally, I was the one who had recorded and loaded the video onto the internet. I quickly disabled it, which generated a message from the parent site saying it was now "private." Because the author of the article so supported the idea of having us perform for tourists and because his research was so superficial and flawed, I offered a critique of it in the comments section that turned into a debate. I eventually gave up when he began to remove my comments in such a way that my newer statements appeared out of context. His responses to my statements demonstrated faulty parallelism, for example, by comparing San Antonio to Mexico and himself to Jesus's disciples and the authors of Roman history. He also confirmed my concerns that there were intentions to commercialize our *danza* by bringing it to a "larger stage." He saw nothing contradictory about the fact that he was trying to make statements without the experience of a *danzante* to qualify him to do so; he essentially said he could make statements about what would be good for the matachines despite not being one himself.

To begin to understand the reporter's association of the dance with entertainment, it would be helpful to first understand the nature of applause. Applause comes from the ancient Greeks and is meant to show the approval of or give encouragement to people who endeavor to perform or entertain. Yet, when applause for matachines comes from the community of devotees, it is not to show approval but to show appreciation for the ability to be in the *Virgen*'s presence, and it is a way of doing something that allows them to feel they are participating. This in fact may be the reason why La Danza Guadalupana de Pablo Olivares Sr. has always asked devout attendees to dance in the part of

Our 2008 dance pilgrimage, like the others predating archdiocesan sponsorship, began at 7:00 a.m. and wended through residential streets on the west and south sides of San Antonio.

the *adoración* after *el viejo de la danza* has been captured. For these reasons, our *danza* could not become a spectacle in the plaza or a tourist attraction. We would effectively make it a source of entertainment. Consequently, it would invite applause and affirm the outsider gaze as a spectacle and tourist attraction in the plaza. If the reporter had his way, we would become a source of entertainment and consequently invite the kind of applause intended for entertainment. That would trivialize and ignore the devotion we *danzantes* invest in our efforts, and, moreover, such appropriation would be for commercial interests.

The 2014 Pilgrimage: Troupe Withdrawal and a Change of Feast Days

The year 2014 saw a number of changes for the Aguilar family. There was a serious medical crisis in the family demanding attention. As well, there were sufficient peripheral responsibilities for them to prevent the scheduling of practices. Tony and I spoke a few days before the pilgrimage, listing the responsibilities, and he discussed some of its challenges that year. He stated that five troupes that had participated in the pilgrimage in years past, that is, prior to Father García's sponsoring of the pilgrimage, had with-drawn one by one from the pilgrimage, though they continued to dance in neighborhood *posadas* and in private backyards. The explanation he gave was that they said, "It didn't feel like a pilgrimage anymore." Consequently, Tony stated that the pilgrimage, "almost didn't happen," and he was only able to save the event by recruiting matachines troupes from nearby towns. The more troupes that participate, the better it is for the strength of our collective prayer through dance. So, it is profoundly ironic that a priest was responsible for this decline in participation. Tony added, in apparent refer-ence to Mission Concepción's involvement with the 2014 pilgrimage, that "they are going to take full control as soon as it's over." In other words, Tony would be relinquishing the organizational responsibilities that had been passed to him from Molly. That was a relief to me, inasmuch as I had seen Molly and then Tony have to deal with the multiple and stressful logistics these responsibilities entailed.

Despite the fact that troupes were withdrawing from the event and were citing a lost sense of spirituality for doing so, Mission Concepción, under the administrative leadership of Father García, publicly declared that the 2014 pilgrimage was in honor of the Feast Day of the Immaculate Conception, which falls on December 8, one day before the Feast Day of San Juan Diego and four days before the Feast Day of *La Virgen de Guadalupe*. This appropriation was evident on two large posters announcing the pil-grimage in front of the mission tourist information center. So, it now had thematically and officially moved away from the story of Juan Diego and *La Virgen de Guadalupe* and would be focused on Mission Concepción. Ironically, one of the large posters at the mission advertised the event as "Native Religious Dance" despite having formally removed its "Native" foundation and made it a celebration of the Feast Day of the Immaculate Conception, which is celebrated by Catholics all over the world. An even more significant change to the pilgrimage was its starting time. As of the 2014 pilgrimage, it began at 2:00 p.m. This is in sharp contrast to our pre-vious starting time at predawn hours.

As we approached the chapel to dance our *veneraciones*, Father García met the troupes and told us repeatedly, "Keep it to five minutes! Pass it down!" He sounded like a backstage manager. When spectators were asked why they had come, they said it was because Father García had told them in mass that the dance was about the Christianization of the Indians and that it was a tradition that the Franciscans started. When confronted with the fact that I, a *matachín*, differed in that view, they insisted I was wrong.

One of the political Hispanic groups who had joined the pilgrimage to promote their campaign to become recognized as Native Americans were chanting the word "yanaguana" while using a central Mexican style *danza*. Yanaguana is a Spanish Colonial–era indigenous word associated with the San Antonio River. They used the word in their effort to "reclaim" their culture (as one of their members told me) and did so with the same inventiveness as Father García's exoticization of the pilgrimage. The people chanting and Father García had more in common with each other than either of them had with the traditional matachines in that both had agendas that were removed from the spirit of the dance.

The 2015 Pilgrimage: Commercialization and Identity Politics

The 2015 pilgrimage began and ended at Mission Concepción for the third year in a row. A week prior to that pilgrimage, I met with Tony to help him train new *danzantes*. He informed me that the person from Mission Concepción who was supposed to organize the pilgrimage asked him only a few weeks before the pilgrimage if he would organize it instead. He agreed with much trepidation because of the short notice. It was a daunting task not only because of the short notice but also because the troupes he had invited from out of town the previous year to replace the withdrawn troupes were not returning. When Tony asked me if I would be dancing in the pilgrimage, I expressed misgivings. I told him I perceived that the pilgrimage had come increasingly under the control of Father García. More specifically, García's collaboration with the business community to develop the mission area for tourism and new residents made me feel that we were being exploited. Most importantly, *La Virgen de Guadalupe* was no longer the focus of the *danza* according to García's recent statements to the mass media. Nonetheless, I also told Tony I would think and pray about it. By the day of the 2015 pilgrimage, I believed that my prayers for guidance were answered in a dream. In that dream I was discouraged from dancing in the "pilgrimage." However, I did go to Mission Concepción to support our *danza* and to see the pilgrimage as non-*danzantes* see it.

Commercialization of the pilgrimage was increased in 2015. Whereas the free sharing of food and refreshments has always been an important component for *danzas* at this time, the local daily newspaper this year had heralded the addition of food venders to the pilgrimage. And, in fact there were food-vending trucks parked in front of the mission as an apparent method of diminishing the church's responsibility to provide food and refreshments to the community of participants and devotees.[2] One was a taco truck and the other was from an upscale hamburger restaurant.

There were noticeably more spectators than before. They included a busload of tourists who were waiting for us along the route, cameras in hand. But there were not as many as seemed to be desired by the local media, which had taken on the role of making the pilgrimage a tourist attraction and entertainment event. One of the participating troupes was a folkloric dance school. There seemed to be new troupes replacing the ones that dropped out. I counted a total of eighteen troupes, including one that had merged with Los Soldados de la Virgen de Guadalupe.

Father García addressed the *danzantes* under the afternoon sun. He told them that, for the first time, the "pilgrimage" would go to the banks of the San Antonio River "because water gives us life" and "our ancestors came from the river." Here it should be noted that an extensive Texas missions inspection report notes that the vast majority of Indians associated with the missions were not even from the present-day San Antonio area (Ortiz 1745). Moreover, most of the dancers were immigrants from Mexico, and the US Army Corps of Engineers had changed the river's route in the twentieth century. Consequently, his words sounded very new age and "spiritual" but had very little basis in reality. He made no mention of San Juan Diego for whom we had originally organized the pilgrimage. Moreover, he made *"la Virgen de la Inmaculada Concepción"* the primary focus of the pilgrimage and the *La Virgen de Guadalupe* a secondary focus, with Christ the King (*Cristo Rey*), added on thirdly.

Father García walked at the front of the pilgrimage, wearing a scallop shell with an image of Mission Concepción on it. The scallop shell worn around the neck is associated with a Spanish pilgrimage from the French border to the Cathedral of Santiago (Saint James) de Compostela in Spain, a distance of approximately five hundred miles. Despite his status as a priest, he had never publicly explained that pilgrims to Santiago de Compostela wear the scallop shells because of the belief that John the Baptist used one to baptize Jesus in the Jordan River. He could have done this when he addressed the crowd at the beginning of the pilgrimage.

Mission staff were wearing scallop shells with the same image of Mission Concepción on them. I asked one if this were the same custom used in Spain and if this was a tradition of the church. She confirmed that it was the kind used by Spanish pilgrims, adding that the church was starting "a new tradition." This form of marketing resonates with Father García's recent public appeals to developers of the area to help him create a "mission experience" for millennial tourists and neocolonists.

By the time we completed our route, there was no doubt in my mind that our pilgrimage for the feast day of San Juan Diego had been appropriated. In the course of the "pilgrimage," I had smelled a tourist cigar, seen politically motivated dancers with their organizational banner, entertainment-seeking tourists in lawn chairs, multiple tables of souvenirs, a busload of tourists, and food trucks replacing communally shared food. We had been consulted by no one about how this might undermine our devotion and intentions. Not by Father García, not by the tour bus company, and not the food truck owners. We had also started and ended at a time completely different from our traditional times.

December 12, 2015

On this feast day of the *Virgen*, we began dancing at 6:30 a.m. We spent the day dancing and going from one church to the next. Our last commitment was at the 7:00 p.m. mass at Mission Concepción. We were supporting the newly formed *danza de matachines* there that Tony had trained only weeks before. Despite the fact that these new matachines had trained and were dancing for the Feast Day of Our Lady of Guadalupe, none of their *trajes* bore her image as is customary. Instead, they had duplicated images of the Immaculate Conception that hangs prominently in the sanctuary of the mission's church.

9

Anatomy of an Appropriated Pilgrimage

It galls us that Western researchers and intellectuals can assume to know all that is possible to know of us, on the basis of their brief encounters with some of us.

—Linda Tuhiwai Smith, *Decolonizing Methodologies*

In the previous chapter I outlined instances of appropriation of our dance pilgrimage during the years it was held at Mission Concepción. One particularly striking observation I made was the shark-like instincts with which institutional systems and public figures zeroed in on the two most important elements in the pilgrimage that were within their reach: autonomy and devotion. I now discuss those two key elements in this chapter because they are crucial to continuity. Their interplay with change reveals how an autonomous, family-based *danza de matachines* troupe like ours can have continuity for many years. I also take a closer look at the instances of appropriation in our dance pilgrimage during its sponsorship by the Old Spanish Missions of San Antonio. I examine instances in which autonomy and then devotion were appropriated—the 2015 pilgrimage being the year of culmination. As well, I examine how authentic matachines responded to the changes with which they were confronted. Ultimately, I assess the ways in which authentic *danza de matachines* troupes responded with resilience.

Appropriation of Autonomy

I would like to remind the reader that, La Danza Guadalupana de Pablo Olivares Sr. has been an *autonomous*, family-based *danza de matachines* troupe from its inception. This autonomy means its leadership has been internal, beginning with its founder. It also means that the troupe's leadership and the troupe itself act independently of outside organizations, even if the troupe collaborates with families, parishes, and the city in order to dance at churches and homes and to have the autonomously organized first pilgrimages. Autonomy is also what gives us the troupe authenticity because that is how the troupe was begun. And, without that authenticity, continuity is compromised indefinitely.

Appropriation of Autonomy by Religious Entities

Our autonomy was undermined when Father García changed our route from the previous years his church sponsored it so that it veered near the San Antonio River. Before Mission Concepción had begun to sponsor our pilgrimages and have them begin and end at that mission, we had a different route every year. So, it was not the change in the route itself that was problematic but the unilateral decision to do so as well as the likewise unilaterally made decision to associate the meaning of the pilgrimage with the San Antonio River. This was never discussed with our troupe, despite ample opportunity for García to have discussed it with Tony and for Tony to then have shared that with the troupe. In fact, García only publicly announced this change and the significance he attached to it thirty minutes before the beginning of the pilgrimage.

Another way our autonomy was compromised was through Mission Concepción's sale of souvenirs. Permission was neither requested nor given to the Mission to set up several tables to sell trinkets such as beverage coasters, Christmas tree ornaments in the shapes of the facades of San Antonio's Spanish missions, imported basketry, lapel pins, and generic ethnic items. No one asked our troupe how we might feel about trivializing our devotion to the *Virgen* with the sale of these items that had nothing to do with our original purpose for the pilgrimage.

Finally, our autonomy was compromised when Father García inaccurately told local news sources and UNESCO officials that the *danza de matachines* had been danced continuously in San Antonio's missions. In fact, a number of parishioners reported that they had been told the same thing during mass, adding that the Franciscans had taught the dance to the mission neophytes. The idea of the Franciscans teaching the *danza de matachines* to *anyone* has no basis in reality. Moreover, I distinctly remember a conversation about the origins of the *danza* with Tony during my early years in the troupe. In that conversation he took exception to a documentary we had seen on public television in which a pundit made that claim. And his position is supported by a lack of evidence proving the Franciscans had such a role. Yet, Father García did not confer with us to find out how we might feel about such a revision of history, let alone to inquire about our views on the dance's origins. Finally, the archdiocese had told us we were on our own when we asked for financial help in paying the city fees imposed on our pilgrimage yet rushed to our aid when its allies in the business community stood to ultimately gain from recognition by UNESCO that we unknowingly facilitated.

The false association of our pilgrimage with the San Antonio River, the exploitation of our pilgrimage as a way of selling tourist trinkets, and the historical revision of our *danza*'s history represent appropriation of our dance pilgrimage by Father García and the archdiocesan organizations he is affiliated with. These are actions that bypass the autonomy our troupe should have maintained even after it began to collaborate with the Old Spanish Missions of San Antonio. What was particularly insidious was the willful feeding of misinformation to UNESCO officials about the *danza de matachines* tradition, that it existed as a continuous presence in the missions when, in fact, it had no continuous *danza de matachines* tradition until our first pilgrimage at Mission Concepción. What makes this deception particularly disrespectful of our autonomy is that it was done for reasons having nothing to do with *La Virgen de Guadalupe* or *San Juan Diego*. Rather, García's intention was that of collectively qualifying the missions for designation as a UNESCO World Heritage Site. Having succeeded in receiving this designation five months earlier, the pilgrimage served to sustain the appearance of what he had claimed.

Appropriation of Autonomy by Commercial Entities

The unprecedented presence of food trucks at the 2015 dance pilgrimage appropriated the aspect of our *danza* whereby food was prepared and shared freely, thus providing a means for further bonding between members of the community of devotees and matachines. Yet, the food-vending trucks, one of which was owned by an upscale hamburger business, were additionally indicative of commodification of the pilgrimage by commercial

The sale of Christmas tree ornaments in the shapes of the missions were one of the ways the archdiocese commercialized our pilgrimage. These were for sale at the 2015 dance pilgrimage on the grounds of Mission Concepción. Photo: Margaret Greco.

entities. One of the most obvious commercial entities is the tourism industry on San Antonio's southside. This was manifest in the sale of mission tourist trinkets that had been distributed by the National Parks Service. It was also evidenced by the tour bus, whose owner, having been informed about the pilgrimage by the mass media, waited for us along the route with a crowd of tourists prepared to take videos and photos. These instances of tourism had not been present when Father García initially hosted our pilgrimage at Mission Concepción. And they were definitely absent during the six consecutive pilgrimages prior to that. Tourism practices in the pilgrimage commodified it by making it a means to generate profits for the business community and revenues for church and public entities rather than dancing for the *Virgen* and recognizing San Juan Diego. In doing so, they appropriated our autonomy. These were not decisions of our making and ran contrary to what we had originally set out to create with our dance pilgrimage.

The gentrification of the communities surrounding the missions is another way in which our dance pilgrimage was commodified. In retrospect, I can see now that it began once the missions came under consideration by

UNESCO as a World Heritage Site. The business community, including land developers and speculators, stood to make large profits through the resultant increase of property values in and around the missions. As well, the city government stood to see increased revenues through increased property taxes. In fact, plans for building an apartment complex adjacent to Mission Concepción were formulated before the UNESCO's International Council on Monuments and Sites could convene in Bonn, Germany, to make their decision about the missions' designation. As in the case of our autonomy being appropriated by tourism, we were not consulted. No one asked us how we might feel about the commodification and exploitation of our dance pilgrimage in order to facilitate gentrification of the missions' barrios.

Appropriation of Autonomy by Political Entities

The autonomy of our 2015 dance pilgrimage was also appropriated by opportunistic political organizations and figures. Some were behind the scenes while others were at the fore. The local Hispanic organizations self-identifying as Native Americans and trying to obtain federal recognition as such were the most visible. Their relationship to the city was similar to ours with the archdiocese. That is, they were kept at a distance until the city and its business community needed to create the appearance of having continuous indigenous traditions around the missions. Once the designation was secured, these self-described Indigenous groups began vying to become the missions' official Indians, so to speak, in order to have greater access to politicians and public funds, and to increase their chances at becoming federally recognized. Their participation during our first pilgrimage at Mission Concepción had been subdued. They were relatively few in number, wore street clothing, and, strangely, they only danced—a *danza conchera* style dance—at the end of the pilgrimage.

In the 2015 pilgrimage, the political agendas of these groups became more pronounced. At least one of these nonprofit organizations carried a banner bearing the name of their group in place of an *estandarte* bearing the *Virgen's* image. Their participants increased in number, and their street clothing was replaced by a hodgepodge of North American Plains Indians costumes and central Mexican style *trajes*. Their physical presence and demeanor in the pilgrimage was primarily oriented to the mass media and to the audience of tourists and onlookers. This was unlike the presence of the typical matachines troupes who participated in our initial dance

There is an anachronistic and cross-cultural assortment of costumes among members of this politically oriented group in the 2015 dance pilgrimage. Members' stances indicate an intention to be telegenic. The imposing presence they self-consciously exude contrasts with the unassuming devotion of the traditional troupes who joined us in the first years of the pilgrimage. These participants walked rather than danced on the pilgrimage route to and from Mission Concepción. Photo: Margaret Greco.

pilgrimages. These politically oriented groups gave one the sense that they were political activists trying to fit in with *danzantes*. It would have helped them to appear a bit authentic and, therefore, less opportunistic if they had worn the kind of *trajes* worn by matachines. Some of them wore a combination of Aztec and Apache dress. Others wore war paint, breechcloths over blue jeans, twentieth century powwow shawls, and appropriated Day of the Dead skull imagery. Upon seeing their war paint, a bystander was heard to ask facetiously if they were setting out to kill the missionaries. As it happens, there is a related saying in Spanish: *El hábito no hace al monje* (The habit doesn't make the monk). Similarly, the regalia does not make the Indian. I had the sense that their costumes were essentially placards. One member of these groups, whom I happened to know, now spoke with an affected, stereotypical Native American accent that I had never heard him use until the day of that pilgrimage. His troupe burned a number of things in a canister while en route, including *copal* (resin incense), sage, and marijuana. The smell of the marijuana was especially pungent, which was ironic since our troupe is opposed to any association with illicit substances.

The opportunistic exploitation of the 2015 pilgrimage by these competing political organizations for their political agendas constituted an appropriation of our autonomy by diluting our overall focus. In addition, these organizations contributed to the mass media's mischaracterization of our pilgrimage as a "parade" and a "march." Moreover, it was done without making their political motives known to us. I should underscore here that we had always politely but deliberately made efforts to keep political elements away from our *danza* and pilgrimage.

By late October 2015, a series of community meetings were being held on the southside by two nascent political bodies designed to monopolize on the economic growth anticipated to result from World Heritage designation. After attending some of these meetings, I noted that one was essentially a panel of aspiring Native Americans, artists, and chamber of commerce types with varying degrees of ties—or not—to the southside. They essentially told residents what was going to happen to their communities, listened to the massive resistance from longtime residents, then shrugged their shoulders indifferently in response. The other political body consisted of four panelists and operated in very similar fashion. It included Father García who, like the moderator, frequently promoted our dance pilgrimage to the public as a tourist attraction. However, the driving force behind these entities and their respective meetings was the city councilwoman of that district, as she had helped to form one of these political bodies and was a member of the other. Members of these entities were allowed to make untenable statements about the surrounding community concerning indigenous history that facilitated continued support of the fictitious relationship between Indigenous peoples in present-day San Antonio and our *danza*. To be sure, descendants of multiple Indigenous cultures have lived in the barrios surrounding the missions for generations. But, as a translator of mission documents, I can see that they were brought from far and wide by the Spanish. And, as I have stated previously, there is no evidence linking them in any way to the *danza de matachines*. Moreover, the individuals most active in asserting themselves as Indians before the city's political system generally have weak ties to the mission area and no more ties to continuous, Indigenous culture than any other Chicano in San Antonio.

At one of the community meetings I attended, a frustrated, elderly veteran angrily addressed panelists and attendees at a library. He wore a shirt with a graphic that suggested he was Native American, and he emphatically accused the panelists of selling out to commercial interests. He also criticized attendees for not being more assertive in their opposition to the changes being foisted onto their communities. He then stormed out of the room before the police could be summoned.

Several *danzas* who had been participating in our pilgrimage had interrupted their participation by withdrawing after the 2013 pilgrimage. They included two especially disciplined *matlachines* troupes. After pressing them for an explanation, Tony learned that they observed that the event no longer felt like a pilgrimage. So reduced were our numbers that the 2014 pilgrimage almost had to be cancelled. Tony could only save it by recruiting troupes from out of town. The elderly veteran's departure from that meeting, in a certain respect, was a typical Native American response to irreconcilable conflict. Coincidentally, it could also be considered a metaphor for the way in which troupes withdrew from the pilgrimage in 2014.

Appropriation of Devotion

Another casualty our troupe experienced during the 2015 pilgrimage was that of our devotion. As a *danza de matachines* troupe, our purpose had been to dance for *La Virgen de Guadalupe* or, as we often refer to her, the *Virgen*. There are, theologically speaking, many different Virgin Marys. And, they are all supposed to be manifestations of the same biblical Virgin Mary. However, for *danza de matachines* troupes, the *Virgen* is a distinctly different person, and we specifically dance for her. In the case of our troupe, this is underscored by the fact that our founder named his troupe La Danza *Guadalupana* de Pablo Olivares Sr.

When we began the pilgrimage in December 2007, the fact that it was in recognition of the newly canonized San Juan Diego had no effect on our devotion to the *Virgen*. He was, after all, the first devotee of the *Virgen*, and his feast day was a mere three days before that of the *Virgen*. Moreover, December pilgrimages for the *Virgen* had been held for her feast day on December 12 for generations. Consequently, San Juan Diego, though important, was still second in importance to the *Virgen*, even within our own troupe. So, our devotion to the *Virgen* remained firmly intact. Among other things, that meant that our *trajes* and *estandarte* retained her image. And, most importantly, she remained as the central inspiration and focus of the dance.

Appropriation of Devotion by Religious Entities

Yet, when Mission Concepción began to sponsor the pilgrimage in 2013, it soon became clear that Father García wanted to exploit his position as sponsoring priest to dilute our devotion to *La Virgen de Guadalupe* and to take San Juan Diego out of the picture completely. Specifically, he made the pilgrimage in honor of the feast day of the Immaculate Conception. That was what his public relations department told the press and online media in advance. This change was particularly clear during Father García's pre-pilgrimage talk before participating troupes, members of the community of devotees, and tourists in 2015. In that talk he gave the Virgin of the Immaculate Conception primary focus and our *Virgen de Guadalupe* secondary importance. There was no mention of San Juan Diego as there had been in the years prior to dancing at Mission Concepción. At one point, as if dubiously attempting to channel the spirit of the Chicano activism of his generation, he raised a fist in the air and shouted, "*¡Viva la Virgen de la Inmaculada Concepción!*" (Long live the Virgin of the Immaculate Conception!), to which Spanish speakers politely answered with an obligatory and somewhat confused "*¡Viva!*" Sadly, outsiders to the dance had no other option but to assume that they were seeing our devotion in traditional rather than hijacked terms. It should be noted that the "Virgin of the Immaculate Conception" is more amenable to Anglos, and therefore, a more tourist-marketable patroness who García chose to replace our *Virgen* in prominence. And this act served to promote tourism to the missions. In fact, the *trajes* of that mission's *danza de matachines* troupe—formed that year—did not bear the image of *La Virgen de Guadalupe* but, rather, the same image of Mission Concepión's patroness that hangs prominently in that church's sanctuary. These are the same *trajes* that troupe wore that year even for the feast day of *La Virgen de Guadalupe*.

The Old Spanish Missions of San Antonio and Mission Concepción, under Father García's leadership, further appropriated our devotion by introducing to it the devotion of St. James. During the 2015 pilgrimage García wore a scallop shell with an image of Concepción's facade on it as a pendant and encouraged parishioners to wear them as well. He explained that he wanted to have a miniature version of Spain's "Camino" pilgrimage. He was quick to add that Spain's Camino is also a UNESCO World Heritage Site. When asked, one staff member explained that the mission was starting a new pilgrimage tradition and was using the scallop shell to allude to a connection between the two pilgrimages. Unfortunately, this initiative by Mission Concepción imposes a "new tradition" on our *danza* that consequently compromised the integrity of our devotion. It diluted our devotion to the *Virgen* further by adding St. James among its official saints that were associated with the pilgrimage.

Associating a five-hundred-mile Spanish pilgrimage route with one that was under a mile—as Father García did during our 2015 pilgrimage—may seem harmless, at first glance. However, his motives were to reframe the original devotion to the *Virgen* in our pilgrimage in a more Christian and European light. To understand this impulse to control devotional direction, it is worth remembering the undeclared political schism between clerics supporting devotion to the *Virgen* and those who viewed it as heretical. Despite the passage of time, this dichotomy persists in the minds of clergy in nuanced ways. I see Father García's wanting to associate our pilgrimage with the Spanish and, therefore, more Christian pilgrimage to Santiago de Compostela as having trajectory in the outrage of Fray Francisco de Bustamante. He as well as the priest in chapter 5 who made fun of our *danza* could easily find sympathy among sixteenth-century Franciscans in Mexico City.

Father García's public reframing of the pilgrimage's devotion to include the Virgin of the Immaculate Conception, St. James, and Christ the King opened it up to other devotions that had nothing to do with our troupe's intentions when it was started. This was evident when political groups seeking federal recognition as Native Americans gathered around a drum they were beating powwow style and chanted the name Tonantzin, an Aztec religious personage having nothing to do with our pilgrimage. It also became evident when I encountered one member of the audience who had no background involving *La Virgen de Guadalupe* but who insisted that the *Virgen* is part of a larger, mother figure composed of all mothers. When I informed her that was not the case, and that I was a *matachín*, she told me I was wrong and launched into a Jungian diatribe, referencing the Hindu deity Ganesh. She told me our *danza* was "a dance to the amalgamated mother." I attempted unsuccessfully to call to her attention the fact that the Jungian psychology she was indirectly citing is a European perspective and that to superimpose it on us is indicative of a colonial mentality. She also advanced the idea that the pilgrimage's lack of authenticity owed to an absence of "ecstatic trance dance" among its participants. *Matachines don't have or need "ecstatic trance dance."* We dance for the *Virgen*, not Hindu deities.

On the feast day of the *La Virgen de Guadalupe*, the *trajes* (suits) worn by these dancers bear images of the Immaculate Conception instead the *Virgen*, another instance of decreased emphasis on the *Virgen* by the archdiocese. Photo: Margaret Greco.

Perhaps the greatest appropriation of our devotion to the *Virgen* at the hands of Father García and his organizations was that our troupe was forced to alter its *veneración*. Specifically, we were prevented from allowing members of the community of devotees to be escorted to the *estandarte* to venerate the *Virgen*. The reason flippantly given for this was time. As mentioned earlier, when we approached the church, Father García shouted to the troupes, "Keep it to five minutes! Pass it down!" A regularly scheduled mass was to start soon. That scheduling conflict begs the question of why he had wanted us to reschedule the pilgrimage for the afternoon to begin with, and the answer is apparently that attracting tourists was more important than letting us keep our troupe's traditional way of venerating the *Virgen*.

Appropriation of Devotion by the Mass Media

Father García, the archdiocese, and Mission Concepción could not have had appropriated the devotion of our pilgrimage without the cooperation of the local mass media, especially print and online sources. And it should be noted that the mass media news sources, as commercial entities, also were stakeholders in the UNESCO debacle. The inroads into the sphere of the *danza* by outside entities have led me to reflect on how our *danza* went from being a ritual practice that was intimate and spiritual to one that was trivialized by the dissemination of misinformation by outside "experts." Where and how does one maintain the integrity of the pilgrimage's original purpose without allowing it to become a source of "colorful" entertainment and a curiosity in the eyes of outsiders?

In answering that question, it is important to note that the *danza* has long been perceived as a "spectacle" by its chroniclers and historians as well as by the observers who have passing familiarity with it at best. This misperception leads me to believe that it has been misinterpreted through lenses of Eurocentric, linear assumptions that also fail to understand it along class lines. It is also important to observe how the dance's integrity was preserved when La Danza Guadalupana de Pablo Olivares Sr. danced in the secular context of the 1968 World's Fair along with other troupes. Although that may seem like a breach of their integrity, the matter was slightly more nuanced than that. The purpose of the World's Fair was to educate about different cultures and countries. It was *understood* by the troupe that its participation was for educational purposes, so they were in a position to freely decide to participate. Similarly, our troupe danced at the San Pedro Park Library and the Bazán Branch Library in 2008 and 2009, respectively. Moreover, in the case of the fair, there could not have been any duplicity on behalf of the fair's talent recruiters because it was obviously a secular event. Dancers would not be trying to summon the presence of the *Virgen*, fulfill *promesas*, or pray for loved ones because they knew the essence of the dance was not going to be the same. When the matachines' commitment to the fair ended, the traditions of Pablo Olivares Sr.'s troupe continued with its integrity intact. I contrast the transparency on the part of the World's Fair talent recruiter with Father García's co-opting our dance pilgrimage, which is a spiritual undertaking for its participants, and marketing it as entertainment for political and commercial—including touristic—interests.

The resiliency of La Danza Guadalupana de Pablo Olivares Sr., that is, its essential immutability over four decades, has not been paralleled by an equally static church. In other words, while the essence of the *danza de matachines* appears to have remained the same, the Catholic Church has undergone numerous changes. While it continues to be a colonial power-broker in San Antonio, it no longer has the same political strength it once had. More importantly, it has undergone a number of changes in attitudes that would seem alien to a sixteenth-century Tlaxcaltecan *danzante*, or any other inhabitant of New Spain. Just as today there exists considerable "disconnect" between matachines and outsiders (for example, tourists, certain clergy, journalists, and intellectuals) with regard to the essence of the *danza*, there were bound to exist such differences of perception between Colonial-era clergy and Tlaxcaltecans who brought the *danza de matachines* with them as far as northern New Mexico (Pohl 2014). Consequently, it is not known if what the Tlaxcaltecans were "converting" other Indians to was even necessarily the Catholicism of the Spanish Colonial era. In 1759, a number of Franciscan clergy from Mission San Francisco de la Espada complained in writing to their prelate that a manual for converting the Texas Indians was needed in an Indigenous language. One of the reasons given was that Indians charged with translating the gospels from Spanish were doing so in such a way that they were "teaching not what they [were] told but what [seemed] correct to them" (García 1759, par. 7). This statement implies that there was a relatively unstable relationship between the presumably converted Indigenous peoples of New Spain and the religious worldview of the Spanish.

Perhaps allowing the dance to be erroneously perceived as a mere spectacle may have in some way obfuscated an essence otherwise unsanctioned by the church. Maybe it's better to let people keep misperceiving the dance while being careful not to become what the mass media tells us we are. After all, mass communication—of which there is more today than in the Spanish Colonial period—is a two-way medium.

As can be seen in this and previous chapters, the mass media, and the internet especially, has proven to be a double-edged sword for La Danza Guadalupana de Pablo Olivares Sr. and its latter formation, *Los Soldados de La Virgen de Guadalupe*. In order to advocate for the pilgrimage to be turned into a form of entertainment to boost tourism, an attempt was made by the previously mentioned local reporter to use a video I loaded online with one of his articles. In that online article, the reporter disseminated a number of inaccuracies, dismissively citing the internet in general as his source, despite its having no shortage of misinformation regarding the *danza de matachines*. It made me wonder if I had been naive in believing that the photos and videos I posted online, as the media person of the troupe, would only be viewed by a handful of sincere and respectful *danzantes* and researchers who genuinely sought empathetic insight into the *danza*.

The print version of the local newspaper gave respectful coverage when our first pilgrimage took place. As the years went by, especially the year of 2014, the degree to which the journalists were outsiders became clearly indicated by the shortcomings of their research and increasingly frequent inaccuracies, for example, that the *danza de matachines* was being "replicated" from missionary times. Moreover, by the time of the 2014 pilgrimage, journalists seemed to be making no sincere attempt to understand the *danza* and, consequently, could not understand our devotion to the *Virgen*. Rather, they sought to give sensational descriptions of it and of the pilgrimage. This includes the periodical *Today's Catholic*, which misinterpreted *el viejo de la danza* to be "a devil" and said the *danza de matachines* was "re-enacting the battle between the Spaniards and the Moors" (Baass-Sowa 2015). The *San Antonio Express-News* inaccurately said the 2014 *danza* at Mission Concepción "incorporated native indigenous music and dance . . . evolving into dancing now replicated in modern times" (Gerlach 2014, A3). What I find most problematic with this information is that it sidesteps what is most important in the dance: devotion to the *Virgen*.

It is telling that, despite the official event's being in observance of the feast day of the Immaculate Conception, one *danzante* was randomly quoted as saying that she was dancing for the *Virgen de Guadalupe* (Gerlach 2014, A3). Other local news media focused on such superficial aspects as how "colorful" our *trajes* were and the "hissing" of our *carrizos*. In other words: inordinate attention was paid to those aspects deemed to be most exotic. Little attention, at best, was given to *La Virgen de Guadalupe*, including in *Today's Catholic*. Even the references to the feast day of the Immaculate Conception gave no explanation about its religious significance. There was greater commentary devoted to the attributes of the *azteca* and *conchera* dancers with their elaborate pheasant headdresses, painted faces, dramatic steps, and deafening drums, despite their being numerically few. They were repeatedly and erroneously referred to as "matachines." These groups were more than happy to pose for reporters' cameras with one *danzante* theatrically and menacingly raising her hand, claw-like, at the reporters, teeth bared. Gone was the collective sense of awe and devotion before the *Virgen* in our earlier pilgrimages. Gone was the seemingly magical vagaries

of the early morning. The dancers and the dance had become more important in newsworthiness than our devotion to the *Virgen*.

Another way the mass media appropriated our devotion was in the manner it characterized our devotion. Its writers would either state or quote
church pundits as using the word *devotion* in a context that implied a mere
faith that could readily be associated with the idea of docile Indians sub-
mitting to the Spanish. It makes for a simplistic, readily marketable sce-
nario, but it is inaccurate. Our devotion to the *Virgen* is not inspired by
blind faith but by a visceral awareness of her presence that takes place when
everything goes right in a *danza*. The mass media's mischaracterization of
the devotion involved in our dance was an appropriation because it was a
misrepresentation of the dance. As well, it was an appropriation because
it was carried out to improve the chances of the missions' receiving World
Heritage designation and then sustaining it. Those are motives that have
nothing to do with the *Virgen*.

Letting Sleeping Dogs Lie to Themselves and Others

In response to the appropriation of our autonomy and devotion, several *danza de matachines* troupes in our pilgrimage withdrew from their
annual participation. It is hard to tell how many withdrew because of the
appropriation of our autonomy and how many because of the appropriation of our devotion. But it is safe to say that when they said it "didn't
feel like a pilgrimage anymore," it was in response to the effects of both
because the two elements are so intertwined. It is also highly likely that the
troupes from out of town who withdrew after 2014 were responding to the
same issues. Some participants remained, however. By the 2015 pilgrimage,
groups that were less invested in the tradition of dancing for the *Virgen* had
grown in proportion to the rest. They included a folkloric dance school
and the aforementioned political groups who did more walking, drumming, and singing to peyote and Tonantzin than dancing for the *Virgen*.
Another group consisted of only a drummer and two dancers who I had
seen years before dancing in a secular, political march. It is quite conceiv-
able, though, that more invested troupes remained not because they agreed
with the changes being foisted on them but because they still carried with
them the colonial dynamic seen in Hill's (1992) previously described interpretation of the Fiesta del Volcán. That is, they perceived that outsiders to
the dance had no grasp of the dance but did not care as long as they could
sustain their relationship with the *Virgen* through the dance.

They Got the Pilgrimage but Not the Dance: Resilience as a Response

The grievances of the withdrawing troupes have considerable validity in that the route, starting in 2013, began and ended at Mission Concepción and was very brief. In fact, it was about one-third of the distance of our previous pilgrimages. This stands in contrast with our past routes that went from one church to another over considerably longer routes. It is also in contrast to our original intentions for dancing at the mission, which was to dance from Mission San José to Mission to Concepción. (A pilgrimage by definition goes from one point to another.) This meant that matachines would dance for the *Virgen* for a much briefer time. And, news that we would be starting at 2:00 p.m. instead of 7:00 a.m. could not have helped matters because of the qualitative loss of energy, intimacy, and the palpability of the *Virgen*'s presence.

Beginning with the 2013 dance pilgrimage, matachines troupes continued to gradually withdraw from the annual event. And, this withdrawal started when it became evident to matachines that aspects of the autonomy and devotion that characterized the dance pilgrimage were being compromised by entities external to the dance. Rather than attempting to engage the structures responsible for these changes, such as the Old Spanish Missions of San Antonio, matachines troupes simply withdrew with the consequence that their absence further threatened the devolved pilgrimage's continuity. In fact, by December 2017, the appropriation was completed when the archdiocese hailed the pilgrimage we started in 2003 as a "procession" along Father García's Camino on a newly paved tourist pathway culminating in dance "in front of the historical pantings [*sic*] of the Virgin Mary" (San Antonio Report 2017). And, in another case of historical revisionism, the archdiocese stated that the event was in its fifth year (San Antonio Report 2017), disregarding the fact that our troupe had started the pilgrimage ten years earlier with considerable blood, sweat, and tears. Interestingly, whereas Molly and then Tony had always placed our troupe at the very end of the pilgrimage, Father García placed himself and his church's troupe at the head of his 2017 procession.

The most telling detail by this point was that his *estandarte* did not bear the powerful image of the *Virgen*. Rather, it bore the image of the Mission Concepción's facade. The image of the *Virgen* imbues the *estandarte* with sacredness. For this reason, Mission Concepción's *estandarte* that year was the ultimate symbol of the church's usurpation of the dance pilgrimage's autonomy and devotion and its replacement of the event with a mere strolling procession consisting of only church-based troupes. I find Father García's expression of devotion to an inanimate building rather than the *Virgen* highly ironic, given the vigilance with which Spanish Colonial clergy punished idolatry among the Indians. Bishop Zumárraga was responsible for burning an Indian convert at the stake for idolatry (Jackson 2014, 14–15).

I relate the withdrawal of troupes from the pilgrimage to the instance when a priest maneuvered to have our dance serve as dinner entertainment at a *posadas* held at a residence. Molly's Aunt Janie abruptly ended our *veneración* on seeing the affront that our dance had become that night. While still at the residence, Molly calmly informed me that we would not return to dance at that residence since that priest was always in attendance. Molly's aunt's abrupt ending of the *veneración* and Molly's decision not to return were essentially the same response as that of the withdrawing troupes. The only significant difference was that the former happened at a residence and, therefore, was on a smaller scale. In neither that case nor that of the appropriated pilgrimage did dancers attempt to confront anyone. Nor were these decisions made publicly, spitefully, or in a huff. In fact, the withdrawing troupes only gave their reason after Tony pressed them for reasons. Although it was not the intention of the withdrawing troupes to place the continuity of the commodified pilgrimage in jeopardy, it was the natural consequence of their efforts to safeguard the integrity and authenticity of their *danzas* by withdrawing. In the same way, the decision by our own *danza*'s leadership to stop the *veneración* at that residence was made for the sake of its integrity and authenticity.

After witnessing the 2015 pilgrimage, I knew I could no longer, in good conscience, participate in any of the ones that might follow as long as our autonomy continued to be replaced by Father García's control over it. Why did this happen? Because it serves colonial entities, at this point in history, to associate the *danza* with the missions and the San Antonio River. This fictionalization occurred because geo-economic circumstances were such that these landmarks could draw increased profits from tourism and development after the missions collectively became a UNESCO World Heritage Site. The fictitious relationship of these landmarks to the *danza de matachines* and our dance pilgrimage provides an outward appearance of an authenticity that commercial entities facilitate in consort with religious, commercial, and political entities as well as with the mass media. This commodified, faux "authenticity" helps to maintain the missions' status with UNESCO and attract investment and development for the area. Paradoxically, not only are the pilgrimage's key elements of authenticity and devotion compromised, but the missions also lose their authenticity as large segments of the missions' descendants are being forced out by these new economic changes. Mission Concepción's director effectively destroyed the pilgrimage, in much the same way that mission prelates destroyed indigenous practices and replaced them with ones they could sanction three hundred years earlier.

The Archdiocese of San Antonio denied our request that it pay the newly city-required insurance. The stated reason for the archdiocese's denial was that it did not sanction the pilgrimage since it was not associated with a particular parish church. In other words: It was an event that enjoyed autonomy from the archdiocese. However, in 2013 Mission Concepción took advantage of this financial challenge by sponsoring it with its expectations that we would accept the changes Father García made to it. Those changes included the public claim that the event was essentially the property of the mission and that it was in observance of the feast day of the Immaculate Conception rather than that of San Juan Diego or *La Virgen de Guadalupe*. This appropriation continued in 2014 and 2015. I should point out that it was sponsorship on the cheap. That is, Father García bypassed the need for insurance and security by having it on a sidewalk instead of in the street as we had been doing.

His motives for sponsoring the pilgrimage were by no means altruistic. The archdiocese's missions and Father García stood to gain prestige and status from the resulting increased corporate presence in the mission area that would result from the then pending decision by UNESCO to make the missions a World Heritage Monument. More tellingly, his archdiocese owns the 12.5-acre property adjacent to Mission Concepción and entered into a long-term lease with a local developer to build a 228-unit gated apartment complex there. The archdiocese began planning for the development with that local firm subsequent to the application for World Heritage (Dimmick 2015). So, Father García's ability to document a supposedly ongoing connection to the past in the form of a traditional and "indigenous" dance pilgrimage served the best interest of not only corporate interests but also of the archdiocese. And, all the local powerbrokers I have referenced in this chapter—religious, commercial, political—worked in tandem with the effect of appropriating the autonomy and devotion to the *Virgen* that had previously characterized our pilgrimage. Consequently, the pilgrimage ceased being a pilgrimage by losing its authenticity. And, this loss of authenticity signified a loss of continuity.

However, it is important to understand that the appropriation of the pilgrimage's autonomy and devotion with its consequent discontinuation cannot be equated with an appropriation of the dance. The troupes who withdrew continued doing what *danza de matachines* and *matlachines* troupes have done for centuries: dancing for the *Virgen*. They left with their autonomy and devotion intact. Withdrawing from the pilgrimage simply meant they had more time to dance for the *Virgen* in their barrios where no one was going to ask them for a permit, insurance, or other fees requested by the city. Nor would they need to comply with Father García's placing himself prominently among them while reciting a rosary. Hundreds of years of devotional and autonomous tradition cannot be discontinued overnight. This resilience exists because during those hundreds of years, we have had time to develop strategies that circumnavigate colonial systems that would appropriate our traditions. As for any troupes who remained to dance in the procession, they could still dance for the *Virgen* and allow spectators to think they were dancing in the Christians and Moors drama. It would be analogous to the Maya Cakchiquels indifferently allowing Spanish colonials to think they were reenacting their defeat in battle when they were actually renewing their relationship with the earth.

Boundaries and Ritual Space

Tourists often enter historic Spanish churches such as San Fernando Cathedral to snap pictures and record videos while people are praying or having mass. (Signage discouraging this has only partly solved the problem.) And this is essentially the very thing that the leadership of the archdiocese has encouraged since the 2012 pilgrimage by promoting the *danza* as a spectacle for tourists. It is also what local journalists have encouraged and promoted. This type of promotion also demonstrates a gross lack of understanding where the intimacy of space is concerned. And, because the journalists cited pundits who trivialized our pilgrimage as a form of entertainment for which we don "costumes," reporters saw nothing wrong with approaching us to ask questions *while we were dancing* and to insert themselves between the columns to photograph us. This violation of the intimacy of our space, much like the cigar smoke and exponentially increasing photography, was symbolic of the presumed entrée outsiders to the dance were made to feel they had because of how we were portrayed by the mass media.

I once worked with someone who grew up in Taos, New Mexico, in the

In 2013 Father García had announced that the dance pilgrimage and subsequent *danza* were for the Feast of the Immaculate Conception. Yet these three members of the community of devotees hold *estandartes* of *La Virgen de Guadalupe* at that event in recognition of her feast day instead. This demonstration of devotion shows that the *danza* is not only resilient but also that it is resilience. Photo: Margaret Greco.

1950s. He recalled riding horseback to the neighboring Indigenous community of Taos Pueblo to visit friends. If during a given visit it became time for a ceremony to begin, nonresidents, he said, were escorted out of the community. Sklar (1999) noted similar boundaries drawn in Tortugas, New Mexico, for example, by one *matachín* leader who limited photography (179). These are the types of boundaries of ritual space from which our pilgrimage would have benefited.

Understanding the Contradictions of the 2013–15 Pilgrimages

A number of questions are raised in this section. How, one might ask, can a priest with no experience as a *danzante* and who grew up in an Anglo parish give so much direction to matachines? As well, one might ask how

We're matachines danza
CHAPTER 9 *at the museum* 373
to convey the fourth

he could make a false, historical claim about matachines to an institution like UNESCO. One might ask how political activist groups become part of a nonpolitical event. Or, one may ask how the mass media can make completely erroneous statements about the *danza*. How, one might also ask, did we wind up attracting a host of such outsiders to the tradition who claim to have a greater knowledge of the dance than we do?

Ironically, to begin to answer these questions, one must start with Father García's previously cited words: "The missions are still doing what they started to do almost 300 years ago" (Ayala 2015, K11). The view he refers to rests on, among other things, having and acting on paternalistic attitudes toward pre-Spanish worldviews. He has adopted the missionary legacy, which has been a supporting component of the colonialization process. In colonial processes and perspectives, Indigenous people, their cultures, and their lands are treated as resources to be exploited, usurped, modified, or destroyed, depending on prevailing political and economic circumstances.

The missions in Texas and their lands were secularized from the 1790s into the 1820s (Torres 1997, xi). My *trastátarabuela* (grandmother from several generations) Paula Ortiz was a mission resident who witnessed the end of the mission era. In the meantime, in the present-day Mexican state of Nuevo León, the ritual dance called *la danza de matachines*, with its origins going all the way back to the *Virgen's* appearance, was still being practiced. It would continue to be practiced when a twentieth-century youth named Pablo Olivares formed a matachines troupe bearing his name. His family and future descendants would carry his traditions into the twenty-first century and into a new country. Furthermore, the *danza* tradition would survive a later attempt to commodify it by the San Antonio Archdiocese.

In Search of Old Mission Matachines

At this point, I was still puzzled by the archdiocese's sudden enthusiastic willingness to be of help in the matachines pilgrimages, regardless of its public statements about the *danza de matachines*. The archdiocese desperately wanted to have a public, historical association with the *danza de matachines* and attempted to establish that association by claiming that *danza* existed in San Antonio's missions.[1] In search of a historical basis for that claim, I carried out extensive research in university and public libraries, the World Wide Web, and in my own materials to no avail. How, I wondered, was the *danza de matachines* tradition associated with the archdiocese's missions? I would not find the answer, but the answer would find me. And, it would take me by surprise.

A Meeting with Father García

By now the reader has been exposed to a range of clerical attitudes toward the *danza de matachines* and our *danza* in particular. These attitudes have comprised a gamut with ridicule and suspicion on one end and a natural respect on the other. In between there have been hints of pragmatic acceptance, good intentions lacking in understanding, and opportunistic affirmation. In order to glean possibly better insights into how Catholic clergy might view the *danza de matachines*, I requested a meeting with Father García. At the 2015 pilgrimage, I introduced myself to Father García as a *matachín* who was writing a book and asked if I could contact him for an interview. He mistook me for a reporter for the *San Antonio Express-News*, saying he welcomed anyone from that paper. He also asked, "Where do you sell your stuff?" I clarified that I did not sell anything and that I was conducting research, not journalism. He then became demure and seemed to become distracted by something else. However, I did contact him by email and arranged to interview him. His roles as the director of the Old Spanish Missions of the archdiocese and pastor of Mission Concepción were especially relevant for this purpose. Father García readily welcomed my emailed request, and we arranged to meet on December 23, 2015. We met in his office housed in a small archdiocesan office building in the north-central part of San Antonio. Coincidentally, it was located a stone's throw from the Oblate School of Theology where my brother had introduced me to the tile, mosaic image of the *Virgen*. Father García allowed me to audio record my interview with him. Something of a public figure in San Antonio, García's charisma was as evident in person as when he spoke to groups of people or on the radio. However, his responses to my questions tended to be indirect, extraneous, and verbose. A direct transcription of the interview, therefore, would have presented the reader with the challenge of discerning his answers among considerably dense material irrelevant to the questions. Moreover, it would not be very revealing to the reader without the context of subtleties such as intonation and body language. For those reasons I have paraphrased the most relevant points of the interview here, incorporating quotes when helpful.

The first question I asked him during our twenty-minute meeting was when his earliest memory was of the *danza de matachines*. He said it had been in Mexico City. At that time, he was a seminarian visiting Mexico's capital with fellow seminarians in the summer of 1971. While there he visited the original shrine to Our Lady of Guadalupe. It was there that he first saw a *danza*. He returned in the 1980s as a priest. But, by that time, he and a colleague went to the Basilica of Our Lady of Guadalupe on her feast day to, "get the full benefit of what they do." He described the plaza in front of the basilica as being "jam packed with Indigenous people, all of them in their different colors. . . . There was one circle after another. . . . Maybe a hundred thousand" dancers he said. These dancers apparently made a great impression on him. He had grown up in an Anglo parish. However, I have never seen a *danza de matachines* troupe use circles in their choreography, as he described. Nor have I encountered any published works in my research that acknowledges the use of circles by matachines. I have observed, however, that circle dance is an integral part of *danza azteca* and *danza conchera*, both of which come from central Mexico.

Father García later celebrated mass and had "special seats" during a *serenata* to the *Virgen* "and the whole thing." He spent four days returning to see the dancers in the plaza. The fact that he misidentified the circles of dancers as matachines underscores the nature of his visit, that is, one as an outsider who did not grasp the relationship between the *danza* and the *Virgen*.

When I asked him how Mission Concepción had come to be the beginning and the end of the dance pilgrimage for the last three years, he said Tony approached one of his parishioners and eventually communicated with him (Father García). More accurately, I introduced Tony to the parishioner for this purpose in 2012. I remember them exchanging their contact information and was glad to have facilitated that contact.

However, at the time I did not know that the Spanish missions in San Antonio were being considered by UNESCO as a cultural World Heritage Site. Nor had I known that Father García actively supported efforts to bring this designation about. This designation was in fact approved by UNESCO in July 2015. In my interview with him, Father García openly stated that he had used the *danza* pilgrimage to help qualify the missions as a cultural World Heritage Site. He said it in response to my asking him to elaborate on a statement he made in the *San Antonio Express-News* that year. The statement had been made in an article titled "Danza to Mary Will Open Winter Feast Days: Colorful Event Set at Mission Concepción" (Ayala 2015, K10). Specifically, he told the newspaper, "The missions are still doing what they were started to do 300 years ago" (Ayala 2015, K11).

In response to my request for elaboration, he brought up UNESCO's designation of the missions, saying:

> We won the designation because we have what they call "outstanding universal value," and those three words mean that there has been continuous life around these structures for three hundred years. That is, the original intent of the missions is still being realized today in reality in the lives of the people and in the way that these missions operate. And, to me the *danza* . . . is what they have been doing for hundreds of years. (D. García, personal communication, December 23, 2015)

As one who had been reading, translating, and researching Spanish mission documents, in addition to the *danza de matachines*, I was concerned with the veracity of this statement. The Spanish missions of present-day San Antonio were decommissioned in the early nineteenth century (Torres 1997, xi). They ceased to function as missions though descendants of mission residents continued to live in the barrios that formed around the missions. More importantly, I had never encountered among mission documents any evidence to indicate that the *danza de matachines* was ever practiced at the missions. In fact, it made little sense that the Indigenous peoples who became mission residents would engage in a dance that came from the sedentary and agriculturally oriented Tlaxcaltecans. To make such an assertion before UNESCO in order to improve chances of obtaining a cultural World Heritage designation is deceptive. When I turned off the digital recorder at the end of the interview, he leaned back in his chair, and in a more relaxed tone, asked what I thought of the World Heritage designation. I expressed doubt that the *danza de matachines* was practiced in the missions during the Spanish Colonial period. He insisted on his claim, though, referring me to a book written by Timothy Matovina (2005) titled *Guadalupe and Her Faithful: Latino Catholics in San Antonio, from Colonial Origins to the Present*. Father García assured me that Matovina cited primary documents placing the *danza de matachines* at the missions during the Spanish Colonial period. Yet, in the interview he acknowledged that they had no matachines when he was assigned to the missions. Nonetheless, I obtained a copy of the book. It contained no information to even approximate such evidence. So, I asked the author by email if in his research he encountered documentation of any dance in the missions. After all, the book was composed mostly of his doctoral dissertation. He replied saying: "There was no reference to the danza de matachines" to be found in the records from the San Antonio Spanish colonial missions (T. Matovina, personal communication, January 18, 2016).

matachine us passing in one
truth from one gender
to another
CHAPTER 9   177

Another observation I made from our interview concerned Father García's response when I asked him how he would characterize the role of the *danza* at the missions and/or in the San Antonio archdiocese. While he did not technically answer my question, I found his response lengthy and telling. He stated that the matachines inspire, but he emphasized that he saw the *danza* as, "a vehicle for passing on the faith and the cultural and spiritual traditions" from one generation to the next. While I and other matachines in our *danza* have occasionally discussed the importance of its continuation, no one has ever spoken of it as a way to pass the Catholic faith from one generation to the next.

His answer did little to counter the indications that he had played a significant role in appropriating the pilgrimage. Furthermore, when I asked what factors he believed to be constituent of a good *danza*, his reply turned into an attempt to explain the *danza de matachines*, saying, "This kind of prayer is putting the whole body in motion. So, the whole body is being offered up to God through the *Virgen*." Because of my years of experience in the *danza*, I found his interpretation of it to be an abstraction couched in dogma and that it was a method and tool of appropriating it.

Mission Concepción, Father García's church and one of the missions under his direction, had only formed its first matachines troupe in late 2015. It was the first mission in San Antonio to have a *danza de matachines* troupe. Since that was his parish, I asked him about a certain image used on their *trajes*. The mission's church has in its sanctuary a large, prominent painting of the Immaculate Conception of the Virgin Mary. The same image in smaller scale also adorns the *trajes* of the newly formed matachines troupe. He told me that the matachines had asked him what type of design their *trajes* should have. His only suggestion, he said, was that it include something unique that would identify them as belonging to Mission Concepción. That is why his church forewent the tradition of having *La Virgen de Guadalupe* on their *trajes*, opting instead for a prominent image of the Immaculate Conception on all the *trajes* of that troupe. Call it parish branding. Had Father García known the traditions and protocol of the *danza de matachines* in San Antonio, he would have reminded them that the purpose of the *danza* is to dance for the *Virgen de Guadalupe* on her feast day and that she should therefore be the central adornment of the *traje*.

Some of the *danzantes* ignored his directive and featured the *Virgen* anyway. However, the *Virgen* should be danced for exclusively on her feast day. That is, there should be no other *virgen* adorning the *trajes* because

One archdiocesan change to the dance pilgrimage was decreased attention to the *Virgen* (Our Lady of Guadalupe). Here in 2017 Father García leads what had become an annual walk. His *estandarte*'s image is of his church's facade rather than the *Virgen*. Photo: Darren Abate. Courtesy of the *San Antonio Express-News*.

the period between her feast day on December 12 and the feast day of the Epiphany on January 6 is considered to be her time for devotion to the exclusion of the other saints and *vírgenes*. This unawareness of traditional San Antonian protocol, on Father García's part, exemplifies the harm to tradition and, therefore, to the authenticity of matachines troupes that occurs when the churches are deferred to for protocol in the realm of the *danza de matachines*. The authority should be the lineage. Our *danza* is one of the very few I have known of in San Antonio that has a familial lineage. Therefore, we have been able to remain, for the most part, uncompromised by direction from church authority figures.

Father García also confirmed what I had perceived about the rescheduling and rerouting of the pilgrimage. That is, after our first pilgrimage at Mission Concepción, he had us change our usual time from 7:00 a.m. to 2:00 p.m. As well, beginning with the first pilgrimage there, he had the route start and end at his church. Of our original starting time of seven, he paternalistically stated, "That was okay, but there were no people to see it. It was just the dancers." His thoughts were, "Why don't we do everything here?" He moved our starting time to seven hours later, "so everybody could come." In other words: 7:00 a.m. was too early for tourists. This demonstrated that he failed to recognize that the *danza* is for the *Virgen* and not for mere spectators. Matachines as well as people in the community familiar with the dance pilgrimage tradition know that its early morning undertaking is a major part of what defines it. To take that away is to diminish its purpose.

The headlines of local news sources, especially the online Rivard Report, partly chronicle the process by which the dance pilgrimage we started in 2007 was appropriated and eventually eliminated. The following is a chronology of headlines that summarizes that process. "600 Matachines to Dance Sunday Morning at Mission Concepción" (Rivard 2013). "Hundreds of 'Matachines' Dancers Coming to Mission Concepción" (Kirk 2014). "Fr. David to Explore Economic Impact of World Heritage Status" (Mathis 2015). "500 Matachines to Descend on Mission Concepción" (Guenther 2016). "Matachines Dancers Celebrate Immaculate Conception Feast Day" (Boyd-Batstone 2016). "Matachines to Carry Out Indigenous Tradition Sunday at Mission Concepción" (Rivard Report 2017). By the time the last of these headlines appeared, the archdiocese ceased claiming that the event was a pilgrimage. Instead, it was referred to as a "walk" and a "procession" that was somehow linked to Spain's ancient five-hundred-mile pilgrimage route to Santiago de Compostela.

A Serendipitous Answer

In addition to communicating that he found no evidence of matachines in his research, Timothy Matovina, the previously mentioned author of *Guadalupe and Her Faithful*, referred me to another source. It was a transcribed and translated Spanish document titled "Instructions for the Mission of Puríssima Concepción of the Province of Texas." (It is contained in a fourth edition book titled *Documents Relating to the Old Spanish Missions of Texas*, Vol. 1, *Guidelines for a Texas Mission: Instructions for the Missionary of Mission Concepción in San Antonio*.) I will refer to the original document and its fourth translated edition as the *Instructions*. Not knowing the specific reason for my inquiry, he believed this document's mentioning of other colonial-era dances might be of interest to me. Having received his answer that there had been no *danza de matachines* in the missions, though, I saw no purpose in reading that book.

Yet, the *Instructions* were brought to my attention to me again in late October 2019. On that day Molly, Tony, my wife, and I met with the new administrator of the missions at the chancery. With Father García now retired, the new administrator had replaced him in directing the missions and now wanted to ask us some questions before formally seeking the archdiocese's approval to pay for the permit and security we needed to have a dance pilgrimage for the feast day of *La Virgen de Guadalupe*. I was also there to show her some of the photographs I had made of our previous *danza* pilgrimages. After we were ushered into a small conference room by chancery staff, she entered and greeted us. She was a tall, blond Anglo member of the Catholic laity. Her dress and manner conveyed a type of upper-class informality that exists in San Antonio.

In the course of conversation, she commented that the *danza de mata-chines* tradition dated back to the mission era. Seeing this as an opportunity to find the long-sought answer to my question about the historical basis for such a statement, I said that my research had not turned up any indication of that. She matter-of-factly insisted that it was documented. Then she left the room and returned with the *Instructions*. Her copy was heavily underscored and flagged, manifesting the efforts to master mission history, which was new territory for her. She added that Father Leutenegger was an "academic" and a "scholar" who had spent years in Mexico "looking at" mission documents and, consequently, was bound to know what he was talking about. I agreed to consult the book after the meeting.

Subsequently, my wife, a cultural anthropologist, casually mentioned that the National Park Service's (NPS) narrative, which it had been using in its public interpretation of mission life, was outdated and highly skewed. The director in a very professional manner asked her to elaborate. And my wife obliged: The media of the NPS used rosy images of kindly, paternalistic *padres* taking in Indians interested in Christianity. This portrayal was inaccurate partly because there was no mention of smallpox epidemics or the circumstances that forced Indigenous populations into mission life such as marauding Lipan Apaches and famine. Nor were the instances of harsh treatment of the Indians mentioned (referenced in *The Alamo Chain of Missions* [Habig 1976], paradoxically).

In response, the director suddenly raised her voice in defense of the NPS's narrative. During her unexpected and anxious defense of the NPS, the room became tense as the rest of us politely listened. Though my wife's observation was casual and accurate, it seemed as if Father García's successor had an unforeseen allegiance to the NPS, which was so spirited that her cooperation with us now seemed tenuous. Then she suddenly became silent, and we continued sitting, surprised, wordless, and tense. She then briefly apologized and resumed with the original purpose of the meeting.

What I learned from her exchange with my wife was that, despite publicity aimed at portraying itself as a source of diversity, there was a line not to be crossed with the Old Spanish Missions of San Antonio. And that line was crossed whenever anyone suggested that mission life for Indigenous peoples was anything but desirable.

Calling Dancers *Matachines* Doesn't Make Them *Matachines*

After the meeting, I examined the *Instructions* and now I find it worth discussing in these pages for what it reveals about the clerical, exploitative misrepresentation of the *danza de matachines* to the unsuspecting public and, ultimately, its exploitation of *La Virgen de Guadalupe* for whom matachines dance. The sixty-sixth of the document's eighty-three numbered paragraphs does describe Indian dancers who the anonymous Franciscan author calls "Matachines" and who dance annually at the rectory door for which they are compensated with "refreshments." In the role of devil's advocate, someone could argue that this confirms what Father García could not prove, that is, the existence of matachines in the missions during the Spanish Colonial period. However, a brief consideration of the details surrounding this paragraph would soundly contradict such an assumption.

As one who has learned the *danza* through a familial lineage, my first tendency is to ask *who* could have taught the *danza de matachines*. Colonial-era Tlaxcaltecans would be a logical answer because, after all, they brought the *danza* from central Mexico all the way to present-day northern New Mexico (J. Pohl, personal communication, September 16, 2014). Yet, the anonymous author of the *Instructions* makes no mention of them. Nor does the Franciscan Fray Francisco Xavier Ortiz mention them to his prelate in his inspection report on Texas missions, a document in which he lists 189 Indigenous groups represented in the missions in 1745 (Ortiz 1745). Nor do the Franciscan friars. Bartholome García and Asifclos Valverde (1759), who in the course of outlining their need for a manual with which to instruct the Indians in catechism, reveal a stratification of Indigenous mission residents along social and linguistic lines without mentioning Tlaxcaltecans.

If there were a narrative about how the *danza* was taught in the missions or how it was brought to them, it would be well known.

Though the original *Instructions* document is undated, the editors of its translation's fourth edition, Benoist and Flores, date it at 1787 (Benoist and Flores 1994, 1), the year found in the personal notes of the first edition's editor (J. de León, personal communication, November 11, 2019). Fathers Habig and Leutenegger in *Management of the Missions in Texas: Fr. Rafael José Oliva's Views Concerning the Problem of the Temporalities in 1788*, wrote that the document, "was written after 1773, not ca. 1760" as it had been "tentatively dated," because the mission would not have been flourishing after 1760 as the document implies (Habig and Leutenegger 1977, 37). The *Instructions* were written by an anonymous Franciscan friar (Benoist and Flores 1994, 1) and was transcribed and translated by Father Benedict Leutenegger of the Franciscan Order of Friars Minor (O.F.M.). He was a Franciscan curator of mission archives and founded the Old Spanish Missions Research Library (Diekemper 2019). The first edition of his translation and additional notes appeared in 1976. I noted errors in the translation made by Father Leutenegger that appear in the first and fourth editions. And the annotations he and successive editors added effectively make the book an interpretation of the original document.

His qualifications to ethnohistorically interpret the document were almost nonexistent. He was not an ethnohistorian, and he was not a *matachín*. The only part of his life spent in the American Southwest was during his fifteen years of work at Mission San José (Diekemper 2019). Yet, Father Leutenegger annotated the original Franciscan author's passing mention of "Matachines" dancing on Christmas Eve on the porch of the friary. He gives a vague description and intriguing history of the dance that do not match anything I have seen in my thirteen years of dancing or my research findings. In addition, he translates *refresco* (refreshment) as wine, apparently because the reader is told that the refreshments given to these dancers after they danced at the rectory door came from a *frasquera* (a box that holds jars, flasks, and/or vials). It is possible that Father Leutenegger assumed that, since the refreshments originated from a *frasquera*, that it was wine, which would have been a presumptive translation on his part. In any case, matachines do not drink wine subsequent to dancing. If anything, we drink coffee or *champurrado* but nothing containing alcohol. Through an indigenous perspective, alcohol and ritual are generally incompatible.

The consumption of alcohol, in this case, wine, would be considered a corruption of and disrespectful to any ritual dance with which it might hypothetically involve. The Aztecs disallowed the consumption of alcohol except among the aged. With the fall of the Aztec Empire, reduced inhibition of alcohol consumption resulted in unprecedented instances of drunkenness among that population. This lamentable development is represented among the dance steps of La Danza Guadalupana de Pablo Olivares Sr. That step is called *El borrachito* (the little drunkard). A version of this dance (*El borracho*) is also danced by some matachines in northern New Mexico (Lamadrid 2000, 58). So, it would be especially untenable to call the *Instructions'* mysterious revelers "Matachines," if Father Leutenegger accurately translated "*refresco*" to "wine."

Even if this were an accurate translation, it would be another reason why these misidentified dancers could not have been matachines. Nor do matachines dance at friary entrances as if trying to curry the favor of a priest. Rather, matachines dance for the *la Virgen de Guadalupe*. It is our way of praying to her. This leads to the strongest negation of the labeling of these colonial dancers as "*matachines*": There is no mention of the *La Virgen de Guadalupe* in relation to the people who Father Leutenegger and the original author misidentify as *matachines*. In fact, though the paragraph is meant to inform about the feast days observed by the mission in December, it does not mention the *Virgen*'s feast day on December 12.

Another part of the paragraph that makes it doubtful that these were matachines is the author's use of the word *Baylar* (*bailar*) as if it were synonymous with *danzar*. Both mean to dance, but *bailar* is casual or social dance whereas *danzar* denotes artistic or ceremonial dance. That is why *danzantes* speak of *la danza azteca*, *la danza conchera*, and *la danza de matachines* instead of *baile azteca*, *baile conchera*, or *baile de matachines*. This distinction does not exist in English without the use of added descriptive words like "social." Consequently, using *bailar* or *baile* in the context of ritual and religious dance is very strange. Those are also the reasons why dancers like the *matachines*, *aztecas*, and *concheros* are called *danzantes* instead of *bailadores*. It is not that the author did not know the difference but that he saw Indians "*baylando*" instead of *danzando*. *Se* can also be used in front of a verb to make it passive, but because the context makes the matachines active, it is not in the passive voice. Otherwise, the translation would be, "It is danced." *Baylarse* would have meant something completely different. It is of note that Father García repeatedly committed the faux pas of using conjugations of *bailar* instead of *danzar* when he addressed *danzantes* and members of the public as he prepared to bless pilgrimage participants in 2015. His choice of words drew politely restrained looks of puzzlement from a number of those gathered. But I think others understood from his English cadence that he struggled with Spanish.

The following is the original paragraph in the *Instructions* that mentions "Matachines" followed by Father Leutenegger's translation:

> *La noche de la Vigilia de Navidad o Nochebuena sacan los Yndios su danza de Matachines, y se están baylando en el Portal del Convento todo el tiempo que el Ministro les permite, quien suele darles su refresco acostumbrado, si la frasquera lo permite y el primer día de Pascua se van a baylar al Presidio a casa del Governador y otras particulares. En algunas misiones tienen sus vestidos al propósito para etas fiestas, en esta y en donde no lo hay, se acomodan con los Paños de rebozo, y camisas de su mugeres. También es regular salga esta danza en la Procession del Corpus por suplemento de los Gigantes.* (Benoist and Flores 1994, 34)
>
> On Christmas Eve the Indians do the dance of the Matachines and go on dancing at the entrance of the friary as long as the missionary allows it. He generally gives them a drink of wine if there is enough on hand. On Christmas day they go and dance at the presidio, the governor's house and other places. In some missions they wear outfits in keeping with the spirit of the feast. When these are not available, they use women's dresses and scarfs. This dance is regularly performed also in the procession of the Corpus Christi instead of using the giant figures. (Benoist and Flores 1994, 35)

The following is a revision of the paragraph I propose. It is not meant to be more accurate in identifying the dancers but to reflect how an outsider to the dance at that time was likely to have seen these misidentified dancers. I have italicized the parts I have revised to also show what a native speaker of Spanish with a degree in that language would approach the translation of this paragraph. My purpose for pointing out the weaknesses of Father Leutenegger's translation is to show the disadvantage he was at to interpret the paragraph ethnolinguistically, a reality further frustrated by his not being a *matachín*:

> On Christmas eve, the Indians engage *in a dance missionaries call* the matachines dance, and they dance at the entry of the *friary, for the missionary allows it and often gives them an expected refreshment if the vial carrier allows it, and on Christmas day they go to the fort to perform at the governor's house and at other private homes.* In some missions they have their costumes for

the purpose of these feasts. In this mission and where there are no such costumes, they *make do with Cloaking cloths* that *cover most of their faces and their wives' shirts. It is also normal for this dance to be in the Procession of the Corpus Christi as a supplement to the Gigantes dancers.*

All four editions of the translation include an annotation by Leutenegger claiming, as if trying to strengthen the author's use of matachines, that matachines later became "societies" of Marian devotion, that the dance involved "simple steps," and that dancers wore masks and multicolored robes. *Danza de matachines* steps, depending on the lineage of the troupe, can be complex. The troupe in my neighborhood has intricate steps. And, there is no shortage of dance forms that use masks. Except for *el viejo de la danza*, matachines in San Antonio do not wear masks. And none wear "multicolored capes." The only thing that suggests that these people were matachines is the presence of the word.

La Virgen de Guadalupe appeared to Juan Diego in 1531, which led to a quickly spreading devotion. And December 12 was designated as her feast day by Pope Benedict XIV in 1754 (Matovina 2005, 11), thirty-three years before these *Instructions* were believed to have been written. Yet, there is not even any mention of her feast day in the entire document. Adding to the unlikelihood of the dancers being matachines is that the missions were facing dire straits by this point in their history. Although the number of Indians at Mission Concepción is not available for 1787 when the *Instructions* were written, in 1788 there were only fifty-one (Habig 1976, 139). As they were not enough of a labor source for the operations of Mission Concepción and its corresponding agricultural fields, its secularization process was formally begun in 1794, with land being parceled out to some of its Indian inhabitants (Habig 1976, 141). Those inhabitants included my eighth great-grandparents who at the time had young children, as evidenced by Spanish Colonial census records published by the University of Texas at San Antonio Institute of Texan Cultures (*Residents of Texas* 1984). Friars were so burdened with working for their survival in the wilderness that they hardly had time for even religious matters (García and Valverde 1759). And the decline of Mission Concepción as indicated by Fathers Leutenegger and Habig would mean there were spare resources and time available for activities like the *danza de matachines* that were not directly related to mission operations. So, it would seem incongruous that there would be time, energy, and resources for the *danza de matachines*.

Another highly problematic factor is that this book involves a Franciscan friar interpreting another Franciscan friar's words. Such a tandem relationship is a liability for ethnohistoric interpretation because it is likely that biases of perspective of the original author have been perpetuated. Consequently, if the original term *matachines* was generically ascribed to a group of dancers by one Franciscan, which is the case here, the translation is much more likely to have remained the same.

Having examined the microfilm version of the original document, it is clear that this erroneous use of the word *Matachines* (Benoist and Flores 1994, 35) lies with the anonymous Franciscan author, and that any effort conceivably made to ethnohistorically interpret the document's use of this anecdote was ultimately bypassed. Moreover, the consequent appropriation of the word *matachines* was enabled by the succeeding editors in all four editions of the *Instructions'* translation. If a continuous lineage of *danza de matachines* tradition had existed in the missions, any number of the highly detailed annual inspections, such as those carried out by Fray Juan Agustín Morfi from 1777 to 1778 (Habig 1976, 61) and Fray Francisco Xavier Ortiz in 1756 (Habig 1976, 56), would have commented on them repeatedly and at great length, especially because its practice would have been interpreted as a concrete marker of successful conversion to Christianity.

It is highly plausible that when the anonymous Franciscan author could not identify the dance these Indians performed on Christmas Eve, he defaulted to the *danza de matachines* because of the acceptance of that dance by the church. It would have been awkward for the anonymous author to say in writing that a possibly pagan dance was performed on mission grounds for a religious event. Word of such a practice would especially be awkward if it reached superiors in Zacatecas where the order's Colegio was located. But, the *danza de matachines*, with its reputation as being a dance of converts, could be assigned to Indian dancers without concern for consequence.

The word *matachines* is often misused by outsiders who confuse them for other *danzantes*. It has also been used by those who see it as a generic term with which to identify all *danzantes* whose *danzas* appear to be indigenous. Just as Father García misidentified the *danzantes* he saw in Mexico City as matachines, and just as local journalists frequently publish photos of *Azteca* dancers, for instance, and call them *matachines*, so did the anonymous Franciscan author of this text in 1787 misidentify the Christmas Eve revelers he describes. There is a pattern among mission officials of using the term *matachines* as a gloss for dancers they cannot readily identify. Father García, like Father Leutenegger before him, and like the author of the *Instructions* before him.

When Father David García stated that the missions were still doing what they were doing three hundred years ago, he could well have been referring to the misrepresentation of unknown dancers as matachines. There were a number of dances in New Spain, including those of the indigenous *mitotes* (T. Matovina, personal communication, January 18, 2016). So, in terms of placing the *danza de matachines* in the missions during the era of New Spain, the *Instructions* document is inconclusive at best.

The dances misrepresented as "Matachines," according to the anonymous Franciscan, also danced in procession on the feast day of the Corpus Christi (Benoist and Flores 1994, 35), which adds to the doubtfulness that these dancers were matachines. The feast of Corpus Christi falls in mid-June (Matovina 2005, 46), long after the feast day of *La Virgen de Guadalupe* or the day of the *Tres Reyes Magos*. To establish that matachines existed in the missions, there would need to be at least two incidents of documentation corroborating each other. But, this document's mention of "Matachines" would not even be strong enough to corroborate reference to matachines in another document. For all the above reasons, it makes sense that Matovina would say he found no evidence of matachines in the missions while being aware of the *Instructions'* reference to "Matachines" that were not matachines. And, because of all these weaknesses in confirming that the dancers were matachines, it would be irresponsible to cite the *Instructions* document in an attempt to establish the presence of matachines in the missions during the Spanish Colonial period.

Yet, the *Instructions* represent a mischaracterization of *matachines* as *danzantes* who will dance for any feast day that clergy ask them to, thus denying their devotion to the *Virgen*. The reality is that matachines have danced for occasions other than the feast day of the *Virgen* at clerical request but out of courtesy and as a favor. Or, in cases like the archdiocese's tacitly prerequisite processions for the feast days of Christ the King and the Immaculate Conception, it is done out of coercion. But as well, an ethnohistoric reading of the *Instructions* points to an equally problematic misrepresentation of matachines in physical terms that continues today. Consequently, journalists, influential bloggers, pundits, and photographers disseminate—often in good faith—images in the mass media of the *conchera* dancers, *azteca* dancers, and Hispanic liturgical dancers. With the archdiocese's sudden apparent concern for the *danza de matachines* and the pilgrimages, I had sought to find out where lies its historical basis for asserting that matachines existed in the missions during the 1700s. Thanks to the *Instructions*, together with the events that brought that book into my hand, I now have the answer. It is that the church has never known what matachines are but from the very beginning have attempted to use its traditions for its own interests.

Insights into the Appropriation of the Dance Pilgrimage

La Danza Guadalupana de Pablo Olivares Sr., during its entire existence, has been an autonomous *danza de matachines* troupe. That is, its trajectory, decisions, organization, and coordination have been made by its members, who have largely been related by blood or marriage. And it has functioned independently of institutions. Father García, the pastor of Mission Concepción and director of the Old Spanish Missions of San Antonio, inserted a number of changes into the traditions that were part of an annual dance pilgrimage organized and coordinated by La Danza Guadalupana de Pablo Olivares Sr. These changes were an appropriation of the dance pilgrimage in the political and economic interests of the archdiocese and local business entities. The appropriation of the dance pilgrimage was an attempted usurpation of the pilgrimage's autonomy by religious and commercial entities and of devotion by religious entities and the local mass media.

Authentic matachines troupes responded to these changes to the dance pilgrimage by withdrawing their participation from the dance pilgrimage and continuing the *danza de matachines* traditions in other ways, such as in neighborhood *posadas* and in the backyards of private homes. The troupes who withdrew from the pilgrimage demonstrated the greatest resilience by recognizing the appropriation and ceasing to participate. The troupes that remained in the pilgrimage were either not as invested in the *danza de matachines* traditions, were coaxed into service at the last minute, and/or were participating in it for the first time. Some of the participating troupes were not *danza de matachines* troupes. Consequently, they recognized no dilemma when the dance pilgrimage and its traditions, both of which come from the realm of the *danza de matachines*, were altered.

In this chapter, I asked how a clergyman with no experience in the *danza* could wield so much decision-making power in our dance pilgrimage, how he could make inaccurate historical claims to UNESCO, how political activism came to exploit this apolitical tradition, and how there could be so many misinterpretations of the *danza* in the local mass media. A casual observer might interpret such questioning as an idiosyncratic manifestation on my part, but I have found that these are all parts of continuous colonial patterns of opportunism and exploitation of the *danza* by powerful institutions, especially church institutions. This is probably best illustrated in the fact that Father García's successor was neither a member of the clergy, Hispanic, or a male, like him. Yet, her roles and responsibilities, as far as the archdiocese was concerned, continued seamlessly after Father García's retirement because her role of exploiting the *danza* for the archdiocese's interests remained the same.

The archdiocese placed itself in a paradoxical situation whereby authenticity eluded it to the extent that it attempted to appropriate the dance. But the archdiocese could not appreciate the parameters of authenticity to begin with. And the archdiocese's appropriation of the dance pilgrimage did not compromise the tradition's resilience because the dance is fluid and matachines know how to maneuver through institutional machinations and imposed limitations such as the ones implemented by Father García. Matachines have been sidestepping such maneuvers since the Spanish Colonial period. Serendipity was an important factor in the *danzantes'* resilience. The resilience of these troops cannot be influenced by institutions because it is virtually random and, consequently, fluid. Serendipity cannot be controlled by institutions either. It places *danzantes* in the right places at the right time in order to continue the *danza*. When unlikely timing and the development of interconnected events benefiting the *danza* occur, it is because the *Virgen* uses serendipity that way. And serendipitous exchanges with the new mission administrator aided me in seeing that the church has never understood who *matachines* are but that it has used them to fulfill roles that serve its interests.

10

Conclusion

The Interplay of Change and Continuity in a *Danza de Matachines* Troupe

On December 12, 2016, the feast day of *La Virgen de Guadalupe*, I decorated my home altar to the *Virgen* then went on an errand with my wife. It was dusk, and we happened to be passing by Woodlawn Lake. Noticing a beautiful, nearly full moon rising above it, we stopped to take a walk around the lake to admire the moon. I noticed the timing of the feast day in relation to Woodlawn Lake, where I had spent countless hours with our troupe training and practicing. For a year I had not heard from Tony or Molly regarding practice or a *danza*. A photo appeared, though, on a local online news source of a few members of our *danza* participating in a pilgrimage, this time from Mission Concepción to Mission San José.

My wife and I admired the moon's beauty and were grateful for the view of it that the wide, open space of the lake afforded us. I was excited that the moon was practically full on the feast day of the *Virgen*. After completing the errand, we went home. It was now dark, and we sat down to dinner; then we heard drumming outside. We went outside to investigate and found that there was a procession of matachines approaching. On one hand, I was not surprised because I had known of a nearby resident who hosted matachines practice. I also had previously heard drumming that sounded like *danza conchera* practice a bit farther away, in another direction. However, I had not anticipated that there would be a *danza de matachines* troupe actually dancing in our neighborhood. Just as I stepped outside, the troupe was dancing as it entered my block and was about fifty yards away. A young man at the front of the line spontaneously shouted, "*¡Viva la Virgen de Guadalupe!*" to which an accompanying group of about forty participants in the street and I emphatically answered, "*¡Viva!*" We had been unaware of this dance procession in our neighborhood because every year I was dancing elsewhere on the *Virgen's* feast day.

My wife and I joined the members of the community of devotees, accompanying the dancers on their way. They stopped to dance at residents' temporary, outdoor altars that had been prepared for the *Virgen's* feast day and for the matachines. Our route circled two blocks before returning to the house. There they danced a *veneración* before an altar dedicated to the *Virgen* in a tent in the driveway. A line of matachines and other participants was formed leading up to the altar. The purpose of the line was to give people a chance to write petitions to the *Virgen* that would be read at one point during a rosary that was to follow. It is on the feast day of the *Virgen* that such petitions are especially made, usually on behalf of loved ones. My wife and I wrote petitions in the notebook then stood at the back of the canopy while the young man who had danced at the front of the line led everyone in praying the rosary.

As it turned out, the rosary was prayed in a very augmented way, that is, with verses of a poem about the *Virgen* declaimed at intervals, right before every *Padre Nuestro* (Our Father). The rosary was also augmented by a Catholic litany, two parts of the Catholic liturgy (specifically, the Kyrie and the Breaking of the Bread), and the singing of "*La Alabanza Guadalupana.*" It is a hymn I have known since my youth. Sklar (2001, 42) notes its use in Tortugas, New Mexico, as well. Finally, it included a prayer for each of the petitions that had been written in the notebook on the altar. Each one was read aloud in Spanish.

There was no deacon or priest present to approve of it. Nor was there any distracting media coverage, tourists, new agers, or curiosity seekers. It was at once public and intimate because of this. Of course, the members of the community of devotees understood it. If there had been mass media present, we would not have been able to have the rosary because of the personal nature of the petitions that were read aloud. Moreover, the decision to dance at night would not have been marketable to financial institutions wanting to commercialize it. The darkness of the night also would have posed a challenge to visual publicity media, particularly photography and videography. Also pleasantly absent were politically motivated dancers who wanted to capitalize on the public and potentially symbolic nature of the *danza* to call attention to their identity causes. There were not even any police paid for by exorbitant fees. The gathering was so institution-free that the troupe did not even seem to have a name.

The intimacy of the *danza* procession and rosary reminded me of *danzas* during my earlier years with La Danza Guadalupana de Pablo Olivares Sr. In other words: It was vastly different from the faux pilgrimages that we had participated in after Father García had commandeered our decision-making processes. I approached the men who had danced at the front of the line and asked who their leader was. They both seemed to think that was a strange question but courteously and sincerely answered in Spanish, gesturing toward the *danzantes* who were taking a brief break. "All of us," the young man answered. I introduced myself as a *matachín* who had a *traje* very much like theirs and asked if I could dance with them next year. Fortunately, their response was enthusiastically affirmative. Having secured membership in a new troupe that maintained the autonomy that our pilgrimage once had, I felt that, like the cycle of the tides brought by the full moon, my experiences with the *danza* had come full circle. Because of this serendipitous encounter, in the next few years I would dance for the *Virgen* not only in that troupe but in yet another one formed by Molly and Tony.

But how did this circle come to completion? Any devotee of *La Virgen de Guadalupe* would say she brought it about. One might wonder, though, *how* she brought it about. My answer would certainly include my continual participation in the *danza* over ten years. I would also need to consider our Tlaxcaltecan forebearers who brought the dance north from central Mexico. They were agricultural people who understood that the universe worked in cycles. And, like other agricultural Indigenous societies, they knew that the land had to be understood and interacted with in cyclical patterns in order for it to help them produce food and otherwise provide for their basic needs. And, just as they observed seasons for sowing, reaping, and other cyclical events and periods, so did they come to recognize the cyclical feast day of *La Virgen de Guadalupe* and her season of heightened devotion from December 12 to the feast of the Epiphany the following month. After all, spiritual phenomena can be cyclical too.

They saw that events, be they sowing of corn or the appearances of the *Virgen*, occur cyclically. So, it makes sense that the music and *danza* of her veneration would also be cyclical. Each dance step consists of a repeated cycle of two to four measures. The patterns that characterize these cycles—though they all are different—are uniform in rhythm until they are interrupted by the final measure whose rhythm is markedly different from that of the preceding measures. After the *matachines* dance that measure, the cycle begins again and is repeated until the *monarca* communicates to the drummer to resume playing the *corridito*. It is equally important to note here that the resumption of the *corridito* at intervals, that is, between each dance step, is itself cyclical. As the final measure of each rhythmic figure departs from the measures before it, so does the dance step change as the dancer bows, spins, or hops, depending on the step being danced. This cyclical nature of the dance steps and the dance itself are the reason why I have often had the unmistakable and visceral awareness that time is transcended during our *veneración* and that I am in the presence of the past. It is at this moment when the *capitanes, monarca, malinches,* line dancers, and *viejo de la danza* seem to bodily bring the participants of that *Virgen*'s original moment in history into the present. I have especially felt this way when the echoes of the drums, *sonajas, carrizos,* and stepping of huarache-clad feet could be heard in echoes. And it should be remembered that echoes themselves are cycles of sound. Admittedly, cycles in music are not that rare, and they appear in contexts that are not associated with bringing the past into the present. However, the drumming rhythm and corresponding steps have a brevity of structure that result in the completion of many more cycles than those more commonplace contexts and musical forms. This cyclical aspect of our dancing and drumming, together with the *Virgen* and the *estandarte,* are why our *danza* summons the *Virgen,* Moctezuma II, his *capitanes,* and other historical figures. It makes sense that, as Molly said, our *danza* was once correlated to the rosary because it is largely composed of similarly repeated prayers with a different one said at intervals of ten other ones. I have seen that authentic *matachines* and *matachín* traditions have ways of circumventing contemporary obstacles (for example, official city approval of processions) by virtual force of traditional perceptions about how the *Virgen* should be venerated and prayed to. These perceptions are characterized by implications of cyclical time, which is not unlike the previously discussed Cakchiquel Mayas' creation of the *Fiesta del Volcán* to continue their traditions.

In my experience, dancing to these rhythms regularly made them part of my corporal memory. They bring one into the *Virgen*'s circle. Matachines acquire the cyclical energy of the *danza*, her *danza*. I relate this dynamic to conversation I had with a grandmother after a *danza* at St. Alphonsus Parish Hall. Over our plates of Mexican food, she told me how her teen-aged daughter had begun training in the *danza* the year before. She added that at night, even though there was no practice, she would go outside to dance. This, she said, was not because she felt a need to improve her technical skills as a *danzante* but because she felt corporally compelled to do so. She intimated that the *danza* was that strong, and her granddaughter had enough heart to hear and respond to it.[1] The granddaughter, who was sitting with us, apparently became self-conscious that her grandmother had revealed this private, internal response she had to the *danza* and wordlessly averted her eyes toward her plate.

Similarly, I have heard the drumming in my dreams and felt it even in situations removed from the *danza*. And, when I was practicing independently in public spaces, it felt natural. But I must emphasize that the drumming and the dance are empty and superficial without devotion to the *Virgen*, or at least without the *awareness* of her. Without her, I could not have truly heard the cyclical drumming patterns of the matachines troupe that evening outside my home while I was dining with my wife. It would not have stirred me the way it did. I can see why, for many people, the calendar revolves around December 12.

This troupe's dancing through my neighborhood's streets exemplified the ability of the dance to morph, in a fluid and often serendipitous manner, in the face of change. This is what the troupes who withdrew from the faux pilgrimages were doing. Even if their troupes had for some reason become fragmented, they would still find the dance . . . or the dance would find them. The nature of that ability to morph is, at its core, the *Virgen*'s response to her devotees in former northeastern New Spain. For over three hundred years it has been a way of maintaining continuity through tactical withdrawals and dissimulation in the face of colonial change.

Glossary of Spanish Terms

The following is a list of Spanish terms that appear in this text. It includes definitions unique to the realm of the *danza de matachines* as it is danced by La Danza Guadalupana de Pablo Olivares Sr. The definitions given here are specific to the contexts in which they are used in this book unless otherwise indicated.

Abuela: Literally grandmother, an *abuela* is a personage specific to New Mexican *danza de matachines* troupes. An exchange with Molly, however, indicates that La Danza Guadalupana de Pablo Olivares Sr. once had a dancer who assumed a similar role.

Abuelo: Literally grandfather, an *abuelo* is a personage specific to New Mexican *danza de matachines* troupes. El *viejo de la danza* appears to be the northern Mexico and south Texas version of this personage.

Adoración: Also known as the *la veneración*, *la devoción*, and *la reverencia*, this is the heart of the *danza de matachines* as danced by La Danza Guadalupana de Pablo Olivares Sr. It is a ritual in which *danzantes* take turns venerating the *Virgen*, culminating in the conversion of the *viejo de la danza*.

Agarrando onda: A phrase used to describe a point in which a repetitive action is acquiring its own consciousness.

Altar* or *Altar Casero: A household shrine that often has more than one spiritual personage as well as photos of loved ones for whom intervention is being requested through prayer. However, if the shrine is to *La Virgen de Guadalupe*, all other saints are removed from the *altar* between December 12 and the feast day of the Epiphany, at which time it is also cleaned and decorated elaborately. For the purposes of being venerated by matachines during pilgrimages, residents may create one outdoors.

Arco: Literally "bow," it is a mock weapon and percussion instrument resembling a bow and arrow. The arrow is represented by a wooden bolt which is a fixed part of the instrument. It is held in place by a hole in the bow that it rests in and by the tension of a strip of bicycle tire tube that is attached to its end. The bolt is partially and rhythmically drawn through the hole in the bow and released. Because the half of the bolt on the inside of the bow is thicker than the front part, it strikes the bow, making a high and short-pitched clave-like sound. Some matachines groups carry their *arcos* behind them, while others carry theirs in front. However, the tradition of our matachines troupe is to carry them at the side, "so they're at the ready" as Molly once put it. They are carried in the left hand, and the right hand, while gripping the *sonaja*, pulls on the *arco*'s bowstring.

Azteca (danza): A type of Indigenous-style dance from central Mexico. It is very similar in dress and form to *danza conchera*. Both dances use elaborate, apparently researched *trajes*, and in San Antonio both types of dances have athletic, circular forms. They also involve rapid and repetitive spinning, and the wearing of pheasant feathers and ostrich plumes as part of their elaborate headdresses.

Barbilla: The fine, green, thickly cropped fringes used as trim on some of the matachines regalia, particularly along the bottom hems the *naguas* and the vests, as well as along the borders of the *capas*.

Barrio: A neighborhood where Spanish is spoken. In San Antonio, this has generally been understood to mean predominantly working-class Chicano neighborhoods where recent immigrants from Mexico and Central America also reside.

Camposanto: Literally, this means holy ground. A closer English translation is graveyard. In San Antonio, this term referred to San Antonio's first Catholic cemetery. In the 1840s, its remains were from present-day downtown San Antonio to the Westside where the site was named the San Fernando Cemetery. Afterward, a second one was started a few miles southwest of it called San Fernando Cemetery No. 2. Spanish-speaking San Antonians often refer to these two sites as *El Camposanto Número uno* and *El Camposanto Número dos*, respectively.

Capa: A red tunic-like poncho worn by the *monarca* and the *capitanes*. The older ones worn in our troupe featured a silver-colored thunderbird on the front and an image of the *Virgen* on the back. Later, Molly's mother made them with green, white, and red sequins forming a serpent devouring a snake on a cactus on the front part of the garment. On the back she sewed a mass-produced, square-shaped fabric with an image of the *Virgen* made mostly of sequins. Both versions of the *capa* were worn by the *capitanes* during my early years in our troupe.

Capilla: Literally, chapel, this is the word used for cave-like shrines in devotees' front yards. They are usually constructed from cement and measure approximately two-and-a-half-feet in length by four feet in height and two feet in depth. They contain a statuette of the *Virgen*.

Capitán: Directly translated, this word means captain. Among matachines, it is used to mean subchief. Tony suggested that they are the equivalent of "generals" under the command of the *monarca*. In fact, through actions such as being the first to venerate the *Virgen* and escorting devotees of the *Virgen*, they carry out leadership roles. Traditionally, line dancers can become *capitanes* after accruing enough experience and showing skill in and understanding of the dance. Ideally, we have two *capitanes* at the head of both files and another two bringing up the rear at the end of the files. Like the *monarca*, they wear *capas* instead of the vest of the line dancers.

Carrizo: A species of light river reed cut and arranged in lengths of about two inches to dangle horizontally in parallel rows on the *naguas*. On our *trajes*, the *carrizos* on each end of the rows had varnished, wooden beads attached to their lower parts, while the rest had trade bells attached instead.

Champurrado: A hot, soupy, and mildly sweet drink with lime-treated corn dough as its base. Other ingredients include chocolate, sugar, and cinnamon. It is served during the December–January holiday season.

Chiles: Any variety of chili peppers.

Compadrazgo: The relationship that exists between a godparent and a godchild's parent. This is characterized by a preparedness to assist the child or child's family in cases of emergencies in addition to the standard role of a willingness to safeguard a child's spiritual formation.

Conchera (danza): An Indian-style dance from central Mexico. Dancers of this tradition dance with bands of large seed husks called *ayayotes* around their ankles. Their dress tends to be more elaborate and pre-Spanish. The *danza conchera* is more athletic than the *danza de matachines*, and it has a circular form. Perhaps for this reason it is often seen as the same as *danza azteca*. However, one *conchera* dancer has told me that *danza azteca* is more "show" oriented. In any case, I have known many San Antonian *conchera* dancers and have observed that their members tend to also be artists, intellectuals, and political activists. They also seem to integrate more prayer into their rituals, including litanies. The singular greatest factor that distinguishes them from *danza azteca* troupes are their use of a ten-string mandolin-like musical instrument called a *concha* (shell), perhaps because the back of it was originally made from an armadillo's shell.

Confianza: Endearing familiarity, trustworthiness, personability.

Copal: a type of solidified tree sap that can be burned as incense. Before, during, and after our pilgrimages, the *conchera* dancers burned this in copious amounts.

Cora': Short for *corazón* or heart, this is used in the context of *agarrando onda* to mean the presence of sentiment in the intention with which a repeated action is made.

Corona: Literally "crown." Headwear used by the matachines except the *viejo* and the *malinches*. In our troupe, this term is used interchangeably with *penacho*, though *corona* was possibly once denoted headwear specific to the *monarca*. See also *Penacho*.

Danza: Literally "dance." In this book, it also the rough equivalent of "dance performance," though without the intention of entertaining. It also refers to the *danza de matachines* as well as to the circular central Mexican Indigenous dance traditions practiced in the American Southwest. Among *danza de matachines* and *danza conchera* troupes, we often use the word *danza* synonymously with troupe.

Danzante: Literally, "dancer." Among matachines this term could refer to a *matachín*, a *conchero*, or an *azteca* dancer.

Devoción: Literally, devotion. See also *Adoración*.

Enchiladas: Shredded chicken, ground beef, or cheese wrapped in corn tortillas and covered in a chili sauce. Two or three are served on a plate, usually with refried beans and Spanish rice.

Estandarte: Also called *la manta* (banner), *estandarte* literally means "standard" in the ceremonial sense of the word. It is the tapestry on which the *Virgen*'s image is carried aloft. The standard bearer is positioned at the center and head of the files with the Mexican flag to its immediate left and the American flag on its immediate right. During the *adoración* it is held stationary. Although the *danzantes* have an image of the *Virgen* on their respective *trajes*, her image on the *estandarte* is the principal one. It is the focal point of the *danza*, especially during the *adoración*. As a *danzante*, I sensed that it held more power than any other icon in the dance. This was indicated not only because of its front-and-center position in the files but also because every dancer and willing devotee pays homage before her image during the *adoración* by kneeling before her and/or kissing her. Ideally, the *estandarte* is handmade and features the name of the *danza de matachines* troupe.

Fiesta: While the term *fiesta* in San Antonio has come to mean a specific, secular celebration organized by the city government in the spring, other definitions include feast day celebration.

Gente: In San Antonio, *gente* or *buena gente* refers to people who share the values and codes of conduct of the barrios. When someone refers to another person as *gente* in a sentence that is otherwise in English, it is understood that the person being referred to is *buena gente* (for example, "I know him; he's *gente*"). Literally, *la gente* means the people.

Lámina: Sheet metal or material cut from sheet metal. Strips of it were once used in the making of the *penachos* of La Danza Guadalupana de Pablo Olivares Sr.

Mal de ojo: The incurring of illness, injury, or damage as a metaphysical consequence of a thing or person being admired for its or their appearance.

Mañanitas: Early morning *danzas* and music in *honor* of the *Virgen de Guadalupe* on the twelfth of December, which is her feast day. See also *serenata*.

Más recio: Louder. *Recio* in south Texas is often used to mean loud.

Mitotes: Through Spanish eyes, *mitotes* were all night dances and/or celebrations that were pagan in nature. The Spanish saw the profession of the Catholic faith and participation in *mitotes* as mutually exclusive practices.

Monarca: "The monarch." Lead dancer who represents Moctezuma II. His position is at the front of the column. He converts to the religion of the *Virgen* after the *capitanes* by bowing or partially kneeling before her image on the *estandarte*. His actions, affect, and seemingly anachronistic presence in the dance defy the historical record concerning his life and presumed defeat by the Spanish.

Naguas: A pair of apron-like vestments worn about the waist. They face the front and back of the dancer and have rows of two-inch segments of *carrizo* dangling in horizontal lines. These rows traditionally cover most of the *naguas*. Francisca Aguilar, Molly's mother, used to make our *trajes* from red flannel that had a red linen lining. She cut and sewed mine and then showed me how to sew on the *carrizos*.

Nicho: A box-like alcove made out of wood and usually painted decoratively. It serves as a miniature indoor shrine. See also *altares caseros*.

Norteño: A man from northern Mexico.

Onda: A Chicano term referring to the occurrence of a repetitive action that has acquired its own consciousness combined with sentiment.

Pan dulce: A generic term used to refer to a vast variety of Mexican pastries. Among other Mexican foods, they are traditionally served by homes and churches that host *danzas*, *pastorelas*, and/or *posadas*.

Pastorela: A centuries-old Mexican play about shepherds traveling to see the newborn Jesus. This has been performed in San Antonio since at least the 1880s. The original length of the play was several hours long but has been shortened in contemporary times. In it the devil attempts to prevent the shepherds from reaching the baby Jesus in a way similar to our *viejo de la danza*'s attempts at distracting the *danzantes* and bystanders from our *adoración* of the *Virgen*. It may be for that reason that on occasion people have misidentified *"el viejo"* as the devil.

¡Pa'trás! ¡Pa'trás!: A command given by one of the *capitanes* for the column to move backward just before ending the dance.

Penacho: Literally, "crest." Headwear used by the matachines except the *viejo* and the *malinches*. In our troupe, this term is used interchangeably with *corona*, though *corona* possibly once denoted headwear specific to the *monarca*. See also *Corona*.

Peregrinación: Pilgrimage (also *peregrinaje*).

Peregrinaje: Pilgrimage (also *peregrinación*).

Promesa: A pilgrimage or act of sacrifice performed for the *Virgen* in gratitude for an intention granted. It is important that people unfamiliar with this custom not confuse it with an attempt at negotiation or bargaining with the *Virgen*. Rather, the supplicant carries out the *promesa* without having stipulated that doing so depended on the granting of a petition.

Posadas: Literally, "inns." This is the pre-Christmas December custom in Mexican and Chicano communities of acting out Mary and Joseph searching for an inn. This is traditionally performed by groups of people singing songs specific to the custom and going to several houses, seeking lodging.

Ranchero: Rural resident. Juan Diego in popular iconography is depicted wearing rural attire. *La Virgen de Guadalupe* is similarly often referred to in popular song and poetry as the *Virgen ranchera*.

Rebozo: Way of wearing a cape or cloak when it covers almost all the face. Hence, the book's translation of *paños de rebozos* should be "cloaking cloths" or blankets or ponchos.

Reverencia: See *Adoración*.

Serenata: Performing music and song for the *Virgen*, usually late at night or early on the morning of December 12. When performed in the morning, this type of veneration may also be called *mañanitas*, not to be confused with the traditional birthday songs known as *Las mañanitas* or *Las Mañanitas michoacanas*.

Sonaja: Rattle. Some troupes use the word *maraca* in its stead.

Tamales: The plural form of *tamal*, this is a Mexican food traditionally consisting of pork meat cooked inside *masa* and wrapped in corn shucks. The *masa* is lime-treated corn dough.

Tiendita: A small store once common in San Antonio barrios. Because they tend to be owned and operated by family members, they often serve as informal social spaces where community-related communication can take place among barrio residents.

Tía, Tío: Aunt, uncle, respectively. It is important to keep in mind that among working-class Chicanos, these terms can be used by default to describe family members who are at least middle-aged and carry the weight of authority associated with their age. These terms are especially likely to be used to describe relationships that are too nebulous or too far removed for the speaker to readily describe with precision (for example, "my mother's cousin" or "my great-grand uncle"). This loose application of terms also happens because roles such people play in the family can be more important than their place in abstract familial schemata.

Traje: Literally, "suit," and for our purposes it means the specific clothing that *danzantes* are meant to wear in their role, whether it be that of a *Malinche, capitán, monarca,* or line dancer. The *trajes* of the *capitanes* and *monarca* are the same: a *capa, naguas, penacho,* and *huaraches.* And, they only differ from the line matachines in that the latter dancers use red flannel vests instead of *capas.* The *malinches' trajes* consist of red, white, and green ankle-length skirts, white blouses, and straw hats. Manuel's *viejo de la danza traje* included a mechanic's jumpsuit covered with multicolored strips of cloth, a ghoulish rubber mask, a bull whip, and a baby doll wrapped in a rabbit pelt with a noose around its neck.

Trastátarabuela / Trastátarabuelo: An anthropological term denoting a grandparent who lived several generations before the present.

Varillas: Bands of tin once used by Francisca Aguilar in making *penachos* for the troupe in the 1970s. They ran along the top of the *penachos* and helped to hold the feathers in place. This is the term that Molly's mother, Francisca Aguilar, used when describing the *trajes* she was making for the troupe at that time.

Veneración: Also see *adoración*. This component of the dance is what Carmen, one of the *malinches*, calls the heart of the *danza de matachines*. It is a ritual in which *danzantes* take turns venerating the *Virgen*. First, we dance a number of steps before the *estandarte*, alternately dividing and rejoining our column. Then, with two files of matachines dancing in place, the *capitanes* approach the *estandarte* by dancing from the end of the files opposite from it. They then genuflect or half-bow before the *estandarte*. Then they escort the *monarca* to venerate her in the same way. The line matachines follow suit two by two. Then finally *el viejo de la danza* is chased by the *capitanes* and made to kneel before the *Virgen*. Afterward, devotees in attendance are asked to venerate the *Virgen* in the same way as the drumming continues. After the last devotee has venerated, the drumming continues as we resume dancing three or four more steps. Then we file out of the space, dancing a backward step called *La Fe* (if indoors). If we are dancing outdoors, we walk backward a few steps while slowly bending into a crouching position and rattling our *sonajas*. We then advance, gradually coming out of our crouching position, raising our arms and *sonajas* into the air, and making sharp, staccato cries.

Viejo de la danza: Literally, "the old man of the dance." Also known as *el viejo*, this *danzante* holds the greatest authority in the troupe. Traditionally, he accrues authority through the experience of dancing as a line *matachín*, *capitán*, and then *monarca*. He has a number of purposes. One is to teach by bad example. He does this by trying to disrupt processions and the *adoración* by scaring bystanders with his whip, frightful mask, and clothing. By carrying a baby doll on a noose, he seems to be saying that only evil people detract from the *Virgen* this way. However, in a dualistic way, he also encourages the dancers with his shouting, and he spaces them so that the line maintains an even, orderly appearance.

Virgen: Literally, virgin, this is a common way for Spanish-speaking San Antonians and immigrants from northern Mexico to refer to *La Virgen de Guadalupe* or Our Lady of Guadalupe.

¡Viva la Virgen de Guadalupe!: An approximate cultural translation of this phrase is "Long Live Our Lady of Guadalupe!" When a devotee of the *Virgen* shouts this, it is in the context of a *danza, serenata,* or dance pilgrimage, and all other devotees who are present respond shouting, "*¡Viva!*" echoing and affirming that sentiment.

¡Vuelta a la derecha!: Literally "(Make a) Turn to the right!" This is a command given by one of the *capitanes* at the front of the line for all the dancers to spin around once clockwise. After the dancers respond, the other *capitán* at the front of the line gives the order to spin around counterclockwise by shouting "*¡Vuelta a la macueca!*" On at least one occasion, I have seen Pablo Olivares Jr. give both commands while drumming.

¡Vuelta a la macueca!: "(Make a) Turn to the left!" This is a command for all our dancers to spin around once counterclockwise. It is shouted by one of the two front *capitanes* after the dancers have spun once clockwise in response to the other front *capitán* giving the command *¡Vuelta a la derecha!* Both commands are given and executed at the end of the *adoración* unless the *danza* is taking place indoors, in which case the *monarca* leads the dancers outdoors at the end of the *adoración.* Note: the word *macueca* is an archaic term still in use in the northern Mexico/south Texas region that means "left" or "lefthanded." See also *¡Vuelta a la derecha!*

Yndio: Spanish Colonial word for Indian. It is also the umbrella term the Franciscan missionaries in Texas used to refer to the native peoples with whom they interacted. Its contemporary spelling is with a lower case *I* rather than a capital *Y.*

Zarape: A traditionally woven Mexican blanket of two or more colors. Often *ponchos* are virtually made from *zarapes,* with the only difference being a hole in the center for the wearer's head.

Notes

Chapter 1

1. The approach I take in this work is akin to the native or insider trajectory in the social sciences. More specifically, by writing through the perspective of an insider, the usual academic concern for objectivity is made irrelevant. And, in the course of writing through the perspective of my lived experiences, I reveal partialities, which is acceptable as long as those partialities are not used as global assumptions. If this book were undertaken by outsiders to the *danza* asking matachines questions, their answers would be considered partial as well, and that would be considered acceptable. However, in this case, I am in a sense interviewing myself as a *matachín*, and therefore my partialities are directly disclosed. The only difference is that I am a *matachín* providing information directly to the reader rather than through a second party.

Chapter 2

1. Although this French surname is pronounced *se-guh*, in Texas its spelling and pronunciation tend to be Hispanicized as Seguín (se-gēn).

2. On occasion, people unfamiliar with the *danza de matachines* refer to the *trajes* or regalia as costumes. But the word *costume* denotes a type of dress worn by someone dressed to appear as someone they are not. When matachines wear *trajes*, it is because we are *matachines*. So, used in the context of dance traditions like the *danza de matachines*, costume implies that the wearers lack authenticity. For that reason, I am careful how I use the word *costume* in this book, and I do not use it to refer to our regalia.

Chapter 6

1. I have a number of other authenticity-related concerns with Cantú's chapter. One is that she attempts to use the concept of *mestizaje* to introduce (2009, 97) and characterize (98) the *danza de matachines*. *Mestizaje* is a term that means a cultural miscegenation among Latin American Indigenous Peoples and people from other cultures. I have heard it used consistently in English-speaking theoretical and theological contexts. But, despite having danced for thirteen years as a *matachín*, I have never heard it used conceptually or expressly among matachines. In my *experience* as a *monarca*, it is irrelevant for understanding the *danza*. Those who participate in or otherwise witness the *danza* either understand it, or they do not. Those who do understand it tend to either to be from Mexico or have familial ties to the dance. But *danzantes* are not concerned with ethnicity or even religious affiliation in relation to the *danza*. What is important is that we are dancing for the *Virgen* and that all those present can experience the transcendental moment that can take place as we dance. Her association of the *danza* with *mestizaje*, an idea hardly on the radar of matachines, suggests limited ethnographic exposure to the dance and, to that extent, a lack of authenticity. If in the unlikelihood that she had been able to cite matachines as having *mestizaje* as a traditional element of their *danza*, it would work in favor of having some authenticity. It would especially be helpful for her in that regard if she had been able to dance consistently with a matachines troupe over the years and presented evidence from her experience that *mestizaje* was a concern for matachines. Curiously, Cantú counts the *danza de matachines* "among cultural practices that are part of the daily life" (2009, 97), when in reality, celebrations when matachines dances are annual and, when they are for the *Virgen*, span her feast day on December 12 to the Feast Day of the Epiphany. Cantú's characterization of the *danza de matachines* as part of daily life, like her use of *mestizaje*, indicates a lack of familiarity with the dance stemming from sufficient ethnographic exposure to and/or experience in the *danza*.

2. Like Cantú, Romero attempts to use the idea of *mestizaje* to describe the *danza de matachines* in relation to the cultural origins of *danza de matachines* (Romero 2009, 186). In addition, Romero offers "the sheer joyfulness of the *danza* and its music" (in Cantú 2009, 203) as the main reason for its continuation. Yet, she does not provide evidence to support this inappropriately subjective statement. This is significantly inauthentic because, though joy is found in the *danza*, I know from experience that there are also moments of considerable solemnity. And, the practices as well as the performances would be grueling enough to militate against the *danza*'s intergenerational survival if not for the *Virgen*'s presence in the dance. Here, presence is our motivation for dancing. Without explanation, she also uses English syntax when referring to the *danza de matachines*. Rather than using, *danza de matachines*, she uses "*matachines danza*" in the title of her chapter and

in its text (Romero 2009, 185, 202) despite the fact that these are Spanish terms that are treated as such by matachines. The fact that Romero is unaware of the varied emotions of the *danza de matachines* and her outsider use of syntax in how she phrases it speak to her lack of quality ethnographic exposure to the dance and certainly to a lack of experience in it. These problems highly undermine any claim to authenticity her work might otherwise have.

Chapter 8

1. This organization's name has since been changed to Las Misiones.

2. As of 2019 the archdiocese was still encouraging the replacement of traditionally, freely shared food with food-vending trucks. It was a suggestion received with disappointment by at least two veteran matachines. The idea was rejected.

Chapter 9

1. The Spanish missions were not under the jurisdiction of an archdiocese but of Franciscans friars. The archdiocese, though, associates itself with the missions insomuch as they were major representatives of the same church at that time.

Chapter 10

1. The grandmother was not a *danzante*, yet, as a devotee to the *Virgen*, she had been close enough to the dance over the years to have accumulated sufficient wisdom concerning it to interpret her granddaughter's response to it. In fact, she may have even been in a better position to interpret her granddaughter's response than her granddaughter herself.

References Cited

Almaraz, Félix D., Jr. 1995–96. "Texas Governor Salcedo and the Court-Martial of Padre Hidalgo." *Southwestern Historical Quarterly* 99 (July–April): 435–64.

Anderson, Carl A., and Eduardo Chávez. 2009. *Our Lady of Guadalupe: Mother of the Civilization of Love*. New York: Doubleday.

Andrews, J. Richard. 2003. *Introduction to Classical Nahuatl*. Rev. ed. Norman: University of Oklahoma Press. Retrieved November 16, 2007, from http://books.google.com/books?id=-IDsW8Ymaig-C&printsec=frontcover&source=gbs_ge_summary_r&cad=0#v=one-page&q&f=false.

Austin, Alfredo López. 1988. *The Human Body and Ideology: Concepts of the Ancient Nahuas*. Vol. 1. Translated by T. O. Montellano and B. O. Montellano. Originally published in 1980. Salt Lake City: University of Utah Press.

Ayala, Elaine. 2015. "Danza to Mary Will Open Winter Feast Days: Colorful Event Set at Mission Concepción." *San Antonio Express-News*, November 22.

Baass-Sowa, Carol. 2015. "Matachines and Mission Concepción—a New Tradition." *Today's Catholic*, January 9, 6.

Benoist and Flores, eds. 1994. "Instrucciones para el Ministro de la Misión de la Purísima Concepción de la Provincia de Texas." San Antonio: Our Lady of the Lake University.

Bonfiglioli, Carlo. 1991. "¿Quiénes son los matachines?" *México Indígena* (March 18): 38–39.

Botello, Robert. 2015. Personal interview with Father García. Digital audio recording. Length 22:00:10. December 23.

Boyd-Batstone, Kathryn. 2016. "Dancers Celebrate Immaculate Conception Feast Day." https://therivardreport.com/matachines-dancers-celebrate-immaculate-conception-feast-day/, December 5.

Brinton, Daniel G. 1890. *Ancient Nahuatl Poetry.* Retrieved November 16, 2012, from www.gutenberg.org/etext/12219.

Cantú, N. E. 2009. "The Semiotics of Land and Place: Matachines Dancing in Laredo, Texas." In *Dancing across Borders: Danzas y Bailes Mexicanos,* edited by N. E. Cantú, O. Nájera-Ramírez, and B. M. Romero, 97–115. Chicago: University of Chicago Press.

Champe, Flavia. W. 1980–81. "Origins of the Magical Dance." *El Palacio* 86, no. 4: 35–39.

"Concerning the Visit of Fray Ortiz." 1745. OLLU Mexican American Research Collections (the Mission Archives), Our Lady of the Lake University, San Antonio, TX. Documents Relating to the Old Spanish Missions of Texas ,Vol. 1., 4th ed.

Cruz, Gilbert R. 1988. *Let There Be Towns: Spanish Municipal Origins in the American Southwest, 1610–1810.* College Station: Texas A&M University Press.

Curcio Nagy, Linda. 2004. "Origins of the Matachines Dance." Retrieved September 12, 2012, from www.townofbernalillo.org/document_center/Departments/las%20fiestas/Chapter_2.pdf.

Deery-Stanton, Phyllis. 1998. "Robert K. Thomas and Chinua Achebe: An Indigenous Perspective on Tribal Society." In *A Good Cherokee, a Good Anthropologist: Papers in Honor of Robert K. Thomas,* edited by Steve Pavlik, 291. Los Angeles: University of California at Los Angeles American Indian Studies Center.

Díaz del Castillo, Bernal. 1994. *Historia de la Conquista de Nueva España.* Mexico City: Editorial Porrúa.

Diekemper, Barnabas. 2019. "Leutenegger, Benedict." https://tshaonline.org/handbook/online/articles/fle89.

Dimmick, Iris. 2015. "Mission Concepción Housing Project Wins Commission Approval." https://therivardreport.com/MISSION-CONCEPCION-HOUSING-PROJECT-WINS-COMMISSION-APPROVAL/, September 15.

———.2017. "Developer of Apartments at Mission Concepción Seeks Slightly Taller Buildings." https://therivardreport.com/developer-o f-apartments-at-mission-concepcion-seeks-slightly-taller-buildings/, July 18.

Dozier, Edward P. 1958. "Spanish-Indian Acculturation in the Southwest: Comments on Spicer." *American Anthropologist* 60: 441–48.

Fernández-Armesto, Felipe. 1987. *The Exploitation of Colonization from the Mediterranean to the Atlantic, 1229–1492.* Philadelphia: University of Pennsylvania Press.

Frye, David. 1996. *Indians into Mexicans: History and Identity in a Mexican Town.* Austin: University of Texas Press.

Fuentes y Guzmán, Francisco A. 1680. Archivo General de Centro América, Guatemala, document A 1.2.9 Leg. 2840 Exp. 25350.

García, Bartholome, and Asifclos Valverde. 1759. "Request for a Manual with Which to Instruct the Indians." Translated by Robert Botello.

Gerlach, T. Jeremy. 2014. "Matachines Dance to Honor the Virgin: 700 Costumed Dancers Perform." *San Antonio Express-News*, December 8.

Gibson, Charles. 1952. *Tlaxcala in the Sixteenth Century.* New Haven, CT: Yale University Press.

———.1964. *The Aztecs under Spanish Rule: A History of the Indians of the Valley of Mexico, 1519–1810.* Stanford, CA: Stanford University Press.

Gibson, Steve. 2002. "The Arocha Family from la Isla de la Palma." Retrieved from http://bexargenealogy.com/islanders/arocha.html.

Guenther, Rocío. "500 Matachines Dancers to Descend on Mission Concepción." https://sanantonioreport.org/500-matachines-dancers-t o-descend-on-mission-concepcion/, November 25.

Guerrero, José Luis. 1994. *Conozca a nuestra Señora de Guadalupe.* Liguori, MO: Libros Liguori.

Habig, Marion. 1976. *The Alamo Chain of Missions.* 2nd ed. Chicago: Franciscan Herald Press.

Habig, Marion, and Benedict Leutenegger. 1977. *Management of the Missions in Texas: Fr. Rafael José Oliva's Views Concerning the Problem of the Temporalities in 1788.* Documentary Series No. 2. San Antonio: Old Spanish Missions Historical Research Library at San José Mission.

Harris, Max. 2000. *Aztecs, Moors, and Christians: Festivals of Reconquest in Mexico and Spain.* Austin: University of Texas Press.

Hill, Robert M., II. 1992. *Colonial Cakchiquels: Highland Maya*

Adaptation to Spanish Rule, 1600–1700. Fort Worth: Harcourt Brace Jovanovich.

Hinojosa, Gilberto, and Gerald Poyo. 1991. *Tejano Origins in Eighteenth-Century San Antonio.* San Antonio: University of Texas Institute of Texan Cultures.

Hobsbawm, Eric, and Terence Ranger, eds. 2005. *The Invention of Tradition.* Cambridge: Cambridge University Press, Cambridge. Originally published in 1983.

"Instructions for the Mission of Puríssima Concepción of the Province of Texas." n.d. OLLU Mexican American Research Collections (the Mission Archives), Our Lady of the Lake University, San Antonio, TX.

Jackson, Jack. 2016. Arocha, Simón de, accessed June 27, 2019, from https://tshaonline.org/handbook/online/articles/far36.

Jackson, Robert H. 2014. "The Miracle of the Virgin of the Rosary Mural at Tetela del Volcán." In *Evangelization and Cultural Conflict in Colonial Mexico,* edited by R. H. Jackson, 1–29. Newcastle: Cambridge Scholars Publishing.

Jones, Oakah, Jr. 1979. *Los Paisanos: Spanish Settlers of the Northern Frontier of New Spain.* Norman: University of Oklahoma Press.

Juan Leal Gorás vs. Martín Lorenzo de Armas, Juan Curbelo, and Francisco José de Arocha. 1735. Roll 8, Briscoe Center for American History. Villa de Béxar de San Fernando. April 14. Bexar Archives Online. www.cah.utexas.edu/projects/bexar/gallery_doc.php?doc=e_bx_000022.

Kirk, Martha A. 2104. "Hundreds of 'Matachines' Dancers Coming to Mission Concepción." https://therivardreport.com/hundreds-matachines-dancers-coming-mission-concepcion-2/, November 27.

Lamadrid, E. R. 2000. "Abiquiú: Genízaros and the Price of Freedom." In *Nuevo México Profundo: Rituals of an Indo-Hispano Homeland,* edited by Miguel Gandert and Enrique Lamadrid, 58. Santa Fe: Museum of New Mexico Press.

Lea, Aurora Lucero-White. 1963–64. "More about the Matachines Dance." *New Mexico Folklore Record* 20: 7–10.

León-Portilla, Miguel. 1963. *Aztec Thought and Culture: A Study of the Ancient Nahua Mind.* Translated by Jack Emory Davis. Originally published in 1956. Norman: University of Oklahoma Press.

"List of Canary Islanders Taken at Quautitlan, November 8, 1730." 2014.

Retrieved from https://bexargenealogy.org/archives/islanders.htm, August 18.

Martínez, Juan Carlos. 1996. *Tradiciones Reineras: Fiestas al fin*, edited by El Norte, 43. Monterrey, Mexico: Ediciones Castillo.

Martínez, Patricia. 2004. "'Noble' Tlaxcalans: Race and Ethnicity in Northeastern New Spain, 1770–1810." PhD. diss, University of Texas, Austin. Retrieved September 16, 2012, from http://reposito-ries.lib.utexas.edu/bitstream/handle/2152/1244/martinezp30074.pdf?sequence=2.

Mathis, Don. 2015. "Fr. David Explores Economic Impact of World Heritage Site." https://therivardreport.com/father-davi d-explores-economic-impact-of-world-heritage-status/, August 14.

Matovina, Timothy. 2005. *Guadalupe and Her Faithful: Latino Catholics in San Antonio from Colonial Origins to the Present*. Baltimore: Johns Hopkins University Press.

Mission Concepción. 2015. Retrieved from http://oldspanishmissions. org/mission-concepcion/.

Moreno, J. 2005. "The Tradition Continues: Los Matachines Dance of Bernalillo, New Mexico." Colorado College.

Morfi, J. A. 1973. "The 'Wretched Village' of San Antonio." In *Foreigners in Their Native Land: Historical Roots of the Mexican Americans*, edited by David J. Weber, 43–44. Albuquerque: University of New Mexico Press.

Ortiz, F. 1745. "Concerning the Visit of Fray Francisco Ortiz to Fr. Juan Fogueras." OLLU Mexican American Research Collections (the Mission Archives), Our Lady of the Lake University, San Antonio, TX.

Pohl, J. 2014. "Across Seas: Cultural Interchange and Social Transformation between Mesoamerica and the American Southwest." Lecture.

Pohl, John, and Charles Robinson, III. 2005. *Aztecs and Conquistadores: The Spanish Invasion and Collapse of the Aztec Empire*. New York: Osprey.

Residents of Texas, 1782–1836, Vol 2. 1984. San Antonio: University of Texas at San Antonio Institute of Texan Cultures.

Rivard, Robert. 2013. December 7. "600 'Matachines' to Dance Sunday Morning at Mission Concepción." http://therivardreport.com/600-matachines-to-danc e-sunday-morning-at-mission-concepcion/.

Rodríguez, Sylvia. 1996. *The Matachines Dance: Ritual Symbolism and Interethnic Relations in the Upper Rio Grande Valley.* Albuquerque: University of New Mexico Press.

Rodríguez Mederos, Antonio. 1745 (October 2). Briscoe Center for American History, University of Texas at Austin. Retrieved from https://www.cah.utexas.edu/projects/bexar/gallery_lg.php?s=0&t=1&doc=e_bx_000069_001.

Romero, B. M. 2009. "The *Matachines Danza* as Intercultural Discourse." In *Dancing across Borders: Danzas y Bailes Mexicanos*, edited by N. E. Cantú, O. Nájera-Ramírez, and B. M. Romero, 185–205. Chicago: University of Chicago Press.

San Antonio Report. 2017. "Matachines to Carry Out Indigenous Tradition Sunday at Mission Concepción," December 2. https://therivardreport.com/matachines-to-carry-out-indigenous-tradition-at-mission-concepcion/.

Sklar, Diedre. 2001. *Dancing with the Virgin: Body and Faith in the Fiesta of Tortugas, New Mexico.* Berkeley: University of California Press.

Smith, Linda Tuhiwai. 2012. *Decolonizing Methodologies: Research and Indigenous Peoples.* London: Zed Books.

Spivak, Gayatri. 1985. "The Rani of Sirmur." In *Europe and Its Others*, edited by F. Barker, P. Hulme, M. Iverson, and D. Loxley, 131. Colchester, England: University of Essex.

Terraciano, Kevin, and Lisa M. Sousa. "The Original 'Conquest' of Oaxaca: Mixtec and Nahua History and Myth." *UCLA Historical Journal* 12 (1992): 29–90.

Thonhoff, Robert H. 2016. "Elizondo, Ignacio." Accessed June 27, 2019, https://tshaonline.org/handbook/online/articles/fel08.

Torres, Luís. 1997. *Voices from the San Antonio Missions.* Lubbock: Texas Tech University Press.

Valeriano, Antonio. 1649. *Nican Mopohua.* Mexico City: La Imprenta de Juan Ruyz.

Valverde, A., and B. García. 1759. "Letter to Joseph Antonio Bernal." April 8. OLLU Mexican American Research Collections (the Mission Archives). Our Lady of the Lake University, San Antonio, TX.

Weigle, M., and P. White. 1988. *The Lore of New Mexico.* Albuquerque: University of New Mexico Press.

Index